REVELATIONS *from* THE REVELATION *of* JESUS CHRIST

CHAPTERS 1-3

A COMMENTARY FOR THE BELIEVER IN THE PEW

REVELATIONS *from* THE REVELATION *of* JESUS CHRIST

CHAPTERS 1-3

A COMMENTARY FOR THE BELIEVER IN THE PEW

REV. DESIRÉ P. GROGAN

Ambassador International

GREENVILLE, SOUTH CAROLINA & BELFAST, NORTHERN IRELAND

www.ambassador-international.com

Revelations from the
Revelation of Jesus Christ, Chapter 1-3
A Commentary for the Believer in the Pew

ISBN: 978-1-64960-013-4
eISBN: 978-1-64960-014-1

Cover Design and Page Layout by Josh Frederick

AMBASSADOR INTERNATIONAL
Emerald House
411 University Ridge, Suite B14
Greenville, SC 29601, USA
www.ambassador-international.com

AMBASSADOR BOOKS
The Mount
2 Woodstock Link
Belfast, BT6 8DD, Northern Ireland, UK
www.ambassadormedia.co.uk

The colophon is a trademark of Ambassador, a Christian publishing company.

This work is dedicated to my maternal Grandparents:

To my Grandfather, the Reverend Ervin Stanley, who persuasively preached the Word of God, so that the 'believer in the pew' could get it and live it! It is his pulpit Bible I hold in my author photo.

and

To my Grandmother, Mamie Hayes Stanley Ash, who though her formal education never went past third grade, was a Spirit-taught 'believer in the pew' whose astute understanding of Scripture was a constant source of revelation and faithful living!

CONTENTS

ACKNOWLEDGMENTS

THERE ARE MANY WHO HAVE MADE this volume possible. Allow me to begin at the beginning of my life by acknowledging my mother, Earlean Stanley Grogan, and my father, William Joseph Grogan, Sr., who diligently and consistently trained me and my siblings in the way we should go, so that as we aged we would not desert our Christian heritage *(a personal paraphrase of Proverbs 22:6)*. I gratefully acknowledge the congregation of the Shiloh Baptist Church of Washington, DC — my home church — and our current pastor, the Reverend Dr. Wallace Charles Smith, under whose pastorate I was not only the first woman to be ordained into the clergy but was permitted to teach the *BOOK OF THE REVELATION* in a weekly Bible study for seven consecutive years, during which many of the *revelations* recorded in this volume were received. I am indebted to the faculty and staff of the Howard University School of Divinity and of the Department of Semitics and Egyptian Languages of the College of Arts and Sciences at The Catholic University of America where my theological and linguistic skills were honed to study the Scriptures with exegetical credibility. I am especially grateful for the support of Dr. Alice Ogden Bellis, Professor of Hebrew Bible at the Howard University School of Divinity, who not only kindled my love for the Semitic languages but encouraged my pursuit in discovering Hebraic influences in the New Testament. I am most grateful to Dr. Sam Lowry and the team at Ambassador International who thought it not robbery to give this "new voice" an opportunity to be heard. I am eternally grateful to God the Father, to our Lord and Savior Jesus Christ, and to the Holy Spirit for making all the above-cited advantages possible and for fueling my faithfulness to the vision of publishing this work.

To God Be All the Glory!

THE PASTOR'S FOREWORD

IT IS AN HONOR TO ENDORSE the exciting work of the Reverend Desiré P. Grogan, *Revelations from the Revelation of Jesus Christ.* Reverend Grogan's preaching and teaching display an unquestioned anointing of the Holy Spirit. For seven years I was privileged to attend a number of the classes she presented at Shiloh where the ideas for this book originated. These classes were always well attended, and I witnessed an amazing effect: The Revelation, arguably one of the Bible's most difficult books, became a real-life tool for people to understand and apply its truths to their lives.

Reverend Grogan does not shy away from the difficult passages, nor does she sugar coat the challenges they offer for all who walk the pilgrim pathway. With all the anxiety facing churches of all denominations, this book provides much practical clarity for a world where the light of truth grows ever dimmer.

Reverend Grogan offers light and hope by wading into the Revelation's perplexity and then showing how its message is a word for us today.

The Reverend Dr. Wallace Charles Smith, D.Min.
Senior Minister, Shiloh Baptist Church, Washington, DC

ENDORSEMENTS

REV. GROGAN HAS PROVIDED A THOROUGH and engaging commentary on the book of Revelation. Though intended for the faithful in the pews, this book provides critical analysis of biblical terms that ministers, and other critical interpreters of the Bible would find useful. She has combined her insights from years of teaching, prophetic ministry, and education in biblical languages and literature to bless those who often don't have access to such a wealth of information. Most useful are the side boxes throughout the chapters that raise contemporary questions for those searching to apply the mysteries of the Bible to the realities of their situations. Read and be blessed!

The Reverend Dr. Gay L. Byron, PhD
Professor of New Testament and Early Christianity
Howard University School of Divinity

DESIRÉ GROGAN'S *REVELATIONS FROM THE REVELATION* of *Jesus Christ* is a carefully crafted commentary that is both a close reading of the first three chapters of the book of Revelation and a highly creative one. Grogan uses the plenary inspiration method, in which the Bible is understood to interpret the Bible, with great ingenuity. Although she often refers to the Greek and occasionally to the Hebrew or Aramaic, she is always careful to provide an English transliteration. Thus, the book lives up to its sub-title: *A Commentary for the Believer in the Pew.*

The Reverend Dr. Alice Ogden Bellis, PhD
Professor of Hebrew Bible
Howard University School of Divinity

REV. DESIRÉ P. GROGAN'S GIFTS OF interpretation and teaching combine to make *Revelations from The Revelation of Jesus Christ - Chapters 1 - 3: A Commentary for the Believer in the Pew*, a well-researched and comprehensive look at chapters in the final book of the bible. It provides her identified readership, the believer in the pew, with in-depth meaning of these first three chapters of Revelation. For many the book of Revelation has long been thought of as the most challenging and darkest book in the bible. Rev. Grogan's passion for teaching Revelation and her clear and expressive writing provide clarity and light. It is that combination of clarity and light that makes this book accessible to the reader. It is also why I enthusiastically recommend Rev. Desiré P. Grogan's *Revelations from The Revelation of Jesus Christ - Chapters 1 - 3: A Commentary for the Believer in the Pew.*

Sandra Jowers-Barber, PhD
Ministry of Deacons
Shiloh Baptist Church, Washington, DC

THE REV. DESIRÉ GROGAN'S *REVELATIONS FROM the Revelation of Jesus Christ* is scholarly, insightful, and original. Rev. Grogan opens the door to the first three chapters of Revelation, making them accessible to those of us who do not know Greek and have never been to seminary. Drawing on her encyclopedic knowledge of the Bible, she grounds her interpretations in the interplay between the Old and New Testaments. Written with great clarity and great joy, Rev. Grogan's work offers a unique and spirit-filled perspective on the messages written to the seven churches and sent to us through the corridors of time. This commentary is an excellent study guide, very helpful to "the believer in the pew."

Antoinette S. Mitchell, PhD
Believer in the Pew
Shiloh Baptist Church, Washington, DC

REV. DESIRÉ P. GROGAN, IN HER book *Revelations from the Revelation of Jesus Christ*, evokes in the "believer in the pew" a heart full of gratitude. The clearly articulated overview, scriptural exploration and interpretation of the original text expertly reveal God's ultimate plan for His faithful servants, as articulated in John's Revelation. This in-depth study of "the messages to the church in every generation" educates the reader through the "revelation knowledge" entrusted to the author. Using scripture to explain scripture, Rev. Grogan guides the reader to an enhanced understanding of Jesus' reign as the ultimate judge, while yet inspiring one to live a faithful, obedient life of "patient endurance." A must read for any Christian wanting to fully comprehend the Revelation text.

Deacon Janice Carter-Bowden
Chair of the Christian Education Ministry
Shiloh Baptist Church, Washington, D.C.

IF YOU ARE A BELIEVER, WHO has avoided reading the important Book of Revelation, because of its strange symbols and imagery, this compelling new book is a Godsend. Rev. Grogan uses clear, precise prose to reveal a sound approach to understanding not only the final book in the Bible, but she opens up the whole Bible, using, and showing the reader how to use a tool called "plenary inspiration." This tool directs the reader to compare the word(s) found in the text under consideration with other places in Scripture where the same words are used. With her rich knowledge of the original Biblical languages, Rev. Grogan provides the truest context for letting the Bible interpret itself. This read will be my go-to guide for many years to come. *Revelations from The Revelation of Jesus Christ* is destined to become a classic in its field.

Carl E. Snead, Esq.
Attorney-at-Law

AUTHOR'S FOREWORD

FOR THE BELIEVER IN THE PEW, the book of *THE REVELATION OF JESUS CHRIST* needs no other introduction than that it is the most avoided book of Scripture that few feel capable of navigating and understanding on their own. The dense amount of imagery and the horrific scenes of judgment are mind-boggling, and how to unpack the meaning of it all remains a mystery for many.

The purpose of this volume is to empower you — the believer in the pew — with the most accessible tool to navigate and understand this last book of Scripture, and that tool is the Bible itself, the Bible in your hand. The God who is speaking and acting in this last book of Scripture is the same God who has been speaking and acting throughout the biblical text (cf. Heb 1:1-2). So, to understand what God is saying and doing in this last book you need to discover where God has said and done it in the biblical text prior to this last book. This approach to studying the book of *THE REVELATION OF JESUS CHRIST*, or any book of the Bible, is called plenary inspiration, where you let the Word of God interpret the Word of God. The Spirit through the Apostle Paul highly commends this method of studying the Word of God for interpretation and understanding:

> *"This is what we speak, not in words taught us by human wisdom but in words taught by the Spirit, explaining spiritual realities with Spirit-taught words" (1 Cor 2:13).*

In other words, the Bible in your hand is its own best reference in studying the Bible, as a whole, and the book of THE REVELATION OF JESUS CHRIST, in particular, since this last book of Scripture culminates all of human and salvation history! I highly recommend that as you read this volume you keep your own Bible open and search the Scriptures to see if what is being said is true, even if it is new to your understanding.

It is my sincere hope and prayer that after you read this volume, the book of THE REVELATION OF JESUS CHRIST will no longer be a feared place of study but an awe-inspiring zone of discovering and re-discovering the majesty and the consistency of the only God Who is worthy to be trusted and obeyed, worshipped and adored — the God Who

> *"so loved the world that He gave His one and only Son, that whoever believes in Him shall not perish but have eternal life" (John 3:16).*

PREFACE

PURPOSE

THE PURPOSE OF THIS VOLUME IS to meet the believer in the pew at the point of his/her exposure to *THE REVELATION OF JESUS CHRIST*, in other words, the English translation, in order to encourage and empower those who may never attend a seminary or learn the original languages of Scripture and to engage the English translation of the biblical canon as its own best reference in understanding this last book of Scripture.

It is important to acknowledge that the many English translations of the Bible as well as the many excellent commentaries on *THE REVELATION OF JESUS CHRIST* are the result of scholarly access to original manuscripts and supporting ancient documents. These manuscripts require the linguistic expertise to translate the Hebrew, Aramaic, and Greek texts into what sometimes proves to be the narrow and nebulous channels of the English language. However, the believer in the pew rarely, if ever, has access to these manuscripts, or the required linguistic ability to navigate these ancient documents, no matter how otherwise well-educated he/she is. What the believer in the pew does have on hand is one (or more) of a variety of English renditions of the Sacred Text produced by biblical scholarship from the original languages. As these translations are produced for the purposes of under girding the believer's salvation and life-long edification in the faith of JESUS CHRIST, we are indeed grateful to God for the scholars who have devoted themselves to this sacred task.

To assist the reader in bridging the linguistic gap between the original languages and the English translations of the biblical text, this volume will include the original language scripts, transliterations, and the phonetic pronunciations of selected Hebrew and Greek terms at various points in the discussion. The purpose will be to highlight the unique contribution the original language brings to the understanding of a text.[1] This is done not to overwhelm the reader but rather to connect the reader to the linguistic world from which the English translations hail.

Though it is not the intent of this volume to give an exhaustive comparison of the various English translations, it is recognized that each has both its merits and its deficits in the attempt to accurately reflect the original languages of the biblical text. Some of the difficulty lies within the syntax of the original language, which may require re-wording to articulate it for sense in the English; and some of the difficulty is encountered in the translation of the clearest of terms in the original language into an English-speaking world for which there is no conceptual or concrete equivalent.

This volume will engage the New International Version (NIV) as the primary English translation for the presentation of the *"revelations"* from *THE REVELATION OF JESUS CHRIST*. References to other English translations will under gird the tasks of exposing agreement, conducting comparisons, or highlighting contrasts that clarify the understanding of the text under discussion and the revelation given. Unless otherwise noted, Scriptural quotes and references will be taken from the NIV.

---

1   See the following section, entitled Original Language Transliterations | Phonetic Pronunciation Accents | Vowel Markings.

METHOD

The *"revelations"* from THE REVELATION OF JESUS CHRIST presented herein were received and recorded while studying and teaching this last book of Scripture over a seven-year period in a year-round, weekly Bible study at my home church. Though only the first three chapters are dealt with in this volume, more volumes in this series will be forthcoming and will include all remaining chapters of THE REVELATION OF JESUS CHRIST.

The studying and teaching method employed during the weekly Bible study of this last book of Scripture was premised upon the Spirit's injunction through the Apostle Paul:

> *"This is what we speak, not in words taught us by human wisdom but in words taught by the Spirit, explaining spiritual realities with Spirit-taught words" (1 Cor 2:13).*

The footnote on this verse in the NRSV gives the following variant readings to the last phrase of the above-cited text: "interpreting spiritual things in spiritual language" or "comparing spiritual things with spiritual." The sense of this injunction is that "God's secret wisdom," which Paul was proclaiming (1 Cor 2:7), was not being taught as a result of human wisdom, but was being taught by the Holy Spirit, whose teaching method is to compare spiritual things with spiritual things. Since the Word of God itself satisfies the definition of "spiritual truths" and "spiritual words" (John 6:63b) in both instances within the above injunction, then comparing the Word of God with the Word of God is the only way to understand and interpret the Word of God.

In philosophical circles, this approach would be denounced as repetitively self-serving. However, as a component of the Protestant Rule of Faith, this approach is referred to as *plenary inspiration*,[2] which

---

2 Charles Hodge, "The Protestant Rule of Faith," in *Readings in Christian Theology* (eds. Peter C. Hodgson and Robert H. King: Philadelphia: Fortress, 1985), 44.

unequivocally affirms that "inspiration extends equally to all parts of Scripture . . . that all books of Scripture are equally inspired . . . [that] all alike are infallible in what they teach . . . and that inspiration extends to all the content . . . not just to moral and religious truths, but extends to statements of facts, whether scientific, historical or geographical."[3] It is because

> "all Scripture is God-breathed . . . " (2 Tim 3:16)

that comparing Scripture with Scripture is the method of biblical study enjoined by 1 Cor 2:13 and results in revelation knowledge derived from the biblical text through the agency of the Holy Spirit. The Apostle Paul confirmed this truth in the following two passages:

> However, as it is written: 'What no eye has seen, what no ear has heard, and what no human mind has conceived - the things God has prepared for those who love him - these are the things God has **revealed** to us **by his Spirit** (1 Cor 2:9, **author's emphases**).

> I want you to know, brothers and sisters, that the **gospel I preached** is not of human origin. I did not receive it from any man, nor was I taught it; rather, I **received it by revelation from Jesus Christ** (Gal 1:11-12, **author's emphases**)

It is this method of biblical study, i.e., comparing Scripture with Scripture, that produced the "revelations" contained herein and which the author presents in obedience to the same injunction God gave to several of the prophets to write down, on a scroll or in a book, what God had revealed to them (Exod 17:14; 24:4; 34:27-28; Isa 30:8; Jer 30:2; 36:2, 28; Ezek 43:11; Hab 2:2; Rev 1:11, 19; 2:1, 8, 12, 18; 3:1, 7, 14; 14:13; 19:9; 21:5).

---

3   Ibid., 44.

The response from the participating parishioners to this approach of studying and teaching *The Revelation of Jesus Christ* was expressed in several different ways, but all in amazement at their ability to navigate and grasp the meaning of this often-avoided book of Scripture for themselves, using the Bible in their hands:

> *"I thought I would never be able to understand this book, but now I can see how the same God who was speaking before is saying the same thing in this book, just on a more graphic scale."*

> *"I love it when we trace a biblical concept from first mention to the Revelation. It makes the Bible seem more connected and less daunting to navigate."*

> *"It was exhilarating to come to a revelation in class and to see that the revelation didn't always have to come from or through the teacher but could come from one of us students. This was a first for me and the turning of the corner in my understanding of the Holy Spirit's ministry in revealing truth."*

What the parishioners discovered and what the readers of this volume need to keep in mind is that revelation knowledge, derived from exercising due diligence in the study of God's Word under the anointing of the Holy Spirit, will indeed update and challenge one's current understanding of God, God's Will, and God's Purposes. This updating dynamic of revelation knowledge supports the truth that the eternal Word of God and the eternal Holy Spirit who teaches it (John 14:26) both serve as the

"spring of water welling up to eternal life" (John 4:14)

from which the updating dynamic of revelation knowledge is drawn. For this reason, this author highly recommends that the reader of this book read it with his/her Bible open, in order to first examine the Scriptures to see if what is being said is true, as the believers in the Berean Church were commended for doing (Acts 17:11); and, as a result, to allow the updating Spirit of revelation knowledge to help you grow in the grace and knowledge of our Lord and Savior Jesus Christ (2 Peter 3:18). The reader will discover that in so doing, he/she will see God, God's Will and God's Purposes more clearly than before (cf. 1 Cor 13:12b).

It is the author's hope, therefore, that three outcomes will be experienced by the reader of this work. The first is that the believer in the pew will be empowered with the courage and the competence to become a credible exegete of the biblical text. The second is that the biblical text and the teaching role of the Holy Spirit will be elevated as the believer's accessible resources to see Jesus with the clarity to obey Him more fervently. And thirdly, that the reader's engaged study of the often-avoided book in Scripture, *THE REVELATION OF JESUS CHRIST*, will reveal the Bible to be its own best reference and the God of Scripture to be the same yesterday, today and forever!

ORIGINAL LANGUAGE TRANSLITERATIONS

PHONETIC PRONUNCIATION ACCENTS | VOWEL MARKINGS

WORDS FROM THE ORIGINAL LANGUAGE OF Hebrew, Aramaic and Greek will first be presented in their original script, followed in parenthesis by their phonetic pronunciation using the English alphabet. Syllables that should be stressed in pronunciation are **bold** and marked with a syllabic accent mark (´).

EXAMPLES

HEBREW/ARAMAIC SCRIPT

אֶהְיֶה אֲשֶׁר אֶהְיֶה (pronounced ĕh-**yĕh**´ ă-**sher**´ ĕh-**yĕh**´)

◄——————————   ——————————►

The Hebrew/Aramaic script is read from right to left (◄——), but its transliteration into English is read from left to right (——►).

GREEK SCRIPT

ὁ μάρτυς (pronounced hŏ **mar′**-tūs)

⸺⸺⸺⸺⸺➤

The Greek script and its transliteration into English are both read from left to right (⸺➤).

VOWEL MARKINGS

The following vowel markings will define long and short vowel sounds in both Hebrew/Aramaic and Greek transliterations:

ā or ay	make or day
ă	hat
â	father
ē or ee	seen
ĕ	met
ī	kind
ĭ	kid
i (ee)	intrigue
ō	whole
ŏ	hot
ū	fuel
ŭ	rut

THE REVELATION OF JESUS CHRIST

AS GIVEN TO THE APOSTLE JOHN ON THE ISLE OF PATMOS - A.D. 95

THEME: JESUS THE CHRIST

THIS LAST BOOK OF SCRIPTURE IS referred to by similar titles in variation, some including Jesus' name, some not. For example, the New International Version (NIV) and the Holman Christian Standard Bible (HCSB) simply title it *"Revelation"* with no definite article. The King James Version and the New King James Version title it THE REVELATION (OF ST. JOHN THE DIVINE) and THE REVELATION OF JESUS CHRIST, respectively. The New American Bible (Catholic Edition) refers to it as THE BOOK OF REVELATION whereas the New Revised Standard and New American Standard Bible translations designate it THE REVELATION to John. THE COMPLETE JEWISH BIBLE (D.H. Stern) labels this last book as THE REVELATION OF YESHUA THE MESSIAH TO JOCHANAN (John).

The common denominator in each of the above-cited English translations, however, is that the opening phrase of this last book of Scripture articulates what can be considered the proper title of the book: *THE REVELATION OF*[4] *JESUS CHRIST* (herein after referred to as *THE REVELATION*), thus establishing that Jesus is the main theme and the main character of the book. Such could very well be said of the whole of Scripture, as the entire biblical record is God's unfolding plan of salvation as personified in and secured by Jesus. However, this title is especially true of this last book of Scripture: for every vision given, every series of symbolism depicted, every act of judgment executed, every parenthetical expression of grace extended, and every liturgical hymn sung is an installation into the unfolding and ultimate revelation of Jesus Christ in His Second Advent, occurring as it will against the backdrop of the culmination of human history and the ushering in of both the Millennial and Eternal Kingdoms.

In this culminating revelation, therefore, Jesus is presented in terms of time, relationships, and offices, as each reveal supporting dynamics of His ultimate work in executing His Father's final judgment upon the world (cf. John 5:22-23).

TIME

Though the Apostle John is led to introduce the Father as

> *"him who is, and who was, and who is to come" (1:4),*

it is the Father Himself who is the first of the Godhead to announce His Eternal relationship to time:

> *"I am the Alpha and the Omega, says The Lord God, who is, and who was, and who is to come, the Almighty" (Rev 1:8).*

---

4 The NIV translation uses the preposition *"from,"* which poses no conflict in meaning. The Greek genitive construction of Jesus' Name allows the translation of the preposition to be either *"of"* or *"from."* Both work.

The Father makes a similar declaration in Chapter 21 within the context of the new heaven and the new earth:

> *"He said to me: 'It is done. I am the Alpha and the Omega, the Beginning and the End . . . '" (Rev 21:6a).*

The upcoming exegetical treatment of the above-cited passages will reveal that it is indeed the Father speaking in each case.

Jesus echoes His Father's Eternal relationship to time in His own words of comfort and encouragement to John after the Patmos Vision:

> *" . . . Do not be afraid. **I am the First and the Last . . .** " (Rev 1:17, **author's emphasis**).*

He repeats this self-declaration in His opening salutation to the church in Smyrna,

> *"These are the words of him who is **the First and the Last . . .** " (Rev 2:8, **author's emphasis**).*

However, it is in the last chapter that Jesus presents Himself as One with the Father in the consummate expression of all three elements of their eternal relationship to time:

> *"I am the Alpha and the Omega, the First and the Last, the Beginning and the End" (Rev 22:13).*

The upcoming exegetical treatment of the above-cited passages will reveal that it is indeed Jesus speaking in each instance.

As Jesus was One with the Father in creation (John 1:1) and *is* One with the Father in salvation (John 6:38-40), so Jesus is herein presented as One with the Father in judgment: for He will execute the final regimen of His Father's judgment, and thus bring the present earth and heaven and all time to an end (John 5:22, 27).

RELATIONSHIPS

The relationships that are revealed in Jesus' ultimate work of judgment fall into at least **three categories:** His relationship to the **churches**, to the **Tribulation Jews and Gentiles**, and to the **Millennial (Davidic)** and **Eternal Kingdoms**.

CHURCHES
REVELATION 1:9 - 3:22

Jesus' initial instruction to John was to

> *"Write on a scroll what you see and send it to the seven churches: to Ephesus, Smyrna, Pergamum, Thyatira, Sardis, Philadelphia and Laodicea" (Rev. 1:11).*

Chapters two and three are Jesus' dictation to John of the content of these letters to each church cited. Though the church is not mentioned from Revelation 4:1 to 22:15, it is again mentioned by Jesus in Revelation 22:16:

> *"I, Jesus, have sent My angel to give you this testimony for the churches . . . "*

As the church is addressed both at the beginning and at the end of THE REVELATION, it is safe to conclude that the seven churches not only received their individual letters, but each other's letters as well as the entire book of THE REVELATION. More about this will be discussed in the upcoming exegetical treatment of the Letters to the churches.

TRIBULATION JEWS AND GENTILES
REVELATION 4:1 - 19:21

Both Jews and Gentiles will be present on the earth to experience the Great Tribulation. All the events depicted between Revelation 4:1 and 19:21 will impact these two groups. However, within these two classifications of the human population, a separation between believers and unbelievers will occur as they place their faith in Jesus the Messiah: 144,000 believing Jews will be sealed (Rev 7:4-9) and an innumerable host of believing Gentiles who hail from every nation, tribe, peoples, and languages will be saved (Rev 7:9, 13-14). The rest, of both unbelieving Jews and unbelieving Gentiles, will experience the Great White Throne judgment and, consequently, the Second Death (Rev 20:11-15).

MILLENNIAL (DAVIDIC) AND ETERNAL KINGDOMS
REVELATION 11:15; 20:1 - 22:21

The millennial kingdom, by designation, is the one-thousand-year reign of Christ upon the earth on the throne of David, in fulfillment of the Davidic Covenant (2 Sam 7:16; 1 Kings 2:4, 8:25, 9:5, 11:36; 2 Chron 6:16, 7:18; Ps 89:4,132:11-12; Jer 33:17; Acts 13:22-23). The millennial kingdom will be inaugurated with Jesus' second coming in conquering glory, at which time He will defeat the two emissaries of Satan, the beast and the false prophet, and will cast both into the lake of fire that burns with sulfur (Rev 19:11-20). During this same one-thousand-year period, Satan will be bound in the bottomless pit, or the Abyss (Rev 20:1-3), and all who had been martyred for Christ during the Great Tribulation period, and possibly Old Testament believers with them (cf. Dan 12:13), will be raised to life to reign with Christ in His millennial kingdom on the earth (Rev 20:4-6).

It is worth noting that those who will be raised to reign with Christ during His millennial kingdom will be raised into bodies that will still be subject to death. According to God's timetable, death, as the last enemy (1 Cor 15:26), will not be destroyed in the lake of fire until after the millennial kingdom has come to a close (Rev 20:7, 14). The issue of death during the millennial kingdom is further corroborated by Isaiah's prophecy regarding the character of life during this time:

> *Never again will there be in it an infant who lives but a few days, or*
> *an old man who does not live out his years;* ***he who dies*** *at a hundred*
> *will be thought a mere child; he who fails to reach a hundred will be*
> *considered accursed (Isa 65:20,* ***author's emphasis****).*

Like those who were resurrected to resume life in death-bound flesh, of whom Lazarus is the most poignant example (John 11:38-44), so those who will be resurrected to reign with Christ in His millennial kingdom may indeed live any length of time within the one thousand years, but will do so while occupying the kind of flesh that will still be subject to decay and death.[5]

Between the end of the millennial kingdom and the beginning of the eternal kingdom, Satan will be loosed for a short season with the mission of deceiving the nations who would have lived under Jesus' one thousand year reign of peace (Isa 26:10; 60:12). The number of defectors is characterized as being "like the sand on the seashore" (Rev 20:7-8). As Satan and his newly amassed army surround the saints and the city of Jerusalem, fire will be sent from heaven to consume them and

> *"the devil, who deceived them, [was] thrown into the lake of burning*
> *sulfur, where the beast and the false prophet had been thrown. They*
> *will be tormented day and night forever and ever" (Rev 20:9-10).*

The Great White Throne will then be set up and the dead who were not raised in the first resurrection will be raised at this time to be judged; and, along with Death and Hades, whoever is not found in the book of Life will be thrown into the lake of fire, also known as the Second Death (Rev 20:11-15).

---

5 This longevity of life while occupying dying flesh can be clearly seen in the genealogies presented in Genesis 5:1-32 and 11:10-25.

First Corinthians 15:25-28 tells us that once the last enemy has been destroyed, i.e., death, then Jesus will surrender the millennial kingdom to His Father and be subject to Him in the eternal kingdom, so that God the Father "may be all in all." The eternal kingdom, as announced in Revelation 21:1 – 22:4, and into which the millennial kingdom will be subsumed, will consist of the following seven new things:

1.   New Heaven – Revelation 21:1; cf. Isaiah 65:17; 66:22; 2 Peter 3:13

2.   New Earth – same references as above

3.   New Jerusalem – Revelation 21:2, 9-27

4.   New People – Revelation 21:27

5.   New Temple – Revelation 21:22

6.   New Light – Revelation 21:23; 22:5

7.   New Paradise – Revelation 22:1-4

HIS OFFICES

Jesus is primarily presented in five official capacities in *THE REVELATION*, as He carries out His Father's final judgment:

1. ASCENDED AND GLORIFIED LORD
REVELATION 1:12-18 – PATMOS VISION

The Patmos Vision (so named for John's location on the Isle of Patmos) is the vision given to John of Jesus in His official capacity as Ascended and Glorified Lord. The characteristics of this vision are a merger of the visions shown to both Daniel (7:9; 10:5-6) and Ezekiel (1:26-28). Given these OT references, we can safely assume that the glory of the current vision is of the glory that Jesus had in His Father's Presence "before the world began" (John 17:5, 24) and to which He was restored in His Ascension and Exaltation (Eph 1:20-21). The descriptive elements of the vision, which will be discussed within the exegetical treatment of Revelation 1:12-18, depict Jesus in His exalted role as Judge, Priest and King, and are cited, in part, in each of the letters to the seven churches to indicate that it is indeed Jesus speaking to His Body.

Another indicator of Jesus' Ascended and Glorified Presence will be a composite "signature" of natural phenomena that will accompany each of His roles at distinct moments in the text. The composite signature of Jesus' Presence will include flashes of lightning, rumblings and peals of thunder, earthquakes, and a great hailstorm (Rev 4:5; 8:5; 11:19; 16:18). These phenomena will be manifested in variation and in increasing intensity during each phase of Jesus' judgment activity. Jesus' signature is introduced in Rev 4:5 and establishes Him as the Eternal Son and Power by whom God the Father created all things (Rev. 4:11; cf. John 1:1-4). It is also worthy to note that aspects of Jesus' signature were evident when God gave the Law at Mt. Sinai (thunder and lightning - Exod 19:16; 20:18), as well as in the earth's response to Jesus' crucifixion on Calvary (earthquake - Matt 27:51b, 54) in fulfillment of that same Law.

2. THE ONLY RIGHTEOUS JUDGE
REVELATION 5:1-14; 16:17-18; 20:1-15

Jesus is inaugurated into His office as Judge in Chapter 5 and completes His work of judgment in Chapter 20. All of the intervening events of judgment that occur between these two chapters (6:1-19:21) are under Jesus' Command: "Moreover, the Father judges no man, but has entrusted all judgment to the Son" (John 5:22). Jesus' office as the Only Righteous Judge is denoted in the Patmos Vision by the "gold sash wrapped around His chest," which is in contrast to the priestly attire of the sash around the waist (Lev 8:7). The gold sash around the chest is equivalent to the Old Testament breast piece, or breastplate, which was worn over the heart of the High Priest, and contained the

Urim and Thummim that were consulted for decisions or judgments (Exod 8:29-30). As the attire of judgment, the significance of the gold sash around the chest is corroborated by the same apparel worn by the angels who will administer the seven bowl judgments of God's wrath (Rev. 15:6).

Of special note is the context of the Seventh Bowl of Wrath in Revelation 16:17-18. Here, Jesus officiates incognito as "a loud voice from the temple, saying, 'It is done.'" His Presence is expressed in a more intense version of His signature, i.e., "flashes of lightning, rumblings, peals of thunder, and a severe earthquake. No earthquake like it has ever occurred since man has been on earth, so tremendous was the quake" (Rev 16:18). Jesus' declaration of His finished work of judgment echoes His similar declaration from the Cross, i.e., *"It is finished"* (John 19:30, *author's emphasis*), where He completed His Father's work of redemption (John 17:4). Jesus' declaration of His finished work of judgment is anticipated in Ezekiel's prophecy against Gog (Ezek 39:1-8), and is uttered again by the Father Himself in the prophetic context of the new Heaven and the new Earth (Rev 21:6).

3. GREAT HIGH PRIEST
REVELATION 8:3-6

Jesus officiates, albeit incognito, as "another angel" (8:3), whose presence and work are validated by the high priestly ministry conducted within these verses (cf. Exod 28:1-43; John 17:1-26; Heb 6:13-20, 7:11-28, 8:1, 10:11-12), as well as by an expanded variation of His signature, i.e., "peals of thunder, rumblings, flashes of lightning, and an earthquake" (Rev. 8:5). Jesus' manifestation as an *angel* in this context is also corroborated by His pre-Incarnate appearances in the Old Testament as "The Angel of the Lord" (Gen 16:7, 9, 21:17, 22:11, 48:16; Exod 3:2, 14:19, 23:20-23; Num 22:22; Judg 2:4, 6:11, 13:3; 2 Kings 19:35; Isa 63:9; Zech 1:12, 12:8; Mal 3:1).

4. KING OF KINGS AND LORD OF LORDS
REV 11:15-19; 17:14; 19:16

The sounding of the Seventh Trumpet is the context in which *Jesus' reign* over the kingdom[6] of this world is *announced* (11:15), and in which a variation of His signature, again, appears, i.e., "flashes of lightning, rumblings, peals of thunder, an earthquake, and a great hailstorm" (11:19). In the Seventh Trumpet context, His official capacity as King of Kings and Lord of lords is assumed. However, His official Title is plainly declared and revealed in the contexts of the First Doom (17:14) and the Battle of Armageddon (19:16).

5. BRIDEGROOM
REVELATION 19:7-10

The Marriage of the Lamb is that of Christ and His bride, the church (cf. Matt 22:1-14; Eph 5:22-32). The Marriage is announced after the fall of Babylon and before Jesus' second coming in conquering Glory and the Battle of Armageddon.

MOVEMENT

All events in *THE REVELATION* move toward the following seven culminating events in their order:

1. The Second Coming of Jesus Christ—Revelation 19:11-16

2. The Battle of Armageddon and the Doom of the Beast and False Prophet—Revelation 19:15-21

3. Satan Bound for 1000 Years—Revelation 20:1-3

---

6 Though the world is composed of many kingdoms, all are considered one kingdom under Satan's temporary rule (John 12:31; 14:30; Eph 2:2). Jesus' defeat of Satan has and will transfer the one kingdom of this world back under the reign and rulership of Jesus. See comments under the *Key Verse* section below.

4.   The Completion of the First Resurrection, the Full Manifestation of the Covenanted Davidic Kingdom, and the 1000-Year (Millennial) Reign of Christ Upon the Earth—Revelation 20:4-6

5.   Satan Loosed, Defeated, and Cast into the Lake of Fire—Revelation 20:7-10

6.   The Second Resurrection of the Wicked Dead and the Great White Throne Judgment—Revelation 20:11-15

7.   The New Heaven, the New Earth, and the New Jerusalem of the Eternal Kingdom—Revelation 21:1—22:5

KEY VERSE

Revelation 11:15 — *. . . The kingdom of the world has become the kingdom of our Lord, and of his Christ; and he will reign for ever and ever.*

As previously mentioned, this key verse of THE REVELATION text is declared during the Seventh Trumpet Judgment and announces the fulfillment of the Davidic Covenant and several prophecies related to Jesus' reign over the earth. In the Davidic covenant, God promised David that he would "never fail to have a man on the throne of Israel" (1 Kings 2:4, 8:25, 9:5; 2 Chron 6:16, 7:18; Ps 132:11-12; Jer 33:17; Acts 13:22-23; cf. 2 Sam 7:16; 1 Kings 11:36; Ps 89:4). As the Seed of David, Jesus is that Man who will sit on the throne of David during His Millennial Reign over Israel and the entire world. This is further corroborated in Jeremiah 23:5-6 and 33:15-17, where Jesus is depicted as that "Righteous Branch" of David whom the LORD will raise up to "reign wisely and do what is just and right in the land" (cf. Luke 1:30-33).

In Daniel 2:44-45 and 7:27, the millennial kingdom over which Jesus will reign is described as a kingdom that will never be destroyed, that will be everlasting in duration, and in which *"all rulers will worship and obey Him."* A similar declaration is made in the concluding chapter of the prophecy through Zechariah:

> *The LORD will be king over the whole earth. On that day, there will be one LORD, and his name the only name (Zech 14:9; cf. Eph 1:20-21; Phil 2:9-11; 1 Peter 3:22).*

Since the fall of Adam and Eve, the kingdom of this world has been under the sway of Satan's rule, thus making the world a kingdom in revolt against the rule of God on the earth (cf. 2 Cor 4:4; Eph 2:1-2). However, the kingdom of this world and its prince, Satan, will be *(and have already been)* defeated (cf. John 12:31, 14:30, 16:11) and will become the kingdom of our LORD and of His Christ forever.

The witness of the current declaration and the prophecies that support it unequivocally establish and endorse that all human history will be brought to its apex in Jesus' reign on the earth for a thousand years as King of kings and Lord of lords!

THREE MAJOR CATEGORIES OF REVELATION (REV 1:19)

After being shown the Vision of Jesus in His Resurrection Glory, i.e., the Patmos Vision, John is instructed to write as an eyewitness under three categories of revelation: "what you have seen, what is now and what will take place later."

FIRST CATEGORY OF REVELATION
"WHAT YOU HAVE SEEN," (REV 1:1-20)

This is a direct reference to the Patmos Vision, or, the Vision of Jesus in His Resurrection Glory (Rev 1:1-20). The Vision, as previously stated, is a fusion of the visionary revelations given to Daniel and Ezekiel (Dan

7:9; 10:5-6; Ezek 1:26-28). As such, the Patmos Vision, which John has now seen with his own eyes, can also be viewed as **what was and now is**, i.e., bringing the past into the present, or impregnating the present with the past.

SECOND CATEGORY OF REVELATION
"What is Now" (Rev 2:1—3:22)

This category encompasses the **letters to the seven churches** in Asia: Ephesus, Smyrna, Pergamum, Thyatira, Sardis, Philadelphia, and Laodicea (Rev 1:4-3:22). The **number seven** is first and formally introduced here as symbolic of the completeness of God's activity. The seven churches, therefore, are **symbolic of the complete Body of Christ worldwide** as well as the **full span of the Church Age**. Since the church came into existence with the death and resurrection of Christ and with the outpouring of the Holy Spirit at Pentecost, then the Body of Christ, as depicted by the seven churches, represents "what is now."

THIRD CATEGORY OF REVELATION
"And What Will Take Place Later" (Rev 4:1—22:21)

This phrase echoes Daniel's praise to God for revealing the content of King Nebuchadnezzar's dream. In Daniel 2:28-29, Daniel declares to the king that

> *"there is a God in heaven who reveals mysteries. He has shown to King Nebuchadnezzar **what will happen in days to come** . . . " (author's emphasis)*

and

> *"As Your Majesty was lying there, O king, your mind turned **to things to come** . . . " (author's emphasis)*.

As the "days to come" and the "things to come" began immediately after the close of Nebuchadnezzar's reign (Dan 2:45), then the future sense of what John is shown is infused with what has been, what already is, and what has yet to be (cf. Eccl 3:15).

This last and larger category of revelation in THE REVELATION text, Chapters 6-19, depicts the Tribulation Period, which will be seven years in duration and equates to the prophecy given to Daniel, regarding the seventieth week in Israel's history (Dan 9:24-27). The last 3½ years of the seven-year Tribulation period, described in Chapters 11-18, are labeled the **Great Tribulation**, as this final timeframe will manifest an escalated and more intense outpouring of God's Wrath in judgment. However, the entire seven-year period is prophetically designated as "a time of trouble for Jacob" (Jer 30:7), which will not only be characterized by unprecedented persecution of the Jewish people but will also be a time of salvation for both believing Jews (Rev. 7:4-8) and believing Gentiles (Rev 7:9-10).

The entire Tribulation period will occur **after** the rapture of the church, as symbolized by the command for John to "come up here" (Rev 4:1) **after** all seven churches have been addressed.[7] The Tribulation Period will be composed of the following **six** events of judgment, featuring **seven** phenomena each. Each event will be followed by a **parenthetical** period (two within the 5th event) that moves the divine activity of judgment to its culmination:

1. The Seven Seals — **REVELATION 4:1 - 8:1**

   a. Parenthetical Period of God's Grace
      REVELATION 7:1-17
      Occurs between the 6th and 7th Seals.

---

7   This view is considered a premillennial view of the second coming of Jesus Christ. An excellent resource on the various views of interpreting THE REVELATION is, as follows: Steve Gregg, ed., *REVELATION: FOUR VIEWS: A PARALLEL COMMENTARY* (Nashville: Thomas Nelson Publishers, 1997), xiii-xv.

2. The Seven Trumpets — **REVELATION 8:2 - 11:19**

    a. Parenthetical Period of Mystery and Prophecy
        REVELATION 10:1-11:14
        Occurs between the 6th and 7th Trumpets.

3. The Seven Personages - **REVELATION 12:1 - 13:18**

    a. Parenthetical Period of Praise/ Proclamation / Harvest
        REVELATION 14:1- 20
        Occurs between the Seventh Person and
        the First Bowl of Wrath.

4. The Seven Bowls (Vials) of Wrath - **REVELATION 15:1 - 16:21**

    a. Parenthetical Period of Worldwide Deception in Preparation
        for the Battle of Armageddon
        REVELATION 16:13-16
        Occurs between the 6th and 7th Bowls of Wrath.

5. The Seven Dooms - **REVELATION 17:1-20:15**
    include the following:

    a. The Doom of Babylon **(17:1 – 18:24)**

        i.   Parenthetical Period of Rejoicing / The Marriage
             of The Lamb / The Second Coming of Christ / The
             Battle of Armageddon
             REVELATION 19:1-19
             Occurs between the first and 2nd Dooms.

    b. The Doom of the Beast **(19:20)**

    c. The Doom of the False Prophet **(19:20)**

    d. The Doom of the Kings **(19:21)**

        i.   Parenthetical Period of the One Thousand Year
             (Millennial) Reign of Christ — including the
             Binding of Satan in the Abyss and the First
             Resurrection
             REVELATION 20:1-6
             Occurs between the 4th and 5th Dooms.

    e. The Doom of Gog and Magog **(20:7-9)**

    f. The Doom of Satan **(20:10)**

    g. The Doom of the Unbelieving Dead
       (the Last Judgment) **(20:11-15)**

6.   The Seven New Things - **REV. 21:1 - 22:7:**
      The New Heaven **(21:1),**
      The New Earth **(21:1),**
      The New Peoples **(21:3-8),**
      The New Jerusalem **(21:2, 9-21),**
      The New Temple **(21:22),**
      The New Light **(21:23-27),**
      and The New Paradise **(22:1-7).**

As a result of combining the above series of six sevens with the letters to the seven churches, the entire book of *THE REVELATION* is composed of seven sevens, denoting God's completed work of judgment and a Sabbath rest!

LITERARY GENRES

Since God is saying and doing for the last time in this last book of Scripture what God has been saying and doing all along in all of the previous books of Scripture, then it stands to reason that THE REVELATION OF JESUS CHRIST would *reflect a mixture of the various genres of declaration* in which God has indeed spoken to God's people throughout biblical history (cf. Heb 1:1).

It should not surprise us, therefore, to discover that THE REVELATION employs the *prophetic*, the *apocalyptic*,[8] the *epistolary*—or letter form— and the *liturgical/poetic* forms that have characterized all previous declarations of God's revelation of Himself to His people.

Since it is God who is doing the talking from Genesis to THE REVELATION, we would do well to consider that the origin and nature of *prophecy*, as clarified in 2 Peter 1:20-21 (NIV), is equally applicable to the origin and nature of the *apocalyptic*, the *epistolary*, and the *liturgical/poetic* genres that frame the whole of Scripture:

> *Above all, you must understand that **no prophecy** [apocalyptic, epistolary, liturgical/poetic declarations] **of Scripture came about by the prophet's own interpretation.** For prophecy [apocalyptic, epistolary, liturgical/poetic declarations] **never had its** [their] **origin** in the human will, **but prophets, though human, spoke from God as they were carried along by the Holy Spirit. (author's amplifications and emphasis)***

The inclusive nature of God's Authorship of Scripture in its various genres is also validated by the clear declaration in 2 Timothy 3:16-17 (NIV):

8   John J. Collins, DANIEL WITH AN INTRODUCTION TO APOCALYPTIC LITERATURE (Grand Rapids, Michigan: Eerdmans, 1984), 4-5. See John J. Collins' definition of "Apocalypse," as defined by the OT apocalyptic works of Daniel and others but is equally applicable to the Revelation as the NT apocalyptic equivalent.

> *All Scripture is **God-breathed** and is useful for teaching, rebuking, correcting and training in righteousness, so that the servant of God may be thoroughly equipped for every good work. **(author's emphases)***

Given the internal testimony of the above-cited Scriptures, we are not only able to deduce that a mixed genre of literary styles is employed to convey *THE REVELATION*, but that this mixed genre includes numerous allusions[9] to both Old and New Testament Scriptures within *THE REVELATION* text that serve as key to its interpretation. Recognition of an allusion to an OT prophecy in *THE REVELATION* does not deny the OT prophecy's original contextual meaning or fulfillment in ancient Judah/Israel, but rather embraces its potential for future meaning and fulfillment. First Peter 1:10-12 asserts that the OT prophets were aware, albeit incompletely, of the dual nature of some of the prophecies received from the Spirit and made great effort to discern the future import of the prophecies entrusted to them.

> *Concerning this salvation, **the prophets**, who spoke of the grace that was to come to you, searched intently and with the greatest care, **trying to find out the time and circumstances to which the Spirit of Christ in them was pointing** when he predicted the sufferings of the Messiah and the glories that would follow. It was **revealed***

---

9 An allusion is defined as an indirect reference to another Scripture and is different from a direct quote in that it is not formally introduced by any of the following formulaic phrases that are commonly used elsewhere in the New Testament: i.e., "it is written" (Matt 4:4,7,10), "you have heard that it was said by them of old" (Matt 5:21, 27, 33, 38, 43), "it has been said" (Matt 5:31), "which was spoken by the Lord through the prophet" (Matt 1:23), "thus is written by the prophet" (Matt 2:6), "which was spoken by the prophet" (Matt 3:3), etc. An allusion may also be a combined quotation of several Scripture references forming one complete sentence or thought. For example, Rev 1:7 is a combined allusion to Dan 7:13, Isa 40:5, and Zech 12:10. Allusions, or indirect references to other Scriptures, particularly Old Testament Scriptures, are abundant in *THE REVELATION* and assume the reader's familiarity with and knowledge of the Scriptures to which reference is being made.

*to them that they were not serving themselves but you, when they spoke of the things that have now been told you by those who have preached the gospel to you by the Holy Spirit sent from heaven. Even angels long to look into these things. **(author's emphases)***

Though biblical scholars affirm the unmistakable presence of the "mixture of genres" in THE REVELATION,[10] the tendency is to attribute this literary "mixture" to John's efforts and not to the Spirit's inspiration.[11] As 2 Peter 1:20-21 affirms, John was not the source of THE REVELATION but only the human instrument through whom THE REVELATION was transmitted. John, in other words, was instructed "to write" (Rev 1:19) what he would be shown, not to invent it.[12] Furthermore, John affirms that he was "in the Spirit" (Rev. 1:10; 4:2) when he received all that he was shown. Hence, John's affirmation concurs with God's declaration that "prophets, though human, spoke from God as they were carried along by the Holy Spirit" (2 Peter 1:21).

A brief survey of each genre will help us to appreciate how God employed the unique mixture of the prophetic, the apocalyptic, the epistolary, and the liturgical/poetic forms to unveil this final revelation of His Son as well as the culmination of salvation and human history:

PROPHECY (REV 1:3, 19:10, 22:7, 18-19)

THE REVELATION is confirmed as a prophetic work by the self-labeling use of the term 'prophecy' in these verses. In the prophetic tradition, THE REVELATION conveys God's perspective on the spiritual state of His people

---

10   D. A. Carson and Douglas J. Moo, AN INTRODUCTION TO THE NEW TESTAMENT (Grand Rapids, Michigan: Zondervan, 1992, 2005), 713-716. Read footnotes #61-68 for additional references to the scholarly discussion on the mixture of genres in the book of the Revelation.

11   Ibid.

12   John is given twelve (12) commands to write (Rev 1:11, 19; 2:1, 8, 12, 18; 3:1, 7, 14; 14:13; 19:9; 21:5) and one prohibition not to write (Rev 10:4). Note other prophets who were commanded to write what had been revealed to them: Moses (Exod 17:14; 34:27-28), Isaiah (30:8), Jeremiah (30:2; 36:2, 28), Ezekiel (43:11), Habakkuk (2:2).

and the world, with commendations for faithfulness and repentance, as well as warnings of judgment against unfaithfulness and unbelief. As many of the prophetic works of the OT (Old Testament) communicate God's wrath against the unfaithful and the unbeliever, so THE REVELATION consummates this intent, first towards the church in her various states of apostasy (1 Peter 4:17-18) and then toward the world in its abject state of sinfulness.

APOCALYPTIC (REV 1:1)

The word 'apocalypse' is translated from the Greek as 'revelation' in both the title and in this verse. The use of the word here is an allusion[13] to Daniel 2:28-29, where 'apocalypse' *(in the various Greek translations of the OT)* is used multiple times in its verbal form to convey the transmission of a prophetic revelation directly from God to Daniel. The book of Daniel is, in fact, the OT equivalent to THE REVELATION as an apocalyptic work. Much of the imagery in THE REVELATION can be interpreted by the imagery in Daniel, as well as by that found in Ezekiel, Isaiah, Zechariah, the Psalms, and several of the other prophets. Each of these prophetic books contains apocalyptic material that will be alluded to throughout THE REVELATION text. THE REVELATION, therefore, is considered an "apocalyptic-prophetic work," which, like the aforementioned prophets, combines both genres as an intensified revelation from God.[14] Though the apocalypse as a genre has a technical definition,[15] suffice it to say

---

13 Remember: an allusion is an indirect quote without a formulaic introduction, e.g., "for it is written," etc.).

14 G. K. Beale, THE BOOK OF REVELATION (Grand Rapids, MI: Eerdmans Publishing Company, 1999), 37-38.

15 John J. Collins, a noted scholar on the Apocalypse, has defined this genre, as follows: "Apocalypse is a genre of revelatory literature with a narrative framework, in which a revelation is mediated by an otherworldly being to a human recipient, disclosing a transcendent reality, which is both temporal, insofar as it envisages eschatological salvation, and spatial, insofar as it involves another, supernatural world" ("Introduction: Towards a Morphology of a Genre," Semeia 14 (1979), 5-8).

that one of the key features of this "apocalyptic-prophetic" genre is its abundant presentation of imagery, as is apparent, for example, in the prophetic books of both Daniel and Ezekiel. Another key feature is a closer look at the source of the revelation, i.e., "God's throne room in the heavenly temple."[16] Though we receive Old Testament glimpses of God's throne and the heavenly temple in Isaiah's call (Isa 6:1) and in Ezekiel's visions (Ezekiel 1. - 2.), we receive greater revelation of God's throne in *THE REVELATION* text with regard to the activity of praise that surrounds it as well as to the activity of judgment that issues from it.

EPISTLE (REV 1:4-8; 2:1, 8, 12, 18; 3:1, 7, 14; 22:21)

THE REVELATION begins and ends in the typical form of a New Testament letter.[17] The epistolary dynamic is re-enforced in the addresses to the seven churches of Asia—all of which are in letter form and are the result of Jesus' command to John to write to each congregation. Since the "main purpose of the epistolary genre elsewhere in the NT is to address problems that have arisen in the various churches . . . then its purpose likewise, [in *THE REVELATION*] is to address contemporary problems among the seven churches by appealing to the hearers' present and future share in Christ's blessings."[18]

LITURGY/ PRAISE & WORSHIP (REV 4:8-11, 5:8-14, 7:11-12, 11:15-18, 14:1-5, 15:2-4, 19:1-8)

As has already been mentioned, one of the key features of the "apocalyptic-prophetic" genre is its closer view of "God's throne room in the heavenly temple,"[19] where the activities of worship and praise

---

16 Beale, *THE BOOK OF REVELATION*, 38.

17 Ibid., 39.

18 Ibid 39.

19 Ibid., 38

as well as of judgment are abundantly evident. These seven (7) cited instances of praise and worship in *THE REVELATION*[20] serve the same purpose in the heavenly throne room as the Psalms served to under gird God's praise and worship by God's people in an earthly tabernacle or Temple. These seven cited heavenly instances of praise and worship also mirror the seven Christological hymns in the New Testament in which Jesus is praised as Redeemer: John 1:1-5, 10-12, 14, 16; Ephesians 2:14-16; Colossians 1:15-20; Philippians 2:6-11; 1 Timothy 3:16; Hebrews 1:3; 1 Peter 3:18-19, 22. Since Jesus has now ascended back to the Right Hand of the Father's Throne and is now seated on His own throne, then praise and worship are accorded to both the Father and the Son in *THE REVELATION* text (cf. John 5:22).

In summary, each genre will be evident throughout *THE REVELATION* text, thus making the genre of this last book of Scripture mixed and unique: "If a letter, it is like no other early Christian letter we possess. If an apocalypse, it is like no other apocalypse. If a prophecy, it is unique among prophecies."[21]

---

20   Krause, Mark S. (x009) "The Seven Hymns of Revelation 4, 5 and 7," Leaven: Vol 17: Iss. 4, Art. 6. Krause divides the seven hymns that occur in Chapters 4, 5 and 7, as follows: Hymn 1: Rev 4:8; Hymn 2: Rev 4:10-11; Hymn 3: Rev 5:8, 9; Hymn 4: Rev 5:11, 12; Hymn 5: Rev 5:13, 14; Hymn 6: Rev 7:9, 10; and Hymn 7: Rev 7:11, 12. This author has also included the Hymns found in 11:15-18; 14:1-5; 15:2-4; 19:1-8, for a total of 11 hymns. Krause also offers excellent discussion and resources on the interpretation of the Greek word λέγοντες (pronounced lĕ'-gŏn-tĕs), which is inconsistently translated "saying" or "singing" in most English translations. However, whether spoken or sung, God's praises are indefatigably declared by the heavenly court. It is easy to imagine a singing choir; consider the majesty of a spoken word choir!

21   J. Ramsay Michaels, *INTERPRETING THE BOOK OF REVELATION*, (Grand Rapids, MI: Baker, 1992), 31-32.

PROLEGOMENA

(PREAMBLE)

REVELATION 1:1-3

1:1 The revelation from Jesus Christ which God gave him to show his servants what must soon take place. He made it known by sending his angel to his servant John, 2 Who testifies to everything he saw – that is, the word of God and the testimony of Jesus Christ. 3 Blessed is the one who reads aloud the words of this prophecy, and blessed are those who hear it and take to heart what is written in it, because the time is near.

THE FIRST THREE VERSES OF *THE REVELATION* serve as the preamble to the entire book. Though the exegetical treatment of these first three verses will be undertaken in the following chapter, they are initially examined here for the following seven introductory insights they afford into this last book of Scripture: The Definition, the Subject, the Source, the Purpose, the Recipient, the Blessing, and the Urgency.

The **Definition** of the book is derived from the Greek word αποκάλυψις (pronounced â-poc-â´-lūp-sees), from which we get the English word 'apocalypse.' Translated in both the title and in the first verse as 'revelation,' the term constitutes an allusion to Daniel 2:28-29, both linguistically and contextually. Linguistically, the Greek word is used multiple times in the Greek translation (Septuagint) of the Daniel text to convey the transmission of a prophetic and direct 'revelation' from God to Daniel.

Contextually, the Greek word is used as prologue to Daniel's God-given explanation of King Nebuchadnezzar's dream of a great statue composed of various metals that was destroyed by a stone cut out without hands. The vision and the interpretation of the dream were given to Daniel as God's 'revelation' of His ultimate judgment upon all the Gentile kingdoms of the world. Likewise, the use of αποκάλυψις in *THE REVELATION* text bears the same linguistic and contextual connotations as that found in Daniel: for the current book is the direct 'revelation' from Jesus to John, and the 'revelation' is of the One who is coming to judge the kingdom of this world. Hence, *THE REVELATION* is defined as the New Testament equivalent to the Daniel text as an apocalyptic work.

The **Subject** of *THE REVELATION*, therefore, is Jesus Christ. Pertaining to His office as Judge, Jesus Himself declares, "Moreover, the Father judges no one, but has entrusted all judgment to the Son . . . and He has given Him authority to judge, because he is the Son of Man" (John 5:22, 27).

The **Source** of *THE REVELATION* is God the Father: for it is the revelation "which God gave Him [Jesus]." A fuller discussion of the nature of this communication between Father and Son will be presented in the following exegetical treatment.

The **Purpose** of *THE REVELATION* is for Jesus "to show His servants . . . " The Greek verb δεῖξαι (pronounced **day'**-xī), translated 'to show,' forms a perfect complement to the Greek αποκάλυψις (pronounced â-poc-â'-lūp-sees), as the apocalyptic genre is characterized by the abundant 'showings' of signs, symbols and imagery. However, much of what John will be shown will trigger associations with and allusions to visions given in the Old Testament that will serve as key to their current use and interpretation. Additionally, the visions John will see are not just for him, but are to be shared with Jesus' servants, the body of Christ, as represented in its worldwide scope by the seven churches of Asia.

As has already been implied in the previous discussion, John is the chosen **Recipient** of *THE REVELATION*. Though there is much scholarly debate as to the identity of John, the assertion in this volume is that the recipient of *THE REVELATION* is the same John who wrote the last Gospel and the three Epistles that bear his name. Though scholars have contended that the use of language and the writing style of John's previous works do not resemble the use of language and the writing style in *THE REVELATION*, this writer and others[22] are persuaded that the difference can be creditably attributed to the difference in genre, i.e., gospel narrative or letters vs. a unique and mixed combination of prophetic utterances, apocalyptic images, epistles and liturgy.[23] This writer also bases the assertion of John's identity upon the theological evidence from John's previous works that is alluded to in *THE REVELATION* text. This internal evidence will be presented in support of John's identity throughout the exegetical sections of this work.

A **Blessing** is pronounced upon those who read aloud, hear and take to heart the words written in *THE REVELATION*. The Greek word translated 'read' implies reading aloud or reading in public worship. The Greek word translated 'hear' bears the same root meaning as that used for the 'hearing' that sires our faith and that comes by the Word of Christ (Rom 10:17). The Greek word translated 'take to heart' carries the following multiple, yet synonymous, meanings: to observe, to obey, to pay attention to, to keep under guard, to keep firm. In summary, the blessing is conferred upon those who will read aloud, hear by faith, and obey what is heard of the words of this prophecy.

Lastly, the **Urgency** of the events that will be disclosed in vision to

---

22   Beale, *THE BOOK OF THE REVELATION*, 34-35; Robert H. Mounce, *THE BOOK OF REVELATION: REVISED EDITION* (Grand Rapids, MI: Eerdmans, 1977), 15, 23: see footnotes in both references for additional corroboration and controversy.

23   See discussion on "mixed genres" in the Overview.

John are expressed as "what must soon take place." This note of urgency constitutes another significant allusion to Daniel 2:28-29 and 45, where the phrases "what will happen in the days to come" (2:28), "what is going to happen" (2:29), and "what will take place in the future" (2:45) express the same idea. The difference, however, is that Daniel was told to seal up the full content of the revelations entrusted to him until the time of the end (Dan 12:4, 9; cf. 9:14). Jesus, on the other hand, announces that what is to come will soon take place. Jesus later instructs John not to seal

> "the words of the prophecy of this scroll, because **the time is near**" (Rev 22:10, **author's emphasis**).

A similar note of urgency is articulated in verse 3 and in Rev 22:10, i.e., "because the time is near." A fuller discussion of what time is near will be presented under the exegetical treatments of these verses.

COMMENTARY

CHAPTER ONE

PROLOGUE
REVELATION 1:1-3

1 The revelation from Jesus Christ which God gave him to show his servants what must soon take place. He made it known by sending his angel to his servant John, 2 Who testifies to everything he saw – that is, the word of God and the testimony of Jesus Christ. 3 Blessed is the one who reads aloud the words of this prophecy, and blessed are those who hear it and take to heart what is written in it, because the time is near.

VERSE 1

"The revelation from[24] Jesus Christ which God gave him to show his servants what must soon take place. He made it known by sending his angel to his servant John,"

THE MOST NOTEWORTHY OBSERVATION IN THE first two phrases of this first verse is that *THE REVELATION* was given to Jesus (Him) by God the Father! What this clearly indicates is that there is direct communication between the Members of the Godhead! Though this may seem an obvious

---

24 The Greek genitive construction of Jesus' Name allows the translation of the preposition to be either *"of"* or *"from."* Both work.

truth, it would be too easy to assume that, since the Father, the Son, and the Holy Spirit are One, their need for direct communication would be unnecessary. However, there are several references which plainly indicate that each Member of the Godhead is informed of the Will and the Intent of the Other only by **hearing and receiving** it from the Other!

Consider, for example, that in clarifying the ministry of the Holy Spirit, Jesus stated that the Holy Spirit "will not speak on His own; He will speak only what he hears . . . the Spirit will take from what is mine and will make it known to you . . . " (John 16:13b, 14b). In other words, the Holy Spirit reveals to us only what He has heard and received from Jesus. Additionally, Jesus declared of His own ministry that it was not of His own making, but rather the revelation of what He had both seen and heard from the Father:

What is remarkable about the intra-communication system between the Members of the Godhead is that it is premised upon the same principle by which faith is sired in the believer: "So *faith* comes from *what is heard,* and what is heard comes through the *word of Christ*" (Rom. 10:17, author's emphases)! In other words, even within the Godhead, each Member must hear and receive BY FAITH what the Other is saying! There should be little wonder, therefore, that "*without faith it is impossible to please God...*" (Heb. 11:6a, *author's emphases*): for it is the very foundation of the communication between the Father, the Son, and the Holy Spirit! It is amazing that the Triune God has required no more of us than what He Himself does! This should inspire us to re-visit the faith passages of Scripture with a fresh anointing upon our understanding!

For I did not speak on my own, but the Father who sent me **commanded me to say all that I have spoken.** *I know that His command leads to eternal life. So* **whatever I say is just what the Father has told me to say** *(John 12:49-50; cf. 6:38; 7:16; 8:28- 9,38A; 14:10, 24,* **author's emphases***).*

Of particular note is Jesus' prophetic declaration that the Father has even greater things to show Him (Jesus) than that which the Father had already revealed to Him:

Jesus gave them this answer: 'Very truly I tell you, **the Son can do nothing by himself; he can do only what he sees his Father doing, because whatever the Father does the Son also does.** *For the Father loves the Son and shows him* **(the Son)** *all he* **(the Father)** *does. Yes, and* **he (the Father) will show him (the Son) even greater works than these,** *so that you will be amazed' (John 5:19-20 -* **author's emphases and clarifying insertions***).*

The implication in these verses is two-fold. Jesus, on the one hand, is affirming His Father's Sovereignty over what He (Jesus) currently knows and does; and, on the other hand, Jesus is confessing His own submission to His Father's prerogative to reveal to Him what He (Jesus) has yet to know and do. **In both cases, Jesus is acknowledging His Father as the sole source of the Revelation of who He (Jesus) is and of what He (Jesus) has yet to do!**

The fact that the Father has more to reveal to Jesus ("greater things than these") clearly implies that Jesus has more to hear and receive from the Father concerning *THE REVELATION* of Himself! The begging question is this: **What was it that the Father had yet to reveal to Jesus concerning Himself?** The answer is **this current Revelation which is being given in this last book of Scripture, and in which all the dynamics of Jesus' second coming are disclosed!** The truth of this is evidenced and anticipated in

Jesus' own prophetic declaration concerning this culminating event of salvation and human history:

> *But about that day or hour no one knows, not even the angels in heaven, nor the Son, but only the Father (Mark 13:32, author's emphases).*

In the Wisdom of God, therefore, **Jesus knew what He did not know,** i.e., the day nor the hour of His own return. However, through faith in God His Father, Jesus the Son **knew that what He had yet to know of this matter would come solely from His Father!** And so it does, as these first two phrases of *THE REVELATION* text reveal!

As was introduced in the previous section (see **Prolegomena**), the purpose of the Father's revelation to Jesus was/is "to show to His servants what must soon take place . . . " Though Jesus uttered lengthy prophecies during His earthly ministry concerning the end times and His second coming (Matt. 24:3-25:46; Mark 13:3-37; Luke 21:7-36), these, in hindsight, were but snapshots of that which would now be more fully revealed to His servants, the churches. Before Jesus' Ascension, His disciples inquired concerning the restoration of the kingdom to Israel; but Jesus replied that "it is not for you to know the times or dates the Father has set by his own authority" (Acts 1:6-7). However, as the Father is now revealing to His Son Jesus the ultimate revelation of all times and of all seasons, so Jesus is charged with revealing the same ultimate revelation to His servants (cf. Rev. 22:6; John 15:15)!

The servant chosen to initially hear and receive this ultimate revelation of Jesus Christ is **John**. As previously mentioned, (see **Prolegomena**), there is much scholarly debate as to the identity of John. However, this writer is fully persuaded, by the internal evidence of Scripture, that this John is the same John who wrote the last Gospel Narrative and the three Epistles that bear his name; who was with Jesus on the Mount of Transfiguration (Matt 17:1-2; Mark 9:2; Luke 9:28-

29); who leaned upon His Breast at the Last Supper (John 13:23-25, 21:20); who was the only male disciple present at Jesus' Crucifixion (John 19:26-27); who, with Peter, was the first of the remaining eleven disciples to view the empty tomb (John 20:3-8); who saw, heard, and ate with Jesus during His post-Resurrection ministry (Matt 28:16-20; Mark 16:14-20; Luke 24:33-53; John 21:1-2, 7, 20-24); who was among the eyewitnesses of Jesus' Ascension (Acts 1:9-11); and who, indeed, received the Holy Spirit while tarrying with the disciples in the Upper Room, in Jerusalem, on the Day of Pentecost (Acts 1:12-14; 2:1-4)! The internal evidence of Scripture to support John's identity will be provided throughout the exegetical treatment of *THE REVELATION* text.

It is to John, the beloved disciple, that Jesus sends His "angel" to signify or to show all that he will see and hear. Though the divine prerogative of commissioning angels to convey God's revelation to His servants is well attested in both the Old and New Testaments, the identity of this "angel" deserves special attention. First, the angel is identified as Jesus' angel under Jesus' command, i.e., "He sent . . . His angel." This observation, on the surface, may seem obvious, as all angels are subject to both Jesus and to the Father (cf. Heb 1:4-7). However, the text does not say that Jesus sent "an angel," but that He sent "His angel," suggesting, through the use of the possessive pronoun (His), a more intimate relationship between the angel and Jesus. Secondly, the angel is being sent by Jesus to John: "He sent . . . His angel to His servant, John." This, too, may appear an obvious observation, inasmuch as all angels are designated as ministers to the heirs of salvation (cf. Heb. 1:13-14). And thirdly, the angel is being sent by Jesus to John, His servant, to "show (or to reveal) what must soon take place." Angels have been sent in the past to reveal what God was going to do before He did it (cf. Gen 18:17; Dan 10:14), and such is the case in this current context.

Given the above three-fold delineation of this angel's identity and ministry, coupled with John's own testimony that

"On the Lord's Day I was in the Spirit" *(Rev. 1:10, **author's emphasis**)*

when he heard and received THE REVELATION, then we can safely conclude that this "angel" is none other than the Holy Spirit: for the Holy Spirit, a.k.a. the Spirit of Truth, is indeed sent by Jesus (John 15:26; 16:7); He is indeed sent to all believers (Acts 2:1-4, 10:44-48); and He is indeed sent "to teach [us] all things and . . . remind [us] of everything I have said to you" (John 14:26), to "guide [us] into all truth" (John 16: 13a), and *"to tell [us] what is yet to come"* (John 16:13c; 1 Cor. 2:9-12; Eph. 3:1-5, *author's emphases and clarifying insertions*)! This conclusion, regarding this angel's identity as the Holy Spirit, is further endorsed by Jesus' reference to this same angel as "My angel" in the last chapter of THE REVELATION:

> It is I, Jesus, who sent **My angel** to you with this testimony for the churches" *(Rev 22:16a, **author's emphasis**)*

Though the appropriation of the term "angel" to the Holy Spirit in this instance is unique to THE REVELATION text, it is itself revelation knowledge that finds its parallel in Jesus' pre-incarnate manifestation as the Angel of the LORD or the Angel of God in the OT (cf. Gen 16:7, 9, 22:11, 48:16; Exod 3:2, 14:19, 23:20-23; Num 22:22-27, 31-35; Judg 2:4, 6:11, 13:3; 2 Kings 19:35; Isa 63:9; Zech 1:11-12, 12:8). Since John will receive from the Spirit what to write to each angel of the seven churches, then it is safe to assume that the Holy Spirit is as much in command over the host of angelic emissaries as God the Father and Jesus the Son, and can take on the form of an angel to carry out His ministry in the New Testament, like Jesus did in the Old Testament. We can further note that it is not to an angel, or heavenly emissary, but to the Spirit – Jesus' Angel - that each church is commanded to have an ear to hear. As Jesus' Angel, the Spirit is the Source and the Communicator of each letter through John to each angel, or heavenly emissary, of the seven churches.

VERSE 2

"Who testifies to everything he saw – that is, the word of God and the testimony of Jesus Christ."

John's faithfulness to what he had already seen and heard during Jesus' earthly ministry had evidently qualified him, in the divine mind, to receive this ultimate revelation of his Lord! He, in the words of the text, had been a faithful witness "to the Word of God and to the Testimony of Jesus Christ," and is credited with this same faithfulness to all that he would be shown, i.e., "who testifies to everything he saw." Such faithfulness is the high call of every believer as "the servants of Christ," and especially of those who are accounted worthy to be called

> **"stewards of God's mysteries.** *Moreover, it is required of stewards that they be* **found trustworthy"** *(1 Cor. 4:1-2 NRSV, author's emphases)!*

What begins, therefore, as an internal disclosure between the Father and the Son is, in turn, transmitted by the Holy Spirit to a faithful servant, through whom THE REVELATION is both published and proclaimed! For by faith, John must hear and receive all that will be shown to him, so that others may read, hear, and take to heart all that is contained in THE REVELATION OF JESUS CHRIST! Such has been the divine design for disclosing the divine mind down through the ages (Deut. 5:22-31, 18:15-19; 2 Kings 17:13; 2 Chron. 24:19; Isa. 6:1-13; Jer. 1:1-19, 7:13,25-26, 25:3-4,26:1-7, 29:19, 32:33, 35:14-15, 44:4-5; Ezek. 1:1-3, 2:1-3:27; Dan. 2:19-23; Matt. 16:13-18; 1 Cor. 2:9-16; Heb. 1:1-3; 2 Peter 1:19-21), and, at the last, is a fitting testimony to the truth that

*"Surely the Sovereign LORD does nothing without revealing **his plan to his servants the prophets**" (Amos 3:7, **author's emphasis**)!*

It would be appropriate at this point to examine how God goes about creating a witness in the earth to heavenly truth. According to His divine prerogative and down through the ages, our Heavenly Father has consistently demonstrated that in order for Him, who dwells in heaven, to get things done in the earth, He must have agreement in the earth (1 John 5:5-11). And in order to get agreement in the earth, the Father has to reveal the heavenly truth that is to be agreed upon. That heavenly truth, a.k.a. revelation knowledge, is then conveyed from God by the Holy Spirit, to a vessel that has been specially chosen (Acts 10:41) and prepared by God to receive and believe the revelation. Once the spirit of the chosen vessel has received and believed the revelation, the Holy Spirit then empowers that vessel with the ability to proclaim that revelation into the earth's atmosphere, thus establishing a witness of agreement in the earth to a heavenly truth!

The biblical text fully attests that through the various and sundry ways in which God spoke or revealed Himself in the past (Heb 1:1-2) — whether through an angel sent to earth with a heavenly message (Judg 13:3-5), or through a prophet who proclaimed "Thus says the LORD" (Isa 66:1; Jer 9:23; Ezek 5:5; Amos 5:4), or even through the mouth of a donkey that was given the good sense to see the angel of the LORD in the road (Num 22:28-33), and whether a heavenly truth was revealed in a vision (Ezek 1:1-28; Dan 8:1-17) or a dream (Dan 4:4-18; 7:1-14) — no matter which vessel or what method God chose in times past, the process was always the same: the revelation proceeded from God, was conveyed by the Holy Spirit, was received into the spirit of a chosen vessel, was believed on in the heart of the vessel, and was then articulated with the vessel's mouth into the earth's atmosphere.

We would not be belaboring the point to consider that the principle and the significance of the Father's need to establish a witness to the ultimate Revelation of His Son in the earth is recorded 1 John 5:5-11, which declares that there are three (3) witnesses that agree in the earth that Jesus is the Son of God: "For there are three that testify: the Spirit, the water, and the blood; and the three are in agreement" (1 John 5:7-8). We can safely deduce that the Spirit in this verse is the same Holy Spirit whom God poured out upon the 120 believers on the Day of Pentecost to be witnesses unto Jesus. But what is the identity of the water and the blood witnesses that must agree with the Spirit's witness here on earth?

With a little detective work, the identity of the water and blood witnesses can be gleaned from three (3) references: Luke 1:34-35; John 19:34 and 1 John 5:6:

1. **Luke 1:34-35** records Mary's visitation from the angel Gabriel:

   *"'How will this be,' Mary asked the angel, 'since I am a virgin?' The angel answered, '**The Holy Spirit** will come on you, and the power of the Most High will overshadow you. So the holy one to be born will be called Son of God'"* **(author's emphasis).**

In other words, God sent the angel Gabriel, from His Presence, down to the earth, not only to reveal to Mary that she had been chosen by God to be the Mother of His only begotten Son and how that would happen, but also to secure Mary's agreement to allow her womb to be the host of that holy child who would be conceived in her by the overpowering presence of the Holy Spirit. Needless to say, if God had not secured her agreement, this holy activity would have been perpetrated in her against her will. God forbid! However, when Mary articulated her response into the earth's atmosphere, "I am the Lord's servant . . . May it be to me as you have said" (Luke 1:38), the Father then had her agreement in the earth to manifest His only begotten Son through the seed of a woman, as previously promised (Gen 3:15) and prophesied (Isa 7:14). With her consent, Mary, in truth, surrendered the water and blood of her own humanity to the Spirit's activity in the birthing process — thus making her a bona fide witness in the earth to the Incarnation of the Son of God, with all three elements of agreement in tact — the Spirit, the water and the blood. As a result, that Holy Child who would be born of her would also be composed of all three (3) witnesses that agree in the earth — the Spirit, by whom He was sired, and the water and blood of Mary's humanity! This is why Jesus, the Son of God, could assert that, even in His humanity, He and the Father are One (John 10:30), because in His Incarnation Jesus constituted the earthly equivalent (the Spirit, the water and the blood) to the heavenly witness (the Father, the Word, and the Spirit) to Himself![25] This is the first clue as to the identity of the water and blood witnesses that **must agree with the Spirit's witness in the earth!** Moving from the cradle to the Cross, our 2nd clue is given in . . .

2.   **John 19:34** – where this same John records what issued from Jesus' pierced body on Calvary:

> *"Instead, one of the soldiers pierced Jesus' side with a spear, bringing a sudden flow of **blood and water**." (**author's emphasis**)*

In other words, Jesus' death mirrored the same elements that constituted His birth from Mary's womb when He shed both blood and water from Calvary's cross, while still full of the Spirit (remember: Jesus did not commend His Spirit into the Father's hands until His

---

25   Though the NRSV, the NIV, the NASB, and the Holman CSB translations do not include the three witnesses that agree in heaven, i.e., the Father, the Word, and the Holy Spirit within the text of 1 John 5:7-8, each does cite in a footnote on these verses that a few later manuscripts do include the heavenly witnesses. However, the heavenly witnesses are included in the text of the KJV and the NLT. The Amplified Bible also includes the heavenly witnesses within the text, but also footnotes its reference to later manuscripts as the source.

seventh and last Word from Calvary – Luke 23:46). The update is that these same elements, i.e., blood and water, characterized Jesus' death as a birthing process, which would indeed result in the new birth of a redeemed humanity composed of all three elements of the earthly witness to who He is: a humanity who, by faith, would be washed in the flow of His blood (1 Peter 1:18-19; Rev 7:14), cleansed by the water of His word (John 15:3; Eph 5:26), and filled with the power of His Holy Spirit (Acts 2:1-4; 4:31)!

This is the 2nd clue as to the identity of the water and blood witnesses that must agree with the Spirit's witness in the earth! And our 3rd clue can be found in . . .

3.   **1 John 5:6** - where John's testimony to Jesus is that He was

> "... the One who **came by water and blood** - Jesus Christ. He did not come by water only, but by **water and blood**. And it is **the Spirit who testifies**, because the Spirit is the truth" (author's emphases)

In other words, John validates the previously-cited evidence that Jesus came into the world, dwelt among us, and exited out of the world with the presence and agreement of all three earthly witnesses in tact: the Spirit, the water, and the blood.

Now when we consider that all three clues refer to Jesus' bodily existence among us, and when we consider that all human flesh – which is the same flesh that Jesus took on among us - is composed of at least 50-60% water, and has blood as its life principal – then let's do the math: The Holy Spirit + any one of us in our water-and-blood flesh who believes = the 3 witnesses that agree on earth that Jesus is the Son of God!

The amazing grace toward us in this equation is that the believing child of God, as an earthen vessel of water and blood, constitutes two-thirds of the three witnesses that must agree in the earth! And it is within these earthen vessels of water and blood that the Spirit, the third member of agreement, takes up residence, in order to complete and empower our witness to Jesus in the earth! This is why Jesus instructed the disciples to tarry for the Spirit before witnessing, so that they could receive the Spirit's power to do so (Luke 24:48-49; Acts 1:8). And as Jesus was, so was John, and so are we who believe: Spirit-filled, water-and-blood vessels, who constitute the three (3) witnesses in the earth that agree that "Jesus is the Christ, the Son of the Living God" (Matt 16:16)!

It is worthy to note that the fraction of two-thirds (⅔) is not an arbitrary fraction in God's witnessing equation. Revelation 14:4 tells us that Lucifer, a.k.a. Satan, drew only one third (⅓) of the stars, or angels, in that angelic rebellion that took place in heaven before the creation of the world. What this means is that two-thirds (⅔) of the angels chose to remain faithful to God and, in fact, constitute the 10,000 x 10,000 and thousands of thousands of angels who surround the Father's throne (Deut 33:2; Dan 7:10b; Rev 5:11). It is apparent, therefore, that in His witnessing business, God has seen fit to reflect the witness of the remaining ⅔ of His faithful angelic host in heaven with the two-thirds witness of any one flesh-and-blood believer within the human family on earth! And since the Holy Spirit constitutes the essential and indispensable third component of agreement in both the heavenly and earthly witness to Jesus, then the witness unto Jesus is both proclaimed and sustained in heaven (Rev 5:11) and in the earth (Acts 1:8) by the Holy Spirit's power! For this reason, Jesus could declare with all accuracy that " . . . there is joy in the presence of the angels of God over one sinner who repents (Luke 15:10)," because the Spirit-empowered witness of just one believing child of God on the earth is equivalent to the Spirit-empowered witness of the entire angelic host in heaven! As the sustainer of both the heavenly and earthly witnesses unto Jesus, it should not be difficult to understand why the only unforgivable sin is blasphemy against the Holy Spirit:

> *And so I tell you, but blasphemy against the Spirit will not be forgiven. Anyone who speaks a word against the Son of Man will be forgiven, but anyone who speaks against the Holy Spirit will not be forgiven, either in this age or in the age to come (Matt 12:31-32; cf. Mark 3:29; cp. 1 John 5:16-17)*

John is clearly and currently engaged in God's age-old business of creating a witness of agreement in the earth to the ultimate revelation of Jesus Christ: for THE REVELATION proceeded from God the Father to God the Son; was conveyed by God the Holy Spirit to a specially chosen and prepared vessel in the earth named John; was received into John's spirit and believed on in his heart; and was published by John, in the power of the Holy Spirit, so that it could be proclaimed by the power of that same Holy Spirit into the earth's atmosphere until Jesus comes again!

VERSE 3

"Blessed is the one who reads aloud the words of this prophecy, and blessed are those who hear it and take to heart what is written in it, because the time is near."

Blessing is pronounced upon those who will read aloud, hear, and take to heart (observe and do) the things written in THE REVELATION, thus implying that this last book of Scripture was always intended to be understood. The difficulties that accompany these three tasks are not to be denied. The text, for example, will be difficult to read, due to the vast amount of imagery contained in it. The text will also be difficult to hear, due to the horrific accounts of judgment that will unfold. And the text will be difficult to take to heart or observe, as the believer who seeks to do so will indeed incur the most vehement opposition from the spirit of the antichrist, which is already in the world (1 John 2:18,22; 4:1-6; 2 John

7). Each of these difficulties has, unfortunately, served as the prevailing reason for neglecting the study of this book. However, embedded in each area of difficulty are the seeds of blessing for those who will read aloud, hear, and observe this ultimate Prophecy with the diligence that befits both the faith and the faithful (2 Tim. 2:15; Heb. 11:6)!

This same blessing is pronounced in the last chapter of *THE REVELATION* but is summarily directed to the one who "keeps (observes, does) the words of the prophecy of this book" (Rev. 22:7). The counsel of Scripture unanimously affirms that it is the doer of the Word who is wise (Matt. 7:24-27); who possesses a good understanding (Ps. 111:10); who is not deceived (James 1:22-25); and who is justified (Rom. 2:13). Such was the requirement of those who were given the Law (Deut. 28:1-2, 15; 29:20); and such is the requirement of those who will "be called great in the Kingdom of Heaven" (Matt. 5:19)! Hence, *THE REVELATION* commences and concludes with the divine blessing that has and will always accompany obedience to God's revealed will!

As we have already noted, (see *Prolegomena*), verse 3 ends on a **note of urgency**, "because the time is near," which is again echoed in the last chapter of *THE REVELATION* (cf. Rev. 22:10b). When we consider that John both received and recorded *THE REVELATION* around A.D. 95, then this note of urgency has actually characterized every generation since then, including our own! The begging question is 'What time is near?' This question is addressed only in part by Jesus' answer to His disciples' question before His Ascension: "Lord, are you at this time going to restore the kingdom to Israel?" (Acts 1:6). Jesus answered, "It is not for you to know the times or dates that the Father has set by His own authority" (Acts 1:7). What the disciples were not to know at that time is fully revealed to John in *THE REVELATION OF JESUS CHRIST*, when the Father reveals that the time that is near is eight-fold in character:

1. The time of the full manifestation of the son of perdition and of the mystery of iniquity - (2 Thess. 2:1-12; Rev. 13:1-18)

2. The time of Jacob's trouble, or, The Great Tribulation - (Jer.30:7; Dan.12:1c; Matt. 24:21; Mark 13:19)

3. The time of the end of the times of the Gentiles - (Luke 21:24)

4. The time of the saving of the Jewish Remnant and the multitude of believing Gentiles - (Isa. 11:11-16; 56:6-8; Jer. 16:14-16; 23:7-8; Ezek. 37:21-28; Joel 2:32; Micah 2:12; 4:1-2,6-8; John 10:16; 17: 20- 21; Rev. 7:1-17; 14:1-5)

5. The time of the second coming of Jesus Christ - (Rev. 19:11-21)

6. The time of the Millennial Reign of Christ upon the earth - (Rev. 11:15; 20:1-6)

7. The time of the Final Dispensation of God's Judgment - (Rev. 20:7-15)

8. The time of the ushering in of the New Heavens and the New Earth - (Rev. 21:1-22:5)!

THE REVELATION, therefore, is, in truth, the consummate fulfillment of every time-honored covenant, prophecy, and promise made by God with His creation! All human history has been moving toward this time, which, by Divine Revelation, is near and now at hand!

SALUTATIONS TO THE SEVEN CHURCHES FROM THE GODHEAD AND JOHN'S DOXOLOGY

REVELATION 1:4-8

4 John, to the seven churches in the province of Asia: Grace and peace to you from him who is, and who was, and who is to come, and from the seven spirits before his throne, 5 and from Jesus Christ, who is the faithful witness, the firstborn from the dead, and the ruler of the kings of the earth. To him who loves us and freed us from our sins by his blood, 6 and has made us to be a kingdom and priests to serve his God and Father — to him be glory and power for ever and ever. Amen. 7 Look! He is coming with the clouds, and every eye will see him, even those who pierced him; and all peoples on earth will mourn because of him. So shall it be. Amen. 8 "I am the Alpha and the Omega," says the Lord God, "who is, and who was, and who is to come, the Almighty.

VERSE 4

"John, to the seven churches in the province of Asia: Grace and peace to you from him who is, and who was, and who is to come, and from the seven spirits before his throne,"

AS IS THE CASE IN THE majority of the New Testament letters, both the writer (John) and the recipients (seven churches) of THE REVELATION are plainly identified. Further clarification as to the identity of both will be taken up in verses 9-11. At this point, however, it is worthy to note that the actual salutation, "Grace and peace to you," is immediately followed by the preposition 'from', indicating that John is both the recipient and the scribe through whom THE REVELATION is being processed for the benefit of the seven churches. As this same salutation can be found, in some variation, in at least seventeen of the New Testament letters, so is found the consistent use of this preposition in denoting the writer to be both the recipient and the scribe of the revelation received 'from' God for the benefit of God's people. A similar indicator is repeatedly expressed by the Old Testament prophets, in such phrases as "Thus says the Lord," or "The Word of the Lord came unto me, saying . . .," indicating that each prophet was both recipient and proclaimer/scribe of the heavenly revelation that had proceeded from God and had been entrusted to them. The point of these observations is to clarify that the recipients and scribes of God's past and current revelations are not the authors of the revelations they received. As already mentioned in the Literary Genres section of the Overview, this truth is unequivocally affirmed in Peter's second letter to the church:

> *Above all, you must understand that **no prophecy of Scripture came about by the prophet's own interpretation.** For prophecy never had its origin in the human will, **but prophets, though human, spoke from God as they were carried along by the Holy Spirit.** (2 Peter 1:20-21, **author's emphases**).*

Coupled with the witness of 2 Peter, the above-cited prophetic phrases (OT) and the preposition 'from' (NT) all serve the purpose of introducing the true Source and Author of the revelations received and recorded in both Testaments — God alone.

Since the above salutation will, in turn, be extended from both the seven Spirits and from Jesus Christ, we can safely conclude that the identity of Him from whom this greeting initially hails is none other than the eternal God and Creator of all life, i.e., the Heavenly Father and First Member of the Godhead, "him who is, and who was, and who is to come."

The characterization of the Father as "him who is" reflects the Name He revealed to Moses in his commission from God to deliver the Hebrews from Egyptian bondage: אֶהְיֶה אֲשֶׁר אֶהְיֶה (pronounced ĕh-yĕh´ ă-sher´ ĕh-yĕh´) — "I Am that I Am" (Exod 3:14). Though the Divine Name (**I Am**) in the Exodus narrative is recorded in the Hebrew imperfect tense, which is more frequently translated into the English as a future tense, for example, "I Will Be What I Will Be," this same imperfect tense lends itself to a present tense translation when applied to the eternal God who occupies past, present, and future. This further characterization of the Father as Him "who was, and who is to come" captures the full flavor of the original Name given to Moses, as well as the truth of the Father's eternal existence.

Though the salutation of grace and peace from the heavenly Father may be well understood, we would not be belaboring the point to emphasize that grace and peace not only denote the character of God, but also express that which He has achieved and extended to the church through the Person and Work of His Only Begotten Son, Jesus the Christ (cf. John 1:14, 16-17, 14:27; Rom 5:1-2; Eph 2:13-18).

The Father's identity is further endorsed by the salutation of grace and peace "from the seven spirits before his throne." In John's vision of the Father's throne, as recorded in Revelation 4:5, these same seven spirits are depicted as "seven lamps of fire burning before the throne." These same seven spirits are also described as "seven eyes" in John's vision of the slain Lamb who has seven horns and who stands in the midst of the throne and its heavenly entourage (Rev 5:6). The specific identity of these seven spirits, however, is defined in Isa 11:2, as outlined in Table 1 below.

The corresponding cross-references,[26] insightfully expound upon each Spirit as the power and character by which the Christ will rule over the restored Davidic kingdom during His millennial reign on the earth:

TABLE 1
THE SEVEN SPIRITS OF GOD

ISAIAH 11:2		CROSS-REFERENCES
1.	The Spirit of the Lord	Isaiah 40:13-14; 42:1; 61:1-3; Micah 3:8; Zechariah 4:6; Luke 4:18-19; Galatians 5:22-23
2.	The Spirit of Wisdom	Proverbs 1-4, 7-9, 21:30, 23:23; Daniel 1:17, 20, 2:19-23; Luke 2:52; Romans 11:33; 1 Corinthians 1:20-25; Ephesians 1:17-18; Colossians 1:9; 2:2-3
3.	The Spirit of Understanding	Proverbs 4:1-13, 7:4, 9:10, 15:32, 16:16, 21:30, 23:23; Isaiah 40:13-14; Jeremiah 9:23-24, 51:15; Daniel 1:17, 20, 2:19-23, 9:22; Luke 2:47, 24:45; Ephesians 1:17-18; Colossians 1:9; 2:2; 1 John 5:20
4.	The Spirit of Counsel	Psalms 16:7, 33:11, 73:24; Proverbs 11:14, 12:15, 15:22, 19:20-21, 21:30, 23:23; Isaiah 9:6, 25:1, 28:29, 40:13-14, 46:9-10; Acts 2:22-23; Romans 11:33-36; Ephesians 1:11; Hebrews 6:17-18

---

26 The cross-references for each of the seven Spirits are not meant to be exhaustive, but an introduction to one's further investigation into the whole counsel of God on each Spirit. The use of an exhaustive concordance, e.g. *Strong's* or the one for your particular translation, will greatly assist in expanding the list of cross-references under each Spirit, and hopefully expand one's understanding in the pursuit.

Isaiah 11:2	Cross-References
5. The Spirit of Might	Deuteronomy 3:24, 4:34, 37, 5:15, 7:8, 19, 21, 23, 10:17; Psalms 24:8, 50:1, 89:13, 93:4, 106:2, 8, 145:4, 150:2; Proverbs 23:11; Isaiah 1:24; 9:6; Daniel 2:19-23; Micah 3:8; Zephaniah 3:17; Matthew 3:11; Mark 1:7; Luke 3:16; Ephesians 1:19-21, 3:16, 6:10-18; Colossians 1:11
6. The Spirit of Knowledge	Psalms 1:6, 46:10; Proverbs 1:7; Jeremiah 9:23-24; Daniel 1:17, 2:19-23; John 8:32, 10:14, 17:3; Romans 8:28, 11:33; 1 Corinthians 8:1-3, 13:9, 12; 2 Corinthians 4:6; Philippians 3:8; Colossians 2:2-3; 1 Timothy 2:3-4; 2 Timothy 1:12, 2:19, 3:15, 2 Peter 1:5-6, 3:18; 1 John 3:2, 5:20; Revelation 2:2, 9, 13, 19, 3:1, 8, 15
7. The Spirit of the Fear of the Lord	Psalms 19:9, 33:8, 18, 34:7, 9, 11-14, 76:7, 85:9, 86:11, 89:7, 96:4, 112:1, 119:120, 145:19, 147:11; Proverbs 1:7, 2:1-5, 3:7, 8:13, 9:10, 10:27, 14:26-27, 15:16, 33, 16:6, 19:23, 22:4, 23:17; Ecclesiastes 3:14; Jonah 1:9; Luke 23:40; 2 Corinthians 7:1; 1 Peter 2:17; Revelation 14:7

All the above spirits constitute the seven-fold fullness of the one Holy Spirit who, under the New Covenant, conducts an eight-fold ministry to the believer and a tri-fold ministry to the world:

In His eight-fold ministry to the believer, the Holy Spirit —

1. Abides in the believer forever as the Holy Comforter (John 14:16-17).

2. Brings to remembrance all things that God in Christ has said (John 14:26).

3. Guides into all truth (John 16:13).

4. Shows things to come (John 16:13).

5. Intercedes on the believer's behalf before the throne of God, "through wordless groans . . .in accordance with the will of God" (Rom 8:26c, 27b).

6. Conforms the believer to the image of Jesus (Rom 8:29; cf. 1 Cor 15:48-49), including the imputation of His righteousness (1 Cor 1:30; 2 Cor 5:21; Eph 4:24), the in-working of His fruit (Gal 5:22-23), the donning of His armor (Eph 6:10-18), and the endowment of His gifts (1 Cor 12.-14.).

7. Seals the believer for the day of redemption (Eph 4:30).

8. The Power by whom the believer will be raised from the dead and raptured out of the earth at the second coming of Jesus Christ (Rom 8:11).

In His tri-fold ministry to the world, the Holy Spirit —

1. Reproves about sin, because they do not believe in Jesus (John 16:9).

2. Reproves about righteousness, because Jesus has gone to His Father, and because the believer nor the sinner can see Him with the naked eye (John 16:10).

3. Reproves about judgment, because the ruler of this world has been condemned (John 16:11).

This same Holy Spirit, in His seven-fold fullness, also sends salutations to the seven churches, as He is the divine agent by whom all believers are baptized into the body of Christ (cf. 1 Cor 12:13) and the one by whom God's grace and peace are administered to the life of each believer in the church (cf. 2 Cor 9:8; Gal 5:22).

VERSE 5A

"And from Jesus Christ, who is the faithful witness, the firstborn from the dead, and the ruler of the kings of the earth."

The salutation of grace and peace comes also from Jesus Christ who is identified by a four-fold testimony, according to the author's translation of the Greek text. Whereas the NIV and others translate the first testimony to Jesus as 'the faithful witness,' the Greek text of verse 5a separates this testimony into two parts, as indicated by a comma between the first two terms: ὁ μάρτυς (pronounced hŏ **mar´**-tūs), ὁ πιστός (pronounced hŏ pees-**tŏs´**), "the Witness, the Faithful One." In Revelation 3:14, the two terms are not separated by a comma in the Greek, thus forming the adjectival phrase that we see in most translations of our current text: ὁ μάρτυς ὁ πιστός καὶ ἀληθινός (pronounced hŏ **mar´**-tūs hŏ pees-**tŏs´** kī â-lay-thee-**nŏs´**), "the Faithful and True Witness." As the number four in biblical numerology depicts God's activity in relationship to the earth,[27] so the separation of the two terms in our current text (Rev 1:5) allows for a four-fold testimony that depicts Jesus' activity in the earth. The first three parts of this four-fold testimony (**The Witness, The Faithful One, The Firstborn of the Dead**) depict who Jesus was and, thereby, His activity in the earth during His first Advent. The fourth part (**The Ruler of the Kings of the Earth**) depicts who He will be and, thereby, His activity in the earth at His second coming.

The first part of the four-fold testimony to Jesus, therefore, is as "the Witness." The Greek word for witness, ὁ μάρτυς (pronounced hŏ **mar´**-tūs), is the word from which the English term 'martyr' is derived. A martyr is defined as "a person who voluntarily suffers death as the penalty of

---

27   E. W. Bullinger, *Number in Scripture: Its Supernatural Design and Spiritual Significance* (Grand Rapids, MI: Kregel Publications, 1967), 123

witnessing to and refusing to renounce a religion."[28] On a much grander scale, this was true of Jesus during His first Advent. The witness that secured His death was His witness to His heavenly Father and, more precisely, to the truth that He and the Father are One (John 10:30; cf. 8:58). As a testimony to Jesus' singular qualification as the Father's Witness, John begins his Gospel by affirming that "No one has ever seen God, but God the One and Only, who is at the Father's side, has made him known" (John 1:18). Jesus Himself confirmed that He was the Witness to His Father by what He spoke:

> **For I did not speak on my own, but the Father who sent me commanded me to say all that I have spoken.** I know that his command leads to eternal life. **So whatever I say is just what the Father has told me to say** (John 12:49-50, author's emphases).

In addition to saying everything His Father told him to say, Jesus was the Witness to His Father by what He did:

> Jesus gave them this answer: "Very truly I tell you, the Son can do nothing by himself; he can do only what he sees his Father doing, **because whatever the Father does the Son also does**" (John 5:19, author's emphases).

The biblical record also affirms that Jesus witnessed a good confession before Pontius Pilate (I Tim 6:13; cf. John 18:36-37), and was obedient in fulfilling His Father's plan of salvation, even to His death on the Cross (Phil 2:8). Jesus articulated the voluntary part of His sacrifice as being part and parcel of His witness and submission to His Father's will:

> The reason my Father loves me is that I lay down my life - only to take it up again. No one takes it from me, but I lay it down of my own

---

28 *Merriam-Webster Collegiate Dictionary.* Eleventh Edition. Springfield, MA: Merriam-Webster, Incorporated, 2003.

accord. I have authority to lay it down and authority to take it up
again. This command I have received from my Father (John 10:17-18).

Jesus, therefore, consummated the legacy of the prophets who preceded Him; who, as witnesses, received, proclaimed and typified the revelations entrusted to them. Jesus, however, holds the singular distinction of being **"The Witness,"** for unlike His predecessors, He personified, declared, revealed and fulfilled His Father's will.

The second part of the four-fold testimony to Jesus is as "The Faithful One." As previously mentioned, many of the biblical versions have placed this testimony in adjectival relationship to 'the Witness' to render "the Faithful Witness" as the translation. However, the Greek word for "the Witness," ὁ μάρτυς (pronounced hŏ **mar´**-tūs), is a noun in the nominative case, which, in turn, is followed by the substantive adjective of the current testimony ὁ πιστός (pronounced hŏ pees-**tos´**), "The Faithful One." In other words, both terms can stand alone as a testimony to Jesus, as the comma between them appears to indicate.

However, the testimony "The Faithful One," can be construed as being in relationship to the previous testimony, thus providing further elucidation on the character of His witness. Jesus was indeed faithful in His witness to His heavenly Father, as the previously cited Scripture references attest. However, just as Jesus consummates the witness of the prophets who preceded Him, so He consummates with singular distinction the faithfulness of the faithful ones who, in every generation before and since, have believed God's Word and obeyed Him.

The third part of the four-fold testimony is to Jesus as "the Firstborn of the dead" ὁ πρωτότοκος τῶν νεκρῶν (pronounced hŏ prō-**tŏ´**-tŏ-kŏs tōn ně-**krōn´**). This characterization is keyed to Jesus' death and resurrection from the grave, which is attested in all four Gospel accounts and is anticipated, among other places, in a psalm of David:

Therefore my heart is glad and my tongue rejoices; my body also will rest secure, because you will not abandon me to the realm of the dead, nor will you let your faithful one see decay. (Psalm 16:9-10)

Though the above reference and THE REVELATION text both bear witness to Jesus, one might wonder if, for example, Jairus' daughter (Mark 5:22-24, 35-42), the widow's son (Luke 7:11-15) or Lazarus (John 11:43-44) could more accurately be considered 'the firstborn of the dead'. All three had died and had been raised from the dead by Jesus before His own resurrection.

The key to this dilemma is found in the account of Lazarus' resurrection and is applicable to the other instances, as well. John's Gospel states that after Jesus "called with a loud voice, 'Lazarus, come out!,'" then "the dead man came out, his hands and feet wrapped with strips of linen, and a cloth around his face" (John 11:43-44). What is significant here is how Lazarus came out of the grave — bound and wearing grave clothes on his body and a cloth on his face. This, in truth, is not how Jesus was raised from the grave: for the discovery of His missing body revealed that the linen cloths that had covered His body and the handkerchief that had covered His head had been left behind in the tomb (John 20:5-7). Furthermore, John makes a point of noting that the handkerchief that had covered Jesus' head lay separate and apart from the linen cloths that had covered His body, possibly as far apart as the natural distance between the head and the trunk of the body. Based upon this evidence, one could safely infer that the body with which Jesus was raised did not require the movement of His grave clothes for Him to rise, thus leaving the grave clothes in a silhouette arrangement of His old body.

However, Lazarus' emergence from the tomb, bound and wrapped in his grave clothes, strongly substantiates the truth that Lazarus was resurrected back into his old body, the 'grave clothes' being symbolic of the flesh that was still bound to the processes of decay and death. In other words, Lazarus would eventually die again and return to the grave. Such would also have been the case with Jairus' daughter and the widow's son: each was raised to resume life in death-bound flesh. This assertion would also hold true for the resurrections that occurred in the Old Testament, as well (cf. Job 1:2; 42:13; 1 Kings 17:17-24; 2 Kings 4:18-37).

Such could also be asserted regarding those who will be resurrected to live during the millennial kingdom. By its very definition, the kingdom will only last a thousand years (Rev 20:4); and death, as the last enemy (1 Cor 15:26), will not be destroyed in the lake of fire until after the millennial reign of Christ has come to a close (Rev 20:7, 14). In describing the condition on the earth during the millennial kingdom, the prophet Isaiah declares the revelation that death will still be a factor:

> *Never again will there be in it an infant who lives but a few days, or an old man who does not live out his years; he who **dies** at a hundred will be thought a mere child; he who fails to reach a hundred will be considered accursed (Isa 65:20, **author's emphasis**).*

The prophetic testimony of the Isaiah passage affirms, therefore, that all those living during the one thousand year reign of Christ may indeed live any length of time within the thousand years, but all will be occupying the flesh that is still subject to death.

Jesus, however, rose from the dead never to die again (Rev 1:17b-18): for the new body with which he was raised and clothed was not bound nor subject to decay and death! It is for this reason that Jesus remained in the earth only a little while (John 16:16) after His resurrection (cf. Acts 1:3). However, the same body with which Jesus was raised is the same new and glorious body that all believers of all ages are promised in the resurrection unto eternal (not millennial) life:

*But our citizenship is in heaven. And we eagerly await a Savior from there, the Lord Jesus Christ, who, by the power that enables him to bring everything under his control, **will transform our lowly bodies so that they will be like his glorious body** (Phil 3:20-21; cf. Rom 8:23, author's emphasis)*

We have, thus far, spoken only of the resurrection unto eternal life, with respect to this change in bodily form. However, we must also consider that even the wicked dead will be raised from their graves unto eternal damnation (cf. Dan 12:2; John 5:28-29). Will they also receive new bodies? The answer is an unequivocal 'Yes!' when we examine the biblical evidence of that reality called "the second death."

Revelation 20:14 acquaints us with the fact that "the second death" and "the lake of fire" are synonymous phrases denoting the final destination of death and Hades (hell), and the eternal state and residence of the devil, the beast, the false prophet (Rev 20:10), and the wicked dead of all ages (Rev 20:15; 21:8). Of this latter group, i.e., the wicked dead, Isaiah prophesies that "their worm will not die, nor will their fire be quenched" (Isa 66:24b; cf. Mark 9:44, 46, 48). Consider, that if the wicked dead were raised to occupy the same flesh in which they died the first death, then the worm that does not die would cease to have something to feed on, and the fire that is not quenched would cease to have something to burn: for the current flesh would eventually be consumed by both elements. Thus, the wicked dead will also receive a new body in their resurrection in order to be fitted for their eternal state of torment. Furthermore, Jesus' parable of the rich man and Lazarus (Luke 16:19-31) unmistakably reveals that, contrary to the notions of the second death being oblivion or annihilation, those who inherit the resurrection unto this eternal state of damnation will be alive enough to feel the pain!

This brings us to the sterling realization that the second death is, in truth, a form of life that is lived outside of the favor of God or under the wrath of God. Those who will experience the second death will be those who chose to remain 'dead' in their trespasses and sins during this life, and who died the first death in that state. Inasmuch as being dead in trespasses and sins is indeed a form of life that is lived under the wrath of God in our present flesh (Eph 2:1-3), then the second death will be the ultimate and eternal reality of that life that will be lived under the wrath of God in a new flesh suited to its eternal and tormenting habitation.

As the "Firstborn of the dead," therefore, Jesus not only "suffered death . . . [that he] might taste death for everyone" (Heb 2:9), but provided in His resurrection the gateway to both resurrections (cf. Dan 12:2; John 5:28-29; 1 Cor 15:20-26): the resurrection to eternal life and the resurrection to eternal damnation, which is also a form of life known as the second death (cf. Rev 20:11-15)! Hence, even in the second death, the heavenly Father remains amazingly true to Himself as the God of all life (cf. Rom 14:9)!

The fourth part of the four-fold testimony is to Jesus as "the Ruler of the kings of the earth" ὁ ἄρχων τῶν βασιλέων τῆς γῆς (pronounced hŏ **ar´**-kōn tōn bâ-sĭ-**lĕ´**-ōn tās gās). The fact that Jesus will ultimately rule over the earth was initially intoned in God's promise to David that he "will never fail to have a man on the throne of Israel" (1 Kgs 2:4; cf. 8:25; 9:5; 2 Sam 7:12-16; 2 Chron 6:16; 7:18; Ps 132:11; Jer 33:17). As Jesus is the biological descendant of David, of whom the promise spoke, His resurrected and eternal life allows Him to be that 'Man' who will rule over the kings of the earth during His millennial reign.

The King James Version translates the Greek word for ruler in this fourth part of the four-fold testimony as prince, which, in turn, ties it to the prophetic titles for Jesus as "the Prince of Peace" (Isa 9:6), "the Prince of princes" (Dan 8:25), and "Prince and Savior" (Acts 5:31).[29] As such,

---

29   Daniel 9:25 bears the translation of "Messiah the Prince" in the KJV, NKJV, NASB, and the HCSB; and "Anointed Prince" in the NRSV and CJB.

the use of the word 'prince' instead of 'ruler' supports the ancient and prevailing tension between Jesus as "Prince over the kings of the earth" and Satan as "the prince of the power of the air" (Eph 2:2).

However, several other English translations engage the literal translation of the Greek word ἄρχων (pronounced **ar'**-kōn), meaning 'ruler' in this fourth part of the four-fold testimony.[30] This literal translation can be tied to Jesus' office and reign as "the Blessed and Only Potentate, the King of kings, and the Lord of lords" (1 Tim 6:15; cf. Rev. 17:14; 19:16).

Both of the above translations work, inasmuch as both denote the truth of Jesus' ultimate reign over the kings and kingdom of this world, as will be later announced in Revelation 11:15:

> *Then the seventh angel sounded his trumpet, and there were loud voices in heaven, which said, 'The kingdom of the world has become the kingdom of our Lord and of his Messiah, and he will reign for ever and ever!'*

VERSE 5B

"To him who loves us and freed us from our sins by his blood,"

These final two phrases of Revelation 1:5 shift from salutation to the beginning of a doxology that concludes with the Amen in verse 6. The presence of the first person plural direct object "us" indicates that the content of the doxology can be viewed as the shared, albeit condensed, version of John's testimony to Jesus, along with that of the seven churches. And as Jesus is the subject of *THE REVELATION* received, it is to Him that the doxology of praise is offered on behalf of those in the earth who believe in Him, i.e., the seven churches.

---

30 The New Revised Standard Version, the New King James Version, the New International Version, the American Standard Version, the New American Standard Bible, and the Complete Jewish Bible.

The doxology of praise is first addressed "To him who loves us . . . " Jesus' love for those who believe in Him is lyrically expressed by Him in the Gospel of John:

> *"Greater love has no one than this: to lay down one's life for one's friends" (John 15:13).*

Though the sacrificial demonstration of Jesus' love for us took place long ago on a cross, its efficacy postures it as a love that is on-going. The truth of this is borne out by the present active participial form of the verb for love in our current text, ἀγαπῶντι (pronounced â-gâ-**pōn'**-tee), which denotes an on-going love. Though the verbal root ἀγαπάω (pronounced â-gâ-**pâ'**-ō), from which we get the word "agape" to express the unconditional love of God, is expressed in many ways throughout the Scriptures, it is employed only here in its present active participial form. Jesus' on-going love for His disciples is reminiscent of His Father's love for Israel:

> *"I have loved you with an everlasting love" (Jer 31:3b).*

The result of Jesus' sacrificial and on-going love for us is that He has "freed us from our sins by his blood." The King James Version employs the translation 'washed' as if the Greek verbal root in this text is λούω (pronounced **lū'**-ō), which means to wash the whole body. Instead, the verbal root that is actually engaged is λύω (also pronounced **lū'**-ō), which means to loose or release or to set free. It is easy to see how the two verbs could have been confused in the original manuscripts. It is worthy to note that though Jesus' love is on-going, as previously mentioned, His death on Calvary, which loosed us from our sins, is a completed act, as the past tense Greek form (aorist active participle) of λύω, i.e., λύσαντι (pronounced **lū'**-sawn-tee), allows us to assert and as the Scriptures repeatedly affirm. The Scriptures also attest that Jesus' completed work on Calvary was eight-fold in character:

1. **Penal** - Jesus' Sacrifice satisfied the penalty of death for our violation of God's Holy Law - cf. Isaiah 25:8a; 53:5; Hosea 13:14; Romans 3:23-25; 5:9; 1 Corinthians 15:55-57; 2 Corinthians 5:21; Galatians 2:16;3:13-14; Revelation 20:14-15; 21:4

2. **Substitutional** - Jesus died on our behalf and in our stead - cf. Leviticus 1:1-4; Isaiah 53:5-7; 2 Corinthians 5:21; Hebrews 2:9; 1 Peter 2:24; 3:18

3. **Voluntary** - Jesus' Sacrifice was secured through His voluntary and unswerving obedience to His Father's Word, even to His death on the Cross - cf. Genesis 22:9-14; Leviticus 1:3,8; 6:8-13; Matthew 20:28; Mark 10:45; John 10:11-18; 12:32; Romans 8:32; Philippians 2:8

4. **Redemptive** - Jesus' Sacrifice paid the price for our redemption, thus satisfying the legal role of Kinsman-Redeemer on our behalf - cf. Genesis 48:16; Exodus 6:6; Leviticus 25:25,47-55; Ruth 3:12-13; 4:1-22; Isaiah 44:22; 47:4; 49:26; 59:20; 60:16; 63:16; Jeremiah 50:33-34; Luke 21:28; Romans 3:24; 1 Corinthians 6:20; 7:23; Galatians 3:13; 4:4-5,31; Ephesians 1:7,12-14; Colossians 1:13-14; 1 Timothy 2:5-6; Titus 2:14; Hebrews 2:9; 9:12-15,22; 1 Peter 1:18-19; Revelation 5:9; 14:3-4

5. **Propitiatory** - Jesus' Holy Sacrifice fulfilled the Holy requirements of God's Holy Law on the sinner's behalf, thus achieving peace between a Holy God and His sinful creation. With His Holiness vindicated and His Law satisfied, God can now justify and show mercy to the sinner who believes in Jesus' propitiatory work on his/her behalf. As a result, God imputes the righteousness of the fulfilled Law to the believing sinner, thus removing the believing sinner from under the condemnation of God's Righteous Wrath for not having kept the Law in times past. Jesus' propitiatory work translates judgment into mercy for the believing sinner –

cf. Leviticus 16:14-15, 20-23; Romans 3:25-26; 2 Corinthians 5:21; Ephesians 2:11-13; Galatians 3:6-12; Hebrews 4:14-16; 1 John 2:2; 4:10

6. **Reconciling** - Jesus' Sacrifice healed the breach between The Holy Creator and His sinful creation, so much so, that believing sinners are now reconciled to the peaceful relationship of friendship and fellowship which characterized the initial relationship between God and humanity before The Fall - cf. Leviticus 3:1-17; 7:11-21; John 15:13-15; Romans 5:10-11; 2 Corinthians 5:18-20; Ephesians 2:13-22; Colossians 1:20-23; Hebrews 2:17

7. **Revelatory** - Jesus' Sacrifice revealed to us the Love of the Father for us - cf. Jeremiah 9:23-24; Matthew 11:27; Luke 10:22; John 1:18; 3:16; 17:3; 1 John 4:9-10,19

8. **Efficacious** - Jesus' Sacrifice is the Power Source of God's eternal Plan of Salvation - cf. John 12:31-33; 2 Corinthians 5:21; Hebrews 9:11-28; 10:1-18 [31]

It is the eighth character of Jesus' one-time death on Calvary, i.e., efficacious, that undeniably attests to the perennial or on-going power of His blood to release believing sinners of every generation from the penalty of their sins., The aorist active participial form of λύω (pronounced **lū'**-ō), i.e., λύσαντι, (pronounced **lū'**-sân-tee) supports this assertion and denotes both the completed sacrificial act of Jesus as well as the continuous efficacy of that act down to the present day. By the same token, the preposition ἐν (pronounced **ĕn**), which introduces the agency of Jesus' blood, i.e., 'by' his blood, also establishes that the blood of Jesus has performed, and continues to perform, that redemptive work of separating the believing sinner from his/her sins.

---

31 The eight-fold character of JESUS' Sacrifice is cited as a Summary Note on Hebrews 10:18 in the following Scofield editions of the English translations of the Bible: Holman CSB, KJV, NASB, and the NIV.

VERSE 6

"And has made us to be a kingdom and priests to serve his God and Father - to him be glory and power for ever and ever. Amen."

The doxology that began in verse 5b continues in verse 6 in hailing Jesus as He who *"has* made *us to be* a kingdom and priests *to serve* His God and Father" *(author's emphasis).* Various translations of this phrase abound:

- **KJV** – "And *hath* made us *kings and* priests unto God and his Father"

- **NAB** – *"Who has* made us a *royal nation of priests in the service of* his God and Father"

- **NASB** – "And He has made us *to be* a kingdom, priests to His God and Father"

- **HOLMAN CSB** – "And made us a kingdom, priests to His God and Father"

- **AMPLIFIED** – "And formed us *into* a kingdom *(a royal race)*, priests to His God and Father"

The original Greek text, however, does not include many of the supplied words *(italicized above)* and is mirrored in the leaner translation of the above-cited Holman CSB version. As such, the phrase reveals that 'a kingdom' is the second of two direct objects of the verb "made" or "formed" (the first direct object is "us"), separated from what follows by a comma. Before the comma in the Greek construction, the emphasis is placed on 'kingdom' to further highlight Jesus' kingship over it, as previously proclaimed in verse 5; while what comes after the comma further delineates the identity of the first direct object "us," i.e., "priests to his God and Father" (cf. Isa 61:6).

According to Biblical history, the office and duties of priest were originally relegated to the head of the family for the building of altars to God and in calling upon His Name. This role is exemplified by Noah (Gen 8:20), Abram (Gen 12:7), Isaac (Gen 26:25), and Jacob (Gen 31:54). Even Job, who was not part of the covenant community, is seen performing both the sacrificial and intercessory duties of a priest over his family (Job 1:5). When the Law was given to Israel at Mt. Sinai, it was with the promise that the whole nation would be a 'kingdom of priests' based upon their obedience to God's Word (Exod 19:6). The people's violation of the Law, through the building of the golden csalf in the wilderness, however, permitted God to confine the priesthood to the tribe of Levi, who responded wholeheartedly to Moses' question, "Who is on the Lord's side?," and who did not shrink from executing three thousand in the nation who had committed the aforementioned idolatry (Exod 32: 26-29). Given Aaron's participation in the event of the golden calf, he and his descendants were surprisingly, yet graciously, granted the perpetual office of high priest, to whom the Levites were given as assistants in the service of the House of God (Num 3:5-13; 18:1-7). However, the judgment in Aaron's exaltation was that he and his descendants would perpetually have their hands in blood — the blood of the sacrifices for his own sins and the sins of the people, whom he had caused to sin in the golden calf incident!

For the remainder of Israel's sojourn under the Old Covenant until the captivities (Assyrian and Babylonian), the Levitical priesthood functioned in overseeing the annual festivals, the daily sacrifices, and the care and keeping of the sacred articles of God's Tabernacle and Temple. The Aaronic high priests alone ministered the blood of the sacrifices within the Most Holy Place, thus typifying the coming High Priest who alone, and only once (Heb. 9:12, 25-26), would shed His own blood, as the sacrificial Lamb, for the sins of His people.

The purpose of this linguistic exercise is that it allows us to connect our current text to the first mention of a theocratic kingdom over which God Himself would rule (Exod 19:6) and where the terms 'kingdom' and 'priests' articulate the new identity of the newly freed Hebrew slaves:

> *"You will be **for me a kingdom of priests** and a holy nation"* **(author's emphasis).**

The theocratic kingdom was expanded to include the human rulership of God's elect when Israel asked for a human king to rule over them like the other nations (1 Sam 8:5-7, 19-20). Though Saul was the first human king to occupy the throne over Israel, it was to David and to his descendants that perpetual rulership was granted in what is known as the Davidic covenant:

> *Your house and your kingdom will endure forever before Me; your throne will be established forever (2 Sam 7:16).*

And it is Jesus, David's Seed, whose millennial and eternal reign as King of kings and Lord of lords will fulfill the Davidic Covenant in perpetuity.

That the theocratic kingdom would be composed of priests, i.e., the whole of God's people, is attested not only in Exodus 19:6, as previously mentioned, but is also confirmed in Isaiah 61:6 and 1 Peter 2:5, 9. Isaiah's text prophesies of the priesthood of the redeemed nation of Israel during the millennial reign of Christ; and Peter's letter affirms the priesthood of all believers during this current age of Grace.

In fulfilling His role as both High Priest and Perfect Lamb during His first Advent, Jesus provided open access to the throne of grace and to the mercy seat for all believers, as inaugurated by the rending of the veil in the temple at His death (Matt 27:51; Heb 10:20; cf. Exod 26:31-34). Both believing Jews and believing Gentiles now constitute the priesthood of all believers who comprise the body of Christ, the church, during this age of grace (Eph 2:11-22), and who offer a four-fold sacrifice to Jesus, the High Priest of their faith:

1.   His/her living body (Rom 12:1; Phil 2:17; 2 Tim 4:6; James 1:27; 1 John 3:16);

2.   His/her continual praise to God (Heb 13:15);

3.   His/her substance and service (Rom 12:13; 1 Cor 16:1-2; 2 Cor 9:6-15; Gal 6:6, 10; Titus 3:14; Heb 13:2, 16; 3 John 5-8);

4.   His/her intercession on behalf of the saints (Eph 6:18; Col 4:12; 1 Tim 2:1).

In His second coming and during the millennial reign of Christ, the Levites who went astray after their idols before the captivities will still be allowed to minister in the millennial Temple as those having charge of the gates to the house and of the care of the house (Ezek 44:10-14). But the Levites of the house of Zadok, who were faithful before the captivities in keeping the charge of God's house, will alone be allowed to enter God's sanctuary to offer the fat and the blood of the sacrifices (Ezek 44:15-16), as well as teach God's people the difference "between the holy and the common", and "show them how to distinguish between the unclean and the clean" (Ezek 44:23). They will also serve as judges, keep God's laws, and hallow God's Sabbaths (Ezek 44:24); and "everything in Israel devoted to the LORD will belong to them" (Ezek 44:29b).

Though this division of the duties of the Levites during the millennial kingdom is reminiscent of the duties they held when first consecrated from among the Israelite nation for the service of God's house, it does not annul Isaiah's prophecy that the entire nation "shall be named priests of the LORD" and "ministers of our God" (Isa 61:6); for, according to the prophecy through Zechariah, one Jew will lead many to the worship of the One True and Living God:

> *This is what the LORD Almighty says: In those days **ten men from all languages and nations** will take firm hold of **one Jew** by the hem of his robe and say, 'Let us go with you, because we have heard that God is with you' (Zech 8:23, **author's emphases**).*

In what is considered His high priestly prayer, Jesus prayed that those whom the Father had given Him would ultimately be with Him and behold His eternal glory (John 17:24). It is only fitting, therefore, that the doxology of both Old and New Testament believer/priests, as articulated by John, would conclude with praise to both Jesus' "glory and power for ever and ever. Amen."[32] The certain reality of Jesus' eternal glory and power, as indicated by the "Amen," is confirmed in Daniel's prophecy:

> *He was given **authority**, **glory** and **sovereign power**; all nations and peoples of every language worshiped him. His dominion is an everlasting dominion that will not pass away, and his kingdom is one that will never be destroyed (Dan 7:14, **author's emphases**).*

---

32   This is the first *"Amen"* that occurs in The Revelation text; the 2nd occurs in the next verse (verse 7). A more extensive treatment of *"Amen"* will be presented in the discussion of Rev 3:14.

VERSE 7

"Look! He is coming with the clouds, and every eye will see him, even those who pierced him; and all peoples on earth will mourn because of him. So shall it be. Amen."

Verse 7 is a fusion of Old and New Testament quotes concerning the second coming of Jesus the Christ. In many instances, Old Testament quotes found in the New Testament are preceded by a formula clause that introduces the quote, e.g., "as it is written." However, the current fusion of quotes appears without introduction as suddenly in the text as the Christ who is due to return. Such an occurrence of an un-introduced quote or fusion of quotes is called an allusion (see note on *'allusion'* in **Overview | Literary Genre**). Each phrase of the allusion reflects both dominant and supportive prophetic utterances that affirm that Jesus is the subject of each element of the textual fusion.

For example, "Look! He is coming with the clouds" receives its dominant prophetic tone from Dan 7:13:

> *In my vision at night I looked, and there before me was one like a son of man, coming **with** the clouds of heaven. He approached the Ancient of Days and was led into his presence."*

According to Jesus' prophecy of His second coming, what Daniel saw in his night visions will ultimately be beheld by all the tribes of the earth:

> *Then will appear the sign of the Son of Man in heaven. And then all the peoples of the earth will mourn when they **see the Son of Man coming on the clouds of heaven**, with power and great glory (Matt 24:30; cf. Mark 13:26; Luke 21:27 - **author's emphases**).*

It was for this testimony that the high priest tore his clothes and accused Jesus of blasphemy during the travesty of his trial:

The high priest said to him, 'I charge you under oath by the living God: Tell us if you are the Messiah, the Son of God.' 'You have said so,' Jesus replied. 'But I say to all of you: From now on you will **see the Son of Man sitting at the right hand of the Mighty One and coming on the clouds of heaven'** *(Matt 26:63b-64; cf. Mark 14:62 - author's emphases).*

The obvious similarities between Daniel's vision and Jesus' prophecy are that Jesus, the Son of Man, is coming again, and that the clouds of heaven will be a part of His arrival. Scholarly debate abounds, however, on the prepositional variation that occurs in relationship to the clouds in the above-cited texts. For example, Daniel's vision reveals that one like a son of man will be coming 'with' the clouds of heaven; whereas Jesus' prophecy in Matthew 24:30 declares that the Son of Man will be coming 'on' the clouds of heaven. This same prophecy is recorded in Mark 13:26 and Luke 21:27 as Jesus coming 'in' the clouds. Also, the above-cited proclamation for which Jesus was accused of blasphemy (Matt 26:64; cf. Mark 14:62) states that the Son of Man will be coming 'on' the clouds of heaven in Matthew's account, but 'with' the clouds of heaven, in Mark's text.

The issue of 'how' the 'one like a son of man' will come has posed translational challenges from both the Aramaic portion of Daniel, in which his vision is recorded, and from the Greek texts. In Daniel 7:13, the preposition עִם (pronounced 'eem') normally carries the meaning 'with,' and is translated by Theodotion (a version of the Greek translation of the Old Testament) and others as 'with,' the clouds of heaven'. This translation is reflected in our current text. However, the Syriac version (another form of Aramaic) of Daniel and the Greek Septuagint (LXX – another Greek translation of the Old Testament) both render "**on** the clouds of heaven" as if reading עַל (pronounced ăl) in this same text instead of עִם

(pronounced eem). This translation is reflected in Matthew 24:30; 26:64, Mark 14:62, and Revelation 14:14, 16. It is possible that because the prepositions עִם and עַל look similar, one is either a corrupted presentation of the other, or another manuscript existed that substantiated, at some point, the עַל pointing. As it stands now, the two (or three including 'in') readings co-exist within the biblical text.

Before leaving the issue of the clouds, and to assist the reader in making up his/her own mind concerning the above-cited translational challenges, several supportive texts illuminate God's use of clouds as a symbolic means of transportation:

> *He makes the clouds **his chariot** and rides **on** the wings of the wind (Psalm 104:3b - **author's emphases**).*

> *After he said this, he was taken up before their very eyes, and a cloud hid him from their sight. They were looking intently up into the sky as he was going, when suddenly two men dressed in white stood beside them. 'Men of Galilee,' they said, 'why do stand here looking into the sky? This same Jesus, who has been taken up from you into heaven, **will come back in the same way as you have seen him go into heaven'** (Acts 1:9-11 - **author's emphases**).*

> *After that, we who are still alive and are left will be **caught up** together with them **in the clouds** to meet the Lord in the air. And so we will be with the Lord forever (1 Thess 4:17 - **author's emphases**).*

So, whether Jesus returns **with, on,** or **in** the clouds, the bottom line is that He is coming again!

In the phrase, "every eye will see Him," the most familiar Old Testament prophecy that connects with our current text (Rev 1:7) is found in Isa 40:5, where 'the glory of the LORD' is a direct reference to Jesus (cf. Heb 1:3):

> *And the **glory of the LORD** will be revealed, and **all people will see it together.***

*For the mouth of the LORD has spoken. **(author's emphases)***

In the following two phrases of verse 7, i.e., "even those who pierced him; and all the peoples of the earth will mourn because of him," Zechariah 12:10b constitutes the prophetic source:

> **They will look on me, the one they have pierced, and they will mourn for him** *as one mourns for an only child, and* **grieve bitterly for him,** *as one grieves for a first-born son (Zech 12:10b - **author's emphases**).*

It is because Zechariah's prophecy was initially addressed to the Nation of Israel that we can safely assert that the Nation is clearly identified as "those who pierced Him." Though the Jews of Jesus' day did not physically crucify Jesus, they did indeed hand Him over to those who could and did, i.e., the Roman government (cf. John 19:6-15). Though the Roman procurator, Pontius Pilate, could find no fault in Jesus worthy of death by crucifixion, the Jewish religious leaders insisted that He be crucified in exchange for the release of a malefactor and murderer named Barabbas (Mark 15:6-15). This level of betrayal is symbolically equated with the notion of 'piercing' Jesus, as much as the spikes that nailed His hands and feet to Calvary's cross. At Calvary, Zechariah's prophecy was fulfilled in part (John 19:36), as both the Jews and the Romans looked upon Him whom they pierced, hanging on the cross. Zechariah's prophecy will receive its ultimate fulfillment, however, at Jesus' second coming, when "every eye will see him" and "all the nations of the earth will mourn" at His appearing.

As "the testimony of Jesus is the spirit of prophecy" (Rev 19:10), and that the test of true prophecy is that it comes to pass (Deut 18:20-22), then the final statements of verse 7 not only affirm that Jesus is the subject of the prophecies that foreshadow His second coming, but that these same prophecies will indeed come to pass: "So shall it be. Amen."

VERSE 8

"I am the Alpha and the Omega," says the Lord God, "who is, and who was, and who is to come, the Almighty." [33]

Though Jesus will later echo some version of this Self-declaration (Rev 1:17, 21:6, 22:12), it is logical to conclude that it is the Father speaking at this point for the following reasons:

"I AM" was the Father's declaration of His Name to Moses (Exod 3:13-15).

"The Alpha and the Omega" reflects the Father's Self-revelation in the following Old Testament passages:

> *Who has done this and carried it through, calling forth the generations from the beginning? I, the LORD - **with the first of them and with the last - I am he** (Isa 41:4 - **author's emphasis**).*

> *This is what the LORD says - Israel's King and Redeemer, the LORD Almighty: **I am the first and I am the last;** apart from me there is no God (Isa 44:6 - **author's emphasis**).*

> *Listen to Me, O Jacob, Israel, whom I have called: **I am he; I am the first and I am the last** (Isa 48:12 - **author's emphasis**).*

"Lord God" is the compound Name first used in Gen 2:4-3:23 and appears as "LORD God." Separately, the Name "LORD" in all capital letters is the translation of the divine names "YAHWEH" or "JEHOVAH" and embraces the Father's Self-Existent and Unchangeable Nature as well as His Covenant-making relationship with His creation. It should

---

33   This verse *does* appear in the Greek text of the Nestle-Aland Novum Testamentum Graece, p. 633. It is in verse 11 that a similar statement is recorded in the mouth of Jesus but does not appear in the Greek text except as a footnote that it did appear in the Byzantine Majority text marked MA, which is the largest of the textual traditions for the book of The Revelation, with commentary by Andreas of Caesarea. See Nestle-Aland Greek NT, pg. 63 for explanation and pg. 633 for the actual textual note.

also be noted that the divine name "YAHWEH" is derived from the Hebrew root verb הָיָה (pronounced hâ-**yâh'**) meaning "to be" and is the Name that was revealed to Moses as "I Am Who I Am" (Exod 3:13-15). The Name "God" is the translation of the divine name "Elohim" and exposes the plural unity of the God of creation, i.e., that the Father, the Son, and the Holy Spirit were active in the beginning when "Elohim" (all three) created the heavens and the earth (Gen 1:1; John 1:1). Hence, the compound divine name Lord God depicts the fullness of the Godhead — the Three in One — as the Sovereign, Omnipotent, Omniscient, Omnipresent God and Creator who establishes covenant relationships with His creation to His Glory!

"Who is and Who Was and Who is to come" is first presented verbatim in John's salutation (verse 4) as the Source of the grace and peace with which he is addressing the seven churches in Asia and around whose throne are the seven spirits. This is also consonant with similar salutations within the majority of the NT letters, in which the grace and peace extended to the church first comes from the Father of our Lord Jesus Christ (Rom 1:7b; 1 Cor 1:3; 2 Cor 1:2; Gal 1:3; Eph 1:2; Phil 1:2; Col 1:2b; 2 Thess 1:2; 1 Tim 1:2b; 2 Tim 1:2b; Titus 1:4b; Philemon 3; 2 John 3).

"The Almighty" is the English translation of the Greek noun παντοκράτωρ (pronounced pân-to-**krâ'**-tor) and is the equivalent to the Hebrew אֵל שַׁדָּי (pronounced El Shă-**dī'**).

All the above titles, regarding the Father, are true of Jesus, "For God was pleased to have all his fullness dwell in him" (Col 1:19). As one with the Father, Jesus is also the Mediator of the New Covenant that was ratified by the shedding of His Blood on Calvary (Heb 8:6; 9:15; 12:24; cf. 1 Tim 2:5) in obedience to His Father's Will (John 10:17-18). Every phrase of this verse constitutes the Name of the Father that has been inherited by Jesus the Son: for Jesus has indeed been given a Name that is above every Name — His Father's Name (Phil 2:9-11; cf. Isa 45:23) — much as a child takes on the name of his/her father as an inheritance. Though the compound Name is not appropriated to Christ verbatim in the New Testament as it is to the Father in the Old Testament, it is intimated in Thomas' response to seeing Jesus' wounds after His Resurrection: "My Lord and my God" (John 20:28). Though the Name "Lord" is not recorded in all capital letters here, it is the translation of the Greek word κύριος (pronounced **kū'-ri-ŏs**), meaning Lord, which is consistently used throughout the New Testament as the Messianic title for Jesus. The appendage of 'the Almighty' reflects the resurrected Jesus' final statement to His disciples before His ascension:

> **All authority** in heaven and on earth has been given to me (Matt 28:18, **author's emphases**)

Unlike His First Advent, in which He came in the weakness of human flesh, Jesus' second coming will be as the resurrected, all-powerful King and Conqueror of His Father's Kingdom (1 Cor 15:24, 28), and He will reign as King of kings and Lord of lords (Rev 19:11-16).

The Father has not only bestowed upon Jesus' the honor of executing judgment at His second coming-

> Moreover, the Father judges no one, but has entrusted all judgment to the Son, **that all may honor the Son just as they honor the Father** (John 5:22-23a – **author's emphasis**)

but has also bestowed His Son His own Name —

> That at the **Name of Jesus** every knee should bow, in heaven and on earth and under the earth, and every tongue acknowledge that Jesus Christ is **Lord** to the glory of God the Father (Phil 2:9-11 – author's emphases).

JOHN AND THE PATMOS VISION
REVELATION 1:9-20

9 *I, John, your brother and companion in the suffering and kingdom and patient endurance that are ours in Jesus, was on the island of Patmos because of the word of God and the testimony of Jesus.* 10 *On the Lord's Day I was in the Spirit, and I heard behind me a loud voice like a trumpet,* 11 *which said: "Write on a scroll what you see and send it to the seven churches: to Ephesus, Smyrna, Pergamum, Thyatira, Sardis, Philadelphia and Laodicea."*

12 *I turned around to see the voice that was speaking to me. And when I turned I saw seven golden lampstands,* 13 *and among the lampstands was someone like a son of man, dressed in a robe reaching down to his feet and with a golden sash around his chest.* 14 *The hair on his head was white like wool, as white as snow, and his eyes were like blazing fire.* 15 *His feet were like bronze glowing in a furnace, and his voice was like the sound of rushing waters.* 16 *In his right hand he held seven stars, and coming out of his mouth was a sharp, double-edged sword. His face was like the sun shining in all its brilliance.*

17 *When I saw him, I fell at his feet as though dead. Then he placed his right hand on me and said: "Do not be afraid. I am the First and the Last.* 18 *I am the Living One; I was dead, and now look, I am alive for ever and ever! And I hold the keys of death and Hades.*

19 *"Write, therefore, what you have seen, what is now and what will take place later.* 20 *The mystery of the seven stars that you saw in my right hand and of the seven golden lampstands is this: The seven stars are the angels of the seven churches, and the seven lampstands are the seven churches.*

VERSE 9

> *"I, John, your brother and companion in the suffering and kingdom and patient endurance that are ours in Jesus, was on the island of Patmos because of the word of God and the testimony of Jesus."*

"I, John" — The recipient and scribe of THE REVELATION was first introduced to us by name in verses 1 and 4. There is much internal evidence that endorses that the current recipient/scribe is the same John of the Gospel Account and of the three Pastoral Letters that bear his name. This evidence will be interlaced into the discussion of the following verses as proof of his identity.

Suffice it to say, at this point, that the recipient/scribe, named John, is characterized in verse 2 as he "who testifies to everything he saw — that is, the word of God and the testimony of Jesus Christ." In our current verse (vs 9), these two dynamics of faithfulness on John's part are introduced by the causal phrase "because of," which translates the Greek word διὰ (pronounced dee-â'), thus indicating that this was the reason that he was exiled to the island called Patmos.[34] A similar characterization of what John saw and heard from Jesus is made in the Gospel account that bears John's name, thus providing a significant link to his identity as the current recipient/scribe:

> *Jesus performed many other signs in the presence of His disciples, which are not recorded in this book. But these are written that you may believe that Jesus is the Messiah, the Son of God, and that by believing you may have life in his name (John 20:30-31).*

Since the John of the Gospel account and of THE REVELATION are the same John,[35] then John will again occupy a similar posture, in order to

---

34 More on the Isle of Patmos in the upcoming discussion.

35 See initial discussion in the Prolegomena chapter, citing John as the 'recipient/scribe' of THE REVELATION

both receive and to write down the many signs that will be shown to him of *THE REVELATION*. In other words, he will, again, provide this final witness to "the Word of God and to the testimony of Jesus Christ" for the benefit of the seven churches.

"Your brother and companion in the suffering and kingdom and patient endurance that are ours in Jesus," — Inasmuch as John is addressing himself to the seven churches (1:4), he identifies himself first as their brother: for all who believe in Jesus are related to Jesus, and to each other, as brothers and sisters in the Body of Christ (Rom 8:29; Heb 2:11-13, 17). Given his posture in exile for his faithfulness to Jesus, John also identifies himself as sharing in the suffering that comes with being Jesus' disciple. The Greek word for suffering in our text, θλίφει (pronounced **thleeph'**-sā), is the same word employed in Jesus' declaration that

> *"in the world you will have* **trouble***. But take heart! I have overcome the world"* (*John 16:33b,* **author's emphasis***)*.

On the island of Patmos, John was experiencing the truth of Jesus' declaration in his exiled posture.

When we consider, therefore, that it was John who recorded the above saying of Jesus in his own Gospel account, using the same Greek word for suffering there as here, then we have additional evidence that the Apostle John, and not some other John, was the recipient/scribe of *THE REVELATION* text. Coupled with this linguistic evidence of John's identity with *THE REVELATION* text is his own experience of persecution, which Jesus promised would be the lot of those whose suffering is the outgrowth of their faithfulness to Him. As one who was more than likely present when Jesus spoke the following words in His Sermon on the Mount, we can safely assert that John's exile experience on the Isle of Patmos was by no means a source of shame for him, but rather a source of joy! For Jesus had pronounced blessing, joy and an eternal inheritance upon those who suffered on His account:

*Blessed are those who are **persecuted because of righteousness**, for theirs is the kingdom of heaven. **Blessed** are you when people insult you, persecute you and **falsely** say all kinds of evil against you **because of me**. **Rejoice** and be glad, because great is your reward in heaven, for in the same way they persecuted the prophets who were before you (Matt 5:10-12, author's emphases)!*

For more about the sufferings, the trials, and the tribulations which accompany the walk of faith and true ministry in Christ, please meditate upon the following passages: John 16:1-4; Acts 9:15-16, 23-25, 13:50-52, 14:19-20, 16:16-26, 20:17-27; Romans 8:18; 1 Corinthians 4:9-13; 2 Corinthians 1:3-11, 4:8-18, 6:1-10, 7:5, 11:23-33; Galatians 2:20; Colossians 1:24; 2 Timothy 3:10-12; Hebrews 11:32-40; James 5:10-11; 1 Peter 2:18-25, 3:13-18, 4:1,12-19.

It is important to note that it was while suffering for the cause of Christ that John was counted worthy to receive THE REVELATION— a revelation that culminates with the second coming of Jesus, with the setting up of His millennial kingdom, with the final judgment of the wicked of all ages, and with the creation of the New Heaven and the New Earth, which shall be the eternal habitation of the redeemed! What we can infer from this is that suffering for Jesus' sake is that holy arena in which we become eligible to receive 'revelation knowledge' and a 'fresh anointing upon our understanding' as to who Jesus is!

Though suffering for Christ is not the only arena in which God blesses His servants with revelation knowledge of Himself or His Son (cf. Matt 16:16-17), it is one of the more prevalently used arenas in which God delivers revelation knowledge to His faithful servants. Consider, for example, that as Stephen was being stoned by the Sanhedrin for his indictment of their stiff-necked resistance to the Spirit down through their generations, God granted him the revelatory vision of the opened heavens, the glory of God, and Jesus standing at the right hand of God (Acts 7:51-60). Hebrews 12:2 tells us that Jesus has now "taken his seat at the right hand of the throne of God." Stephen, however, saw Jesus standing, as if in standing ovation to Stephen's faithfulness. Consider also that at least four of the New Testament Letters written by the Apostle Paul (Ephesians, Philippians, Colossians, and Philemon) were written from the exile experience of prison; and in them is contained the revelation of the church as that part of the kingdom of God that was previously hidden from the prophets of old (Eph 3:1-12; cf. Rom 16:25-27; Col 1:24-27; 2 Cor 12:7). The key to Stephen's, Paul's, and John's inheritance of revelation knowledge was not only their suffering for Jesus' sake, but also their faithfulness in the midst of it. Because Jesus has promised to be "with (us) always, to the end of the age" (Matt 28:20b), then we can be assured that He will reveal Himself to us, even during our trials and tribulations, if we remain faithful!

John was not only a brother and a companion in the persecutions suffered by all true believers, but he was *also a brother and companion in the kingdom of Jesus Christ*! The kingdom of Jesus will be the culminating reality of divine, or heavenly, authority in the earth — an authority that originates in God and is bestowed by God upon humanity. This divine authority was first bestowed upon Adam and Eve over God's creation (Gen 1:26-28). Through the sin of disobedience to the revealed Will of God, Adam and Eve, as the primordial representatives of humanity, lost their dominion and authority to Satan who, in turn, became "the prince of this world" (Matt 4:8-10; John 12:31, 14:30, 16:11; 2 Cor 4:4; Eph 2:2). The Flood was God's response to the escalation of sin and rebellion against His authority in the earth, after which divine authority was invested into human government (Gen 9:6; cf. Rom 13:1-7). Though divine authority remains the charter of all human government, its failure was first seen at the tower of Babel. Far from being in accordance with God's will, human unity and governance showed itself, from the beginning, to be self-willed and self-ingratiating (Gen 11:1-9).

Hence, God's call to Abraham (Gen 12:1-4) was for the purpose of creating a distinct people through whom His divine authority in the earth could be worked out and reinstated. The distinctiveness of Abraham and his descendants — the Nation of Israel — resided in their definition as a theocratic kingdom — a kingdom of people who acknowledged God alone as their King and Sovereign and, as such, would be the light of God's Sovereignty to the Gentile nations that surrounded them (Exod 19:5-6). A cursory review of Israel's history, however, reveals their abdication of this high call by desiring a human king to rule over them like the other nations (1 Sam 8:4-7, 19-22). Though their desire for a human king constituted a rejection of God as their only King, God, nevertheless, agreed to His people's request and allowed Saul, son of Kish, a Benjamite, to be anointed as their first king (1 Sam 1:1, 20-26). As in the beginning, the purpose of this human leadership was the same: the king was to rule by God's authority according to God's Law. Out of all of the kings that succeeded Saul — whose kingship, like Adam and Eve, failed through disobedience (1 Sam 13:8-14, 15:19-35) — it was to David that God made an everlasting covenant that his house, his kingdom and his throne would be established forever (2 Sam 7:16), and that David "will never fail to have a man on the throne of Israel" (1 Kgs 2:4, 8:25, 9:5; 2 Chron 6:16, 7:18; Pss 89:4, 132:11; Jer 33:17; Acts 13:22-23).

The Resurrected Jesus is Sole Heir to this everlasting covenant, for in His Incarnation Jesus "as to his human nature was a descendant of David" (Rom 1:3; cf. Jer 23:5; Matt 1:1-6, 22:41-45; Luke 1:32-33, 3:23-31; Acts 13:34; Rev 3:7, 5:5, 22:16). The covenant made with David in the Old Testament, therefore, comes unchanged into the New Testament in the Person of Jesus Christ, the Seed of David and the Promised Messiah of Israel. During His First Advent, Jesus came to the lost in the house of Israel (Matt 10:6; 15:24), preaching that the kingdom was at hand, due to His Presence among them (Matt 4:17; Mark 1:14-15).

With His rejection by the Jewish religious leaders, Jesus then announced that part of the kingdom that had been hidden from the prophets of old — that part that fills the time period between His first advent and His second coming. That part is the church (Matt 16:18-19) and that time period is known as the church age, or better, the age of grace: for it is during this time that Gentiles, who were formerly not a part of the covenant promises of Israel, will be grafted into the kingdom (Rom 11:1-25), as fellow citizens and joint heirs with the Jews, by the blood of Jesus (Eph 2:11-22). His Death and Resurrection, coupled with the outpouring of the Holy Spirit at Pentecost (Acts 2) launched the church age, during which "the full number of the Gentiles" (Rom 11:25), or the calling out of Gentile believers, will be completed. Afterwards, the true church will be raptured out of the world as the first stage of Jesus' second coming (1 Thess 4:16-17). Jesus is, therefore, both the Promised Messiah of Israel and the "Head over all things to the Church" (Eph 1:22-23).

The raptured church, therefore, will not be present for the events of the Great Tribulation that will occur on the earth as prologue to the second stage of Jesus' second coming. However, the church, as addressed in the up-coming letters to the seven churches, and as the human representatives of divine authority in the earth at this time, is warned of her need to be ready for the imminent event of the rapture. The raptured church will be present when Old Testament and tribulation saints are resurrected to live upon the earth during the 1000-year reign of Christ, in fulfillment of the Davidic Covenant, and will co-reign with Christ, judging the twelve tribes of Israel (Rev 3:21; cf. Matt 19:28; Luke 22:28-30).

Jesus' resurrection from the grave insures that He will reign on the throne of David as God's Sovereign Ruler over all the kingdoms of this world during the millennial kingdom (Dan 2:44-45, 7:27; Zech 14:9; Rev 11:15). Satan, in turn, will be bound in the bottomless pit during Jesus' 1000-year reign (Rev 20:1-3). The millennial kingdom will then be followed by Satan's loosing from the bottomless pit and by Jesus' eternal confinement of Satan, death, Hades, and the wicked dead of all ages in the lake of fire (Rev. 20:7-15). Lastly, Jesus will deliver up His kingdom to the Father that "God may be all in all" (1 Cor 15:24-28) for all eternity!

As a sharer in the kingdom of Jesus, therefore, John further identifies himself as heir to the same glorious inheritance as that which has been promised to all believers in the kingdom of Jesus Christ — who, through faith in Him, have been made " . . . heirs of God and co-heirs with Christ — *if* indeed we share in his sufferings in order that we may also share in his glory" (Rom 8:17; cf. Acts 14:21-22; 2 Tim 2:12, *author's emphasis*).

The necessary bridge between suffering with Christ and reigning with Him in glory, however, is *"the patient endurance"* of Christ. The Greek word for 'patient endurance', ὑπομονῇ (pronounced hū-pŏ-mŏ-**nay**'), occurs ten times in its present form prior to its use in *THE REVELATION* text. It denotes the character by which fruit is born in the life of the believer (Luke 8:15), the necessary ingredient of faith (James 1:2-4; 2 Peter 1:6), the means by which believers possess their souls while suffering (Luke 21:19), the divine effect of tribulations (Rom 5:3-4; 2 Cor 1:6), the character of the mature in Christ (Titus 2:2), and the hallmark of true ministry (2 Cor 6:4; 12:12; 2 Tim 3:10). The Greek word ὑπομονῇ occurs in variant forms in other Scripture passages, but carries the same meanings previously noted (Rom 2:5-11, 8:25, 15:4-6; Col 1:11; 1 Thess 1:2-4; 2 Thess 3:5; 1 Tim 6:11-12; Heb 10:35-37; James 1:2-4; Rev 2:2-3,19, 3:10).

One of the best and most succinct profiles of Jesus' patient endurance is recorded in Isaiah's prophecy of the Suffering Servant (Isa 53:4-9). The quality of patience that Jesus manifested while suffering the injustices outlined in the Isaiah text can only be effected within the believer by the indwelling power of the same Holy Spirit who indwelled Jesus! When we consider that Jesus was given the Holy Spirit without measure (John 3:34), and that patience, or longsuffering, is itself a Fruit of the Spirit; and when we consider that Jesus' patient endurance secured for him the Victory over sin, death, hell, and the grave (1 Cor 15:55-57; Rev 1:18), then we can firmly assert that the patient endurance of Jesus is that quality of patience which keeps us faithful while suffering and bestows upon us the power to endure and overcome!

Bound up in the Greek word for 'patient endurance', ὑπομονῇ (pronounced hū-pŏ-mŏ-**nay'**), are also the notions of expectation, hope and perseverance. In the Letter to the Hebrews, where the same Greek noun, in its genitive construction, is also translated 'perseverance', the writer commends Jesus as the believer's sole example of how to "run with *perseverance* the race marked out for us" (Heb 12:1c, *author's emphasis*), with the same expectation of hope and victory:

> *Fixing our eyes on Jesus, the pioneer and perfecter of faith. For the joy set before him he endured the cross, scorning its shame, and sat down at the right hand of the throne of God (Heb 12:2).*

This same Greek noun, ὑπομονῇ (pronounced hū-pŏ-mŏ-**nay'**), will be used in its current form two more times during the unfolding events of THE REVELATION, in the call for patient endurance, coupled with faith, on the part of the saints (cf. Rev.13:10, 14:12). It will also be employed in a variant form as a commendation to the church in Ephesus (Rev 2:2-3), embracing the same meaning.

The place of John's exile was an island called Patmos, located in the

Aegean Sea and known for its volcanic and extremely rocky terrain. "On account of its rocky, barren, and desolate nature the Roman government used the island as a place of banishment for criminals. The prisoners were compelled to work the mines of the island. The Roman Emperor Domitian (A.D. 81-96) banished the Apostle John to the island [around] A.D. 95,"[36] most likely because his faithful witness to the Word of God and to the testimony of Jesus Christ included John's 'disturbing' proclamations of the truth that Jesus alone is King of kings and Lord

---

36   Merrill F. Unger, THE NEW UNGER'S BIBLE DICTIONARY, Chicago: Moody Bible Institute, 1988, 967.

CONSIDER: If a rash of persecutions broke out against the church in your city, would there be enough evidence to convict you of being a Christian? Would you boldly continue to live out and lift up the Good News of JESUS Christ (Rom 1:16), or would you try to hide the Light of His Testimony under a bushel of fear (Matt 5:14-16)? Would you continue to be strong in The Lord and in the power of His might (Eph 6:10-18), or would you faint under pressure and compromise your faith (Prov 24:10)? Would you continue to boldly proclaim JESUS as your Lord and Savior (Ps 119:46 Luke 12:8-12; Acts 26:1-29; Rom 10:9-10), or would you recant that you never knew Him just to save your own skin (Matt 26:69-74)?

For more about the fearlessness that should characterize our faithfulness to God's Word and to the Testimony of Jesus Christ, please meditate upon the following passages: Psalms 2:11-12; 27:1-3; 37:1-40; 56:4,10-11; 64:1; 112:1-10; 118:6; Proverbs 29:25; Isaiah 51:12-16; Hebrews 13:5-6; 1 John 4:18. For more about being a faithful witness, please read the following: Proverbs 14:5; 1 John 5:7-12; Rev.1:5; 3:14; 20:4.

of lords — a truth that would have placed him in direct opposition to and in violation of the decree for emperor worship. However, John's apparent refusal to recant revealed his faithfulness to the One who said, "Everyone therefore who acknowledges me before others, I also will acknowledge before my Father in heaven; but whoever denies me before others, I also will deny before my Father in heaven" (Matt 10:32-33). John's faithfulness also revealed his correct perspective on whom to fear: "Do not fear those who kill the body but cannot kill the soul; rather fear him who can destroy both soul and body in hell" (Matt 10:28). In short, John's banishment to the Isle of Patmos was solely due to his fearless faithfulness to the Word of God and to the testimony of Jesus Christ, and it was in this posture that he received all that is contained in *THE REVELATION*!

VERSE 10

"On the Lord's Day I was in the Spirit, and I heard behind me a loud voice like a trumpet"

Though imprisoned on the Isle of Patmos, John was still free "in the Spirit" to worship the Lord. It was John himself who recorded Jesus' update on True Worship:

> *Yet a time is coming and has now come when the **true worshipers** will worship the Father in the Spirit and in truth, for they are the kind of worshipers the Father seeks. God is spirit, and his worshipers **must worship in the Spirit and in truth** (John 4:23-24 – **author's emphases**).*

When we consider that the Spirit has not only been sent to guide us into all Truth and to show us things to come (John 16:13), but that He has also been sent to be our Comforter who abides with us forever (John 14:16,18), then we can safely assert that the "comforting truth" that the

Spirit imparted to John in the time of his exile might well have been that litany of assurances articulated by the Apostle Paul, which is accessible to Spirit-filled believers of every generation who are suffering for the cause of Christ:

> *Who shall separate us from the love of Christ? Shall trouble or hardship or persecution or famine or nakedness or danger or sword? As it is written, 'For your sake we face death all day long; we are considered as sheep to be slaughtered.' No, in all these things we are more than conquerors through him who loved us. For I am convinced that neither death nor life, neither angels nor demons, neither the present nor the future, nor any powers, neither height nor depth, nor anything else in all creation, will be able to separate us from the love of God that is in Christ Jesus our Lord (Rom 8:35-39).*

The designation "the Lord's Day" was applied to the first day of the week by the early church, in celebration of Jesus' Resurrection. On one level, it would not be far-fetched to conclude that John knew what day it was, even in his exile, for the Spirit would have been able to place him in 'spiritual' community with all other believers who observed this day as their day of worship. On another level, however, the Lord's Day could have been any day of the week for John: for the true worship of God, in Spirit and Truth, can be done anytime, anywhere, and under any circumstance, even in our exile experiences. In short, being 'in the Spirit' makes every day 'the Lord's Day' (cf. Col 2:16-17)!!!

Being in the Spirit not only allowed John to worship the Lord in the midst of his exile experience, but it also empowered him to hear the Lord's Voice — "a loud Voice like a Trumpet." John, again, had been privileged to record Jesus' pronouncement that "My sheep hear My Voice" (John 10:27; 10:3) and that they "know His Voice" (John 10:4); and that for these reasons they follow Him. When we consider, therefore, that even our faith in Jesus "comes from hearing the message, and the message is heard through *the Word of Christ*" (Rom. 10:17, *author's emphasis*), then we can unequivocally assert that it is the Spirit who empowers us to hear the Lord's Voice: for faith itself is a Fruit of the Spirit (Gal 5:22), and the Word of God — who is Jesus (John 1:1-2) — is that truth into which the Spirit has been sent to guide us and out of which He will show us things to come (John 16:13)! Because John is a believer who will be shown the things to come — as evidenced by the full scope of THE REVELATION — then we can firmly conclude that John's capacity to hear the Lord's Voice is a direct result of him being in the Spirit of the Lord!

For more about The Voice of The Lord, and those who have heard and will hear it, please meditate upon the following passages: Genesis 3:8-10; Exodus 4:8; 15:26; Numbers 7:89; Deuteronomy 4:12,33,36; Isaiah 66:5-6; Ezekiel 1:24-25,28; Daniel 4:31, 10:9; Joel 2:11; Micah 6:9; Habakkuk 3:16; Matthew 3:17, 17:5, 27:46,50; Mark 1:11,9:7,15:34,37; Luke 3:22,9:34-36,23:46; John 5:25, 10:3-5,16,27,. 11:43, 12:28; Acts 9:4; 10:13,15, 22:6-9, 26:14; Hebrews 3:7,15, 4:7; 2 Peter 1:17-21; Revelation 3:20, 4:1, 18:4, 19:5-6.

The fact that 'the voice' heard is Jesus' voice is initially defined by John's characterization of the voice: "a loud voice like a trumpet." The Lord's Voice has been characterized in several ways throughout Scripture: as Thunder (Job 37:1-5; 40:9; Ps 29:1-11; 77:18; Rev 10:3-4; 14:2); as a Gentle Whisper (1 Kings 19:12); as the Sound of Rushing Waters (Rev 1:15; 14:2); as a Mighty Voice (Ps 68:33); as a Loud Voice (Matt 27:46,50; Mark 15:34; Luke 23:46; John 11:43; 1 Thess 4:16; Rev 12:10; Rev 16:1,17; 21:3); as a Majestic Voice (Isa 30:30); as a Roar (Jer 25:30; Joel 3:16); as a Shout (Jer. 25:30;); as the Voice of an Archangel and as the Trump Call of God (1 Thess 4:16).

The characterization of the Lord's Voice as a trumpet sound has occurred, and will occur, at strategic points throughout the biblical text. The giving of the Law on Mt. Sinai, for example, was accompanied by the voice of the trumpet (Exod 19:13,16,19; 20:18-19; cf. Deut 5:22-27); the Lord's Return for the church will be accompanied by the sound of the trumpet (1 Thess 4:16); John will, again, hear the voice of the trumpet when it is time for him to receive the revelation of "what must take place after this" (Rev 4:1); and it will be the sound of the trumpets which will inaugurate the escalated agenda of God's final judgment upon the earth during the Great Tribulation Period (Rev 8:1 — 9:21; 11:15-19).

Coupled with these vocal manifestations of the Lord's Voice, the trumpet sound has also served to symbolize both the Word of God and the messenger who proclaims it (Isa 58:1; Jer 6:17; Ezek 33:1-20). Whether the Word is one of prophecy or of promise, of revelation or of judgment, the trumpet sound has been employed to denote the clear proclamation of the Word and Will of God! When we consider, therefore, that Jesus is the Word of God and that He was sent to both reveal and to proclaim God's Word; and when we consider that He is now about to proclaim, in John's hearing, the consummate revelation of Himself as the fulfillment of all prophecies and promises, revelations and judgments, then we can safely deduce that the "loud voice like a trumpet" is indeed the voice of our Lord and Savior Jesus Christ! The fact that the voice heard is Jesus' voice is further endorsed by the content of the succeeding proclamation (vv11,17-20) and by the vision of the Lord in His Resurrection Glory, whom John is allowed to behold in the Spirit (vv12-16) — the evidence of which will be discussed in the following verses.

VERSE 11

"which said: 'Write on a scroll what you see and send it to the seven churches: to Ephesus, Smyrna, Pergamum, Thyatira, Sardis,

Philadelphia and Laodicea.'"

The King James Version and the Living Bible translation begin this verse with an expanded echo of verse 8: "I am Alpha and Omega, the First and the Last." However, the Greek text and most ancient manuscripts do not include it, but move straight to Jesus' command to John to write what he sees to the seven churches.[37]

The first piece of evidence that this is Jesus speaking is His command to John to "write (what John sees) on a scroll." From Moses to the writers of the New Testament, God in Christ has issued repeated commands for His Word and Will to be written down (cf. Exod 17:14, 34:27; Deut 17:18-20; 1 Chron 28:19; 2 Chron 26:22; Neh 9:38; Isa 8:1; 30:8; Jer 30:2, 36:2, 17-18, 28, 32; Ezek 43:11; Hab 2:2; Luke 1:3; John 1:45; 2 Cor 2:9). John is here being given the first of twelve commands from Jesus to write what he is shown (Rev 1:19, 2:1, 8, 12, 18, 3:1, 7, 14, 14:13, 19:9, 21:5). There is only one occasion in which John is forbidden to write what he hears (Rev 10:4) — a subject that will be discussed later in its context.

The second piece of evidence that this is Jesus speaking is the command to write "what you see." The Greek verb "to see" is engaged in its present active indicative form, which allows it to also be translated "what you are seeing." The significance is that the latter rendition of the verb, "what you are seeing," embraces not only John's current vision of Jesus in His Resurrection Glory, which he will be shown first (see verses 12-16 below), but also all that he will be shown thereafter of Jesus' various

---

37   Though an abbreviated version of this self-describing phrase, "I am Alpha and Omega, the First and Last," does appear in verse 8 in the Greek text (Nestle-Aland Novum Testamentum Graece), it does not appear in the Greek text here in verse 11, except as a footnote that it did appear in the Byzantine Majority text, marked MA (MA), which is the largest of the textual traditions for the Book of the Revelation with commentary by Andreas of Caesarea. See Nestle-Aland Greek NT, pg. 63 for explanation of the MA citation and pg. 633 for the actual textual note.

roles in the execution of His Father's final judgment as a progressive unfolding of visions to be viewed and written down.

The third piece of evidence that this is Jesus speaking is His command to John to send what he writes "to the seven churches." Let us re-visit Jesus' conversation with His disciples when He asked them, "Who do you say I am?" It was Peter who answered, "You are the Christ, the Son of the living God." To this, Jesus responded,

> "Blessed are you, Simon son of Jonah, for this was not **revealed** to you by flesh and blood, but by My Father in Heaven. And on this **Rock** I will build my church, and the gates of Hades will not overcome it." (Matt 16:15-18, **author's emphases**).

It is in Jesus' response to Peter's answer that several truths become self-evident. First, Peter's answer is defined by Jesus as *revelation knowledge*: for Jesus states that His identity had not been *revealed* to Peter by flesh and blood, but that Jesus' Father in Heaven had *revealed* this knowledge to Peter. This is what *revelation knowledge* is — direct intelligence from the Father to the believer concerning Jesus, with no intervention of human wisdom. Secondly, it would be upon the *revelation knowledge* given to Peter of Jesus' True Identity, i.e., *Jesus is the Christ, the Son of the Living God"* that Jesus would build His church. In other words, it is the *revelation of Jesus' True Identity* that defines the *Rock* upon which His church will be built! As often misunderstood, Jesus would not have built His church upon the mortal vessel used to receive the revelation, i.e., Peter, as some assert, but rather upon the revelation itself: for both the Source (the Father) and the Substance (the Son) of the revelation are eternal.

Let us further confirm this point by noting that Peter's name in Greek is πέτρος (pronounced **Pě'-trŏs**), meaning a piece of a rock and is, of course, masculine in gender. However, the Rock upon which Jesus will build His Church is the Greek word πέτρα (pronounced **Pě'-trâ**), meaning a massive rock and is feminine in gender. Peter would have automatically known that Jesus did not intend to build His Church on him. Additionally, since Peter was the recipient of a direct revelation from the Father concerning Jesus, then it is equally as important to note that the Greek term for revelation, i.e., αποκάλυψις (pronounced â-poc-â'-lūp-sees) is also feminine in gender, thus confirming that it would be upon the Rock of the Revelation — the 'Petra' of the 'Apokalupsis' — of who Jesus is (not upon Peter) that Jesus would build His Church — a.k.a. the bride of Christ! This same Greek word for revelation is employed in the title of this last book of Scripture, i.e., **the Apokalupsis** or **Revelation of Jesus Christ**!

Thirdly, the church that is to be built upon the revelation knowledge that Jesus is the Christ, the Son of the Living God, is the only church against which the gates of hell will not overcome! The reason for this is that revelation knowledge comes only through the Holy Spirit (1 John 2:27). The Holy Spirit is the Spirit of Truth (John 14:17, 16:13) who teaches (the church) all things, and brings to (the church's) remembrance whatever (Jesus) has said to (her) — (John 14:26); guides (the church) into all truth . . . and shows (the church) things to come (John 16:13). Because the Truth that the Holy Spirit reveals is only of Jesus (John 16:14-15), who is the Truth (John 14:6), then his Ministry empowers the church's capacity to receive revelation knowledge concerning Jesus! As such, the Holy Spirit operates as the church's 'immune system' against the lies of the anti-Christ, whose presence is already in the world (1 John 2:18-26, 4:1-3).

As it was by the revealing power of the Holy Spirit that Peter received the initial revelation of Jesus' True Identity, so it is by the revealing power of that same Holy Spirit that John is now being given the ultimate revelation of Jesus Christ, as recorded in this last book of Scripture! This ultimate revelation was to be addressed to "the seven churches" — each of whom was to receive the entire text of *THE REVELATION*, which included their letter, every other church's letter, and all that is recorded to the end of the book![38] This is affirmed first by Jesus' consistent refrain within each letter:

> "Whoever has ears, let them hear what the Spirit says to the **churches**" (2:7; 11, 17, 29; 3:6, 13, 22, **author's emphasis**).

Each church's full receipt of the entire *Revelation* is also affirmed in His concluding declaration in Rev 22:16:

> "I, Jesus, have sent my angel to give you this testimony for the churches."

Having shed His Blood on Calvary for the life of His church, Jesus addressed each church on the authority of being her Foundation (1 Cor 3:11), her Chief Cornerstone (Eph. 2:20), her Capstone (Matt 21:42; Mark 12:10; Luke 20:17; Acts 4:11; 1 Peter 2:7), and the Head over everything for the church (Eph 1:22-23; Col 1:18)!

VERSE 12

> "I turned around to see the voice that was speaking to me. And when I turned I saw seven golden lampstands,"

The voice that John initially heard in verse 10 was now the object of his attention, as he turned to see to whom the voice belonged. The first thing that captured John's attention, however, was the sight of "seven golden lampstands." Jesus will interpret the lampstands in verse 20 as the seven churches to whom John was to write. A fuller discussion of the church as a lampstand will be given at that point.

---

38 Mounce, *THE BOOK OF REVELATION REVISED*, 56.

VERSES 13-16
THE PATMOS VISION: JESUS IN RESURRECTION GLORY

"And among the lampstands was someone like a son of man, dressed in a robe reaching down to his feet and with a golden sash around his chest. The hair on his head was white like wool, as white as snow, and his eyes were like blazing fire. His feet were like bronze glowing in a furnace, and his voice was like the sound of rushing waters. In his right hand he held seven stars, and coming out of his mouth was a sharp, double-edged sword. His face was like the sun shining in all its brilliance."

Verses 13-16 have often been referred to as John's 'Patmos' Vision, so-named after the island on which he was exiled when he received it. However, John's vision can be more aptly acknowledged as The Vision of Jesus in His Resurrection Glory! The fact that this current vision is anticipated by similar visions given to both Ezekiel and Daniel (Ezek 1:26-28; Dan 10:5-6) allows us to not only affirm that Jesus, in His Resurrection, was returned to His former Glory (John 17:5), but to also attest that these previous visions provide us with unmistakable evidence of the current manifestation to John. All three visions are cast in the language of a simile, using words such as "like" and "as" to describe the awesome elements of Jesus' Glory. Table 2 shows a comparison of the current vision with that of the prophetic passages, and reveals that, though closest in similarity to the Daniel vision, The Vision of Jesus in His Resurrection Glory appears more complete than its Old Testament counterparts.

TABLE 2
THE VISION OF JESUS IN HIS RESURRECTION GLORY
PROPHETIC COMPARISON

EZEKIEL 1:26-28; 8:2	REVELATION 1:13-16	DANIEL 7:(9),13; 10:5-6
A figure like that of a man	One like [the] Son of Man	One like a son of man
	Dressed in a robe reaching down to His feet	Dressed in linen; body like chrysolite
His waist up he looked like glowing metal, as if full of fire . . .	Golden sash around His chest	Belt of the finest gold around His waist
	His head and hair were white like wool, as white snow	(7:9) - The Ancient One . . . hair of His head was white like wool (attribute of the Father appropriated to the Son in His Resurrection Glory)
	His eyes . . . like blazing fire	His eyes like flaming torches
From there [his waist] down he looked like fire;	His feet . . . like bronze glowing in a furnace	His arms and legs like the gleam of burnished bronze
Ezekiel heard the voice (but no description is given – 1:25)	His voice was like the sound of rushing waters	His voice like the sound of a multitude
	In His right hand . . . held seven stars	

EZEKIEL 1:26-28; 8:2	REVELATION 1:13-16	DANIEL 7:(9),13; 10:5-6
	Out of His mouth came a sharp, double-edged sword	
And brilliant light surrounded him. Like . . . a rainbow on a rainy day . . . was the radiance around him	His face . . . like the sun shining in all its brilliance	His Face like lightning

Daniel's apocalyptic visions, along with other prophetic passages of judgment, have served and continue to serve as keys not only to the interpretation of John's current vision, but also to the interpretation of other dynamics of this final apocalypse. Inasmuch as the common context of Daniel's, Ezekiel's and John's visions is that of divine judgment, we can safely assert that the vision of Jesus, which John is allowed to behold, is of Jesus as Judge: for judgment will be His primary activity throughout THE REVELATION text. As we examine the above-cited ten dynamics of Jesus' Resurrection Glory, not only will our references to Daniel & Ezekiel be expanded upon but we will discover that there is New Testament support for several of the dynamics, thus connecting Jesus' Resurrection Glory with both prophecy and fulfillment, with both foreshadowing and full manifestation.

The first dynamic of Jesus' Resurrection Glory is the description of him as "one like the Son of Man." This terminology is reminiscent of Daniel 7:13a, where, in a night vision, Daniel "saw one like a son of man, coming with the clouds of heaven," to whom everlasting dominion and glory and a perpetual kingship was given, so that all nations and peoples of every language would serve Him (Dan 7:14). Though the Greek manuscript of THE REVELATION text and the Hebrew manuscript of Daniel's text reflect the indefinite article that appears in our current text i.e., "one like *a* son of man . . . ,"[39] most translations employ the definite article, i.e., 'one like *the* Son of Man', either within the text or as a footnote, possibly in deference to Jesus' abundant use of the title with the definite article in reference to Himself in each of the four Gospels. It is safe to conclude that Jesus is not only the 'one like *a* Son of Man' in Daniel's text, but he is also '*the* Son of Man' who comes to judge all the peoples of the earth in our current text.

In the second dynamic of Jesus' Resurrection Glory, Jesus is described as wearing a "robe reaching down to his feet." Daniel's vision indicates that Jesus was clothed in linen. However, it is from the list of holy garments made for Aaron the high priest and the Levitical priesthood (Exod 28 and 39) that we receive insight into the most likely interpretation of Jesus' long robe. First, there was a linen tunic that was worn by both the high priest and the Levitical priests (Exod 28:40-43; 39:27-29), which, according to Leviticus 8:7, was donned first (after the linen undergarments, we assume – Exod 28:42-43, 39:28; Lev 6:10) as the garment that covered the entire body from neck to ankles. After the tunic, Aaron, the high priest, was dressed in a robe called the robe of the ephod. This robe did not extend to the ankles, but fell just below the knees, so that the bottom portion of the first tunic was still visible.[40] The robe of the ephod was all blue in color and its hem line was adorned with an alternating arrangement of pomegranate tassels made of blue, purple, and crimson yarn and bells made of pure gold (Exod 28:31-35; 39:22-26).

---

39   David H. Stern, COMPLETE JEWISH BIBLE (Clarksville, MD: Jewish New Testament Publications, Inc., 1998). This translation also records this messianic title exactly as it occurs in Daniel's text, i.e., without a definite article, to show the unmistakable connection between the two texts as prophecy and fulfillment.

40   Merrill F. Unger, THE NEW UNGER'S BIBLE DICTIONARY (Chicago, IL: Moody Bible Institute, 1988), 1030.

Regarding the long robe Jesus is wearing in John's vision, there is no mention of the robe's color, adornments or type of material, as is explicitly indicated in the above-cited description of the OT priestly wardrobe. The more likely interpretation of Jesus' long robe, therefore, would be to equate it to the first tunic, which was worn by both the high priest and the Levitical priests for the following three reasons. First, this OT priestly tunic was a long robe reaching to the ankles, which fits the description of Jesus' long robe in the current vision. The OT priestly tunic was also seamless, as indicated by the Hebrew word translated 'woven' (Exod 39:27). Jesus wore a seamless robe during His earthly ministry, as evidenced by the garment for which the Roman soldiers cast lots at the foot of Jesus' Cross (John 19:23-25). Secondly, in light of the lack of evidence regarding the color and type of material of Jesus' long robe, we can safely assume from the following Scriptures that Jesus' long robe was both white and linen (Dan 7:9; Matt 17:2; Mark 9:3; Luke 9:29; Rev 3:4-5, 18, 4:4, 6:11, 7:9, 13, 15:6, 19:8, 14).[41] Thirdly, inasmuch as white linen or a white robe will be the garment of the overcomers in the church in Sardis (Rev 3:4-5) and will also be given to the saints under the altar during the 5th Seal (Rev 6:9-11); and inasmuch as white linen will be the wedding attire of the bride of Christ (Rev 19:7-8) and the uniform of the armies of heaven who will return with Christ during His second coming (Rev 19:14), then Jesus is first seen in His Resurrection Glory wearing the same garment as those who are faithful to Him and who are also characterized as priests who will co-reign with Him in His Father's kingdom (Rev 1:6).

Throughout Scripture, white linen uniformly symbolizes both the righteousness of God and the righteous deeds of the saints. Since Jesus is the Righteous Judge into whose hands God the Father has given "authority to judge because he is the Son of Man" (John 5:27), then it

---

41 Note that Jesus' white robe will be dipped in blood when He returns on a white horse – Rev 19:13.

would be both consistent and appropriate to characterize His long robe as linen in composition, white in color, and seamless in structure, since it is identically worn by both the High Priest as well as by the priesthood of believers!

In the third dynamic of Jesus' Resurrection Glory, the "golden sash around His chest" reflects the breastpiece of judgment that was worn across the chest of the Old Covenant high priest (Exod 28:15-30) for the purpose of bearing the judgment of the people of Israel before God. Though Aaron and his sons wore a sash (referred to as a girdle in the KJV) around the waist made of "finely twisted linen and of blue, purple and scarlet yarn—the work of an embroiderer—as the LORD commanded Moses" (Exod 39:29), it was only Aaron the high priest who wore the breast piece across his chest. We can safely infer, therefore, that the golden sash across Jesus' chest is one of the first indications that Jesus' wardrobe is the wardrobe of the Righteous Judge and that the golden sash across His chest constitutes the glorified insignia of His magisterial office in executing the judgment of His Father upon the world.

It is worthy to note that the OT breastpiece also included gold in its composition, along with the blue, purple, and crimson yarn and finely twisted linen (Exod 28:15-30, 39:8-21). Among other adornments, it also hosted twelve stones engraved with the names of each tribe in Israel. Such adornments clearly identify the OT high priest as judge only of the Nation of Israel. However, in the current vision, the sash across Jesus' chest picks up only the gold dynamic of the OT breastpiece, and does not include the twelve engraved stones. As such, we can conclude that Jesus' ministry as righteous Judge will not only be perfect in its execution (gold) but universal in scope.

The golden sash across the chest will also be the attire of the seven angels who will execute the judgment of the Seven Bowls of Wrath (Rev 15:6), thus corroborating the interpretation that the golden sash and its position across the chest symbolize the wardrobe of judgment in both instances!

In the fourth dynamic of Jesus' Resurrection Glory, the reference to Jesus' "hair on his head was white like wool" is reflected in Daniel 7:9, where one called the Ancient One, or the Ancient of Days (KJV), is described as having hair as "white like wool." As the Ancient One is interpreted as being the Father, it is safe to conclude that a similar description would be attributed to His Resurrected Son, since He is as 'ancient' as His Father (cf. John 1:1-2; 8:58). In addition to signifying 'ancientness,' the color white is often used to signify both holiness and righteousness, attributes that befit both the Father and the Son as well as the character of their judgment (cf. Ps 50:3-4, 6).

The fifth dynamic of Jesus' Resurrection Glory, "his eyes were like blazing fire," engages the imagery of the fire that will test and judge the works of God's people under both Covenants (Mal 3:2-3; 1 Cor 3:13) as well as judge those who have not obeyed or believed the Word of God under either Covenant (Isa 66:15-16; 2 Thess 1:7-8).

The sixth dsynamic of Jesus' Resurrection Glory, "his feet were like bronze glowing in a furnace," reflects His prophetic capacity to tread "the winepress of the fierceness and wrath of Almighty God" (Rev 19:15b) in the day of His vengeance (Isa 63:1-3).

The seventh dynamic of Jesus' Resurrection Glory, which characterizes Jesus' voice "like the sound of rushing waters," is indicated by similar imagery in Ezekiel's vision of the return of the Glory of the God of Israel, who is Jesus, to the millennial Temple:

> *Then the man brought me to the gate facing east, and I saw the glory of the God of Israel was coming from the east.* **His voice was like the roar of rushing waters;** *and the land was radiant with* **His** *glory (Ezek 43:1-2 – author's emphases).*

In Daniel's vision, the voice of the "man clothed in linen . . . " is characterized thusly:

> *"and **His voice** like the **sound of a multitude**" (Dan 10:6e – author's emphases).*

A similar characterization is recorded in Rev 14:2a, where in John's vision of the Lamb standing on Mount Zion, accompanied by 144,000 sealed saints, he hears a

> ***"sound from heaven** like the **roar of rushing waters** and like a loud peal of thunder" (author's emphases).*

This same voice, rendered as a singular noun, is also attributed to "a great multitude, like the roar of rushing waters and like loud peals of thunder (Rev 19:6b). The Lord's voice is also characterized as thunder in Psalm 29.

Critical to the interpretation of Jesus' voice is the fact that "rushing waters" in both the Ezekiel and Revelation passages is more accurately translated from the Hebrew and Greek texts as "many waters." Jesus' voice as "the sound of many waters" receives additional meaning from the Hebrew and Greek words for 'sound' as well as from evidence within *THE REVELATION* text on the definition "many waters." The Hebrew word קוֹל (pronounced kōl) and the Greek word φωνή (pronounced phō-**nay'**) not only carry the meanings of 'voice' and 'sound', but can also mean 'language,' which, of course, is conveyed on the waves of voice and sound. If Jesus' voice, as language, is likened to the sound of many waters, then "many waters" must be the *multiplicity of languages* spoken by the human family (Gen 11:1-9), and even by nature itself (Ps 19:2-4). This interpretation of the "many waters" as languages is firmly endorsed in Revelation 17:1 and 15, where the "many waters" are interpreted within the text as "peoples, multitudes, nations and *languages*." Based on this internal evidence, Jesus' voice, as the sound of many 'languages,' can and will be heard and understood by any language spoken by humanity and nature (cf. Ps 19:1-4).

Since Jesus is the Righteous Judge of all who dwell in heaven and on the earth, then His universal capacity to communicate in any language means that all will hear His commands and His judgments in their respective language. Consider that God inaugurated the plurality of languages at the Tower of Babel to disperse the people from their building project (Gen 11:1-9). However, on the Day of Pentecost, this same multiplicity of languages was used to proclaim the mighty acts of God for the ultimate building project of His church (Acts 2:1-21)! Not only were many languages spoken by the anointed disciples, but those languages were spoken with clarity, as each nation present heard and understood their own language coming from the lips of unlearned, yet anointed, Galilean disciples (Acts 2:5-11).

The above-cited interpretation represents a beautiful blend of Jesus' voice as both Trumpet sound (Rev 1:10) and as the sound of many waters: for as trumpet sound, Jesus' judgments and commands will be declared with clarity; and as the sound of many waters, all languages will hear the clarity of His judgments and commands. Consider that it will be this unique blend of Jesus' voice as trumpet and sound of many waters [languages] that will be evident when He

> "descends . . . with a **shout**, with the **voice** of an archangel, with the **trump** of God" (1 Thess 4:16 KJV, **author's emphases**),

when the dead of all language groups will hear His voice and be raised from their graves (John 5:25, 28)! Consider also that in the current context of judgment, Jesus' voice as trumpet sound and as the sound of many 'languages,' will be the vehicle with which He will wield the instrument of His righteous judgment: the sharp, double-edged sword that comes from His mouth!

Before examining the sharp, two-edged sword that comes from Jesus' mouth, which constitutes the ninth dynamic of the vision John saw of Jesus in his Resurrection Glory, we will proceed to discuss the eighth element of the vision, which states that "in his right hand he held seven stars." This and the seven golden lampstands are the only elements of His Resurrection Glory that Jesus personally defines for John in verse 20 of this same chapter: "the seven stars are the angels of the seven churches." The fact that these seven stars are held in His right hand indicates both His possession of and His authority over these stars. More importantly, Jesus' possession of and authority over these stars or angels also point to His superiority over them: for they are His creation and He is their Creator. As a result, the stars or angels serve Jesus and execute His commands as obedient servants. The identification of these stars as the "angels" of the seven churches will be discussed, in turn, within the exegetical treatment of verse 20.

The ninth dynamic of Jesus' Resurrection Glory, as previously mentioned, is the "sharp, double-edged sword" that comes from Jesus' mouth. Hebrews 4:12-13 aptly characterizes the word of God as the sharp, double-edged sword that has the surgical capacity to divide "soul and spirit, joints and marrow . . . and judges the thoughts and attitudes of the heart." Ezekiel 21:1-24 and Revelation 19:15 also reveal that God's sharp sword is used as a weapon of judgment and destruction.[42] We can

---

42 In Ezekiel 21:9, the double-edged characteristic of the sword is implied by the repetition, "A sword, a sword is sharpened." Though the sword in the Ezekiel passage represents Babylon as his instrument of judgment against His own people (21:19), it foreshadows God's judgment through Jesus against all unrighteousness. In Rev 19:15, the double-edged characteristic of the sharp sword that proceeds from Jesus' Mouth is implied, rather than explicitly stated; however, we can safely assume its connection to this current Vision.

safely conclude that, in His Resurrection Glory, Jesus, whose Name is the Word of God (Rev 19:13), will come the second time as both Judge and Conqueror: judging the thoughts and attitudes of the heart and repaying "to each person according to what they have done" (Rev 22:12). This truth was only partially proclaimed during His First Advent (cf. John 5:22, 27), but is now fully revealed in *THE REVELATION* given to John.

The tenth and final dynamic of the John's vision of Jesus' Resurrection Glory is "His Face ... like the sun shining in all its brilliance." Daniel recorded his vision of "the man clothed in linen" as having a "face like lightning" (Dan 10:6b). What was probably most convincing to John about this tenth dynamic was its striking similarity to the transfigured vision of Jesus' glory, which he, Peter, and James beheld, in a moment, on the Mount of Transfiguration (Matt 17:1-9; Mark 9:2-9; Luke 9:28-36). Though the three cited Gospels record the appearance of Jesus' clothes in His Transfiguration as "white as light," "dazzling white," and "as bright as a flash of lightning," only Matthew's Gospel records that Jesus' transfigured "***Face*** shone like the sun" (Matt 17:2, ***author's emphasis***). Just as John, and the others, saw Jesus exuding the dynamics of His Pre-Incarnate Glory on the Mount of Transfiguration, so John now beholds Jesus in all the dynamics of His Resurrection Glory, thus validating for John, and for us, that the Father indeed answered Jesus' High Priestly petition that He be returned to His former Glory:

> *And now, Father, glorify me in your presence with the **glory I had with you before the world began** (John 17:5 – **author's emphases**).*

Additionally, John records Jesus' response to Peter's query concerning John's future. Peter asked Jesus, "Lord, what about him (John)?" And "Jesus answered, 'If I want him to remain alive until I return, what is that to you? You must follow me!'" (John 21:21-22). As the text goes on to clarify, Jesus did not say that John would not die before He returned, but that Jesus could cause John to remain or tarry in the flesh until He came. What we can deduce from Jesus' statement and John's current vision is that Jesus did allow John to tarry in the flesh long enough to return to him in this current vision of Himself in Glory! Given Jesus' total Revelation of Himself to John, it is equally evident that John was due to be among those who

> *"will not taste death before they* **see** *that the kingdom of God has come with power" (Mark 9:1; Luke 9:27,* **author's emphasis***)!*

Of a certainty, John was shown, in vision, the Kingdom of God coming with power, as he was on the Isle of Patmos, in the Spirit, on the Lord's Day!!!

For more about the visible manifestation of God's Glory, please meditate upon the following passages: Genesis 12:7, 17:1, 18:1, 26:2, 24, 35:9; Exodus 3:2-10; 1 Kings 8:10-11; 2 Chronicles 5:13-14; Isaiah 6:1-10; Ezekiel 40:1-4.

VERSE 17

> *"When I saw him, I fell at his feet as though dead. Then he placed his right hand on me and said: "Do not be afraid. I am the First and the Last."*

John's postural response to the Vision of Jesus in His Resurrection Glory, i.e., "fell at his feet as though dead," is, depicted throughout Scripture (see Scripture references in the textbox) as typical, historic, and prophetic: typical, in that it is the only posture befitting a sinner before a sinless God; historic, in that it is the repeated posture of all who have encountered God's Glory, first hand, down through the ages; and prophetic, in that it anticipates the posture of all creation, as prophesied by God Himself and as echoed by the apostles of the New Testament:

*By myself I have sworn, my mouth has uttered in all integrity a word that will not be revoked: '**Before me every knee will bow; by me every tongue will swear** (Isa 45:23; Rom 14:11; Phil 2:9-11; Rev 5:13 – **author's emphasis**).*

For further evidence of the response of God's servants (including the demonic) to the visible manifestation of His Glory, please meditate upon the following passages: Genesis 17:3; Numbers 16:20-22, 44-45; 20:6; Deuteronomy 9:18,25; Joshua 5:14; Judges 13:20; 1 Kings 18:38-39; Ezekiel 1:28; 3:23; 43:1-5; 44:4; Matthew 2:11; 17:5-6; Mark 3:11; 5:22; 7:25; Luke 5:8,12; 8:26-28,41; 17:5-6; Acts 9:3-4; Revelation 4:9-10; 7:11; 11:16.

Jesus, in turn, lays His right hand upon John — a gesture which both quickens and empowers him. This gesture, however, is significant for another reason. If you will recall, Jesus was holding the seven stars in his right hand in the Vision (1:16). There is no mention of Jesus switching the seven stars to His left hand in order to place His right hand on John. Considering that the seven stars are the seven angels who will transmit Jesus' message to each church, and that the right hand often symbolizes power and authority, then by placing His right hand on John, with the seven stars still in His right hand, Jesus was conferring the same power to John as to the angels to declare His message to the seven churches.

Jesus' first words to John, i.e., "Do not be afraid," are also as typical, historic, and prophetic as John's posture: typical, in that a sinner does become acutely aware of his/her sinfulness in the presence of a Holy God and is, therefore, afraid (Isa 6:5); historic, in that God's Glory has always elicited fear in the hearts of both believer and unbeliever alike;

and prophetic, in that the God who elicits fear is also the God who has, and will, speak words of comfort to His people (cf. Isa 40:1).

For a rehearsal of God's words of comfort to His servants, please meditate upon the following passages: Genesis 15:1; 21:17; 26:24; Isaiah 40:1-2; 41:8-13; 43:1-7; 44:1-8; 54:4; Jeremiah 30:10-11; 46:27-28; Daniel 10:12,19; Haggai 2:1-5; Zechariah 8:13-15; Luke 1:30-33; 2:10-14; 5:9-10; 8:49-50; 12:32; Acts 27:23-24; 2 Corinthians 1:3-7.

Verse 17 concludes with a variation of Jesus' self-declaration, i.e., "I Am the First and the Last," thus re-affirming Himself as One with the Eternal God and Father of all creation (review discussion on v8).

VERSE 18

"I am the Living One; I was dead, and now look, I am alive for ever and ever! And I hold the keys of death and Hades."

In tandem with His initial declaration, as previously cited, Jesus further distinguishes Himself as the eternal Son of God in what we might call a trilogy. For example, in the first phrase, "I am the Living One," Jesus declares Himself as He who has always lived — placing Him in eternity past. The second phrase, "I was dead," implies His life in the flesh which did indeed end in His physical death — thus placing Him in time; and the third phrase, "And now look, I am alive for ever and ever," unequivocally affirms His Resurrection from the grave, having been raised never to die again (cf. Rom 6:9), thus placing Him in eternity present and future. Jesus concludes His Testimony by asserting His victory over Satan, in that He (Jesus) now possesses "the keys of Death and of Hades," — keys that were previously held (by divine permission) by a now defeated foe (cf. 2 Tim 1:8-10; Heb 2:14-15)!!!

VERSE 19

"Write, therefore, what you have seen, what is now and what will take place later."

Jesus, again, re-iterates His command to John to write what he sees and, in doing so, gives to us the three major structural units of the entire book of *THE REVELATION*. John, in other words, is commanded to write "what [he] has seen" — a direct reference to the Vision of Jesus in His Resurrection Glory (Chapter 1); he is to write "what is now" — a direct reference to the letters to the seven churches (Chapters 2-3); and he is to write "what is to take place later" — an allusion to Daniel's use of a similar phrase in a similar context of judgment (Dan 2:28, 45) and a direct reference to all that occurs in Chapters 4 to 22 of *THE REVELATION* text, culminating in the creation of the New Heavens and the New Earth.

VERSE 20

"The mystery of the seven stars that you saw in my right hand and of the seven golden lampstands is this: The seven stars are the angels of the seven churches, and the seven lampstands are the seven churches."

Jesus interprets the imagery of the seven stars and the seven golden lampstands for John. Both are classified as 'mysteries,' a term that constitutes an allusion to Daniel 2:28-30, where end-times are also the focus of the text. Though the seven lampstands are plainly defined as the seven churches, it becomes necessary to identify who the angels are, why they are characterized as stars, and what their relationship is to Jesus, to the churches, and to John.

First, let us explore Jesus' characterization of the angels of the seven churches as "stars." It is worthy to note, for example, that Lucifer's name in the Hebrew language (הֵילֵל – pronounced hĕ-**lel´**) means "morning star" and, as such, gives revelatory evidence of the primordial tension between him and Jesus who is called the "Bright Morning Star" (Rev 22:16). It is also worthy to note that though the dynamics of Satan's expulsion from heaven are amply recorded in Isaiah 14:12-17 and Ezekiel 28:11-19, it is in Revelation 12:3-4b, 7-13 that we learn that Satan drew only one-third of the 'stars' (angels) of heaven in his rebellion. This means that the remaining two-thirds of the angelic host, i.e., the 10,000 x 10,000 . . . (Ps 68:17; 104:3b; Dan 7:10; Rev 5:11), remained, and continue to remain, faithful to God! Just as Satan (a.k.a. Lucifer, the fallen "morning star") has an army of fallen angels or demons who, with God's permission and for a short time, execute Satan's agenda of rebellion and apostasy, so God has an army of righteous angels who minister God's truth, righteousness, and holiness on behalf of believers (cf. Heb 1:14). However, God's army of angels outnumbers Satan's army two to one!

Thus, it is a matter of divine logic that not only are those whom Jesus commands in heaven called stars, deriving their name from his more Glorious Name, i.e., "Bright Morning Star,"[43] but He, who created the stars (for angels are created beings), is superior to the stars or angels He

As a battle strategy, the ratio of two righteous angels to one unrighteous angel bears fruit in our understanding when we consider that Gabriel needed Michael's help to withstand the 'prince' of Persia (Dan 10:13); that JESUS sent out His disciples two by two with authority and power over evil spirits (Mark 6:7); that in the mouth of two or three witnesses a truth is established (Deut 19:15; John 8:17-18; 2 Cor 13:1;); that if two agree about "anything you ask for, it will be done for you by my father in heaven" (Matt 18:19); and that where "two or three come together in My Name, there am I with them" (Matthew 18:20).

---

43   An analogy can also be drawn from the name 'Christian' (Acts 11:26), as derived from the name of the 'Christ," our Head, Lord and Savior.

created, including the fallen ones, as is plainly declared in Hebrews 1:4-7. Therefore, the stars or angels are servants of Jesus and Jesus is their Commander and Chief.

Secondly, as their Commander and Chief, Jesus has apparently assigned each of the seven angels/stars to one of the seven churches in Asia Minor for the purpose of communicating revelation knowledge concerning Him. This should not be hard to imagine: for just as fallen angels are also referred to as stars (Rev 12:4), are given jurisdiction over pagan nations (Dan. 10:12-13) and are the inspiration of apostasy (2 Cor 11:13-15), so righteous angels who, for the first time in Job 38:7, are called "morning stars" by God Himself, and are called "stars" by Jesus in our current text, are appointed to have jurisdiction over the redeemed of the Lord (Ps 91:11-12; Dan. 12:1), and to impart the Truth of God in Christ (Dan. 10:14, 21; Heb 1:13-14). The relationship of these righteous stars or angels to the churches, of whom Jesus is Head, is as "ministering spirits sent to serve those who will inherit salvation" (Heb 1:14; cf. Ps 104:3-4).

Thirdly, with respect to the righteous angels' relationship to John, we would do well to consider the prophetic testimony that in the resurrection "those who are wise will shine like the brightness of the heavens, and those who lead many to righteousness, [will shine] *like the stars for ever and ever*" (Dan 12:3 — *author's emphasis and clarifying insertion*).[44] We need to first affirm that the "stars" implied in the second phrase of this verse are not the celestial bodies of the sky (which would be easy to assume not only because of the allegorical reference to the

---

44   The parenthetic insertion of [will shine] in the second phrase of Dan 12:3 is the author's acknowledgment of a common literary technique in Hebrew prophecy and poetry called 'gapping,' whether of the subject, the verb, or of a preposition. In this case, the verb "will shine" is gapped in the second phrase. In other words, "will shine" is not explicitly stated but is implied in the second phrase and carries the same meaning of its explicitly expressed parallel in the first phrase. However, this is where the parallelism between the two phrases ends.

"heavens" in the first phrase but also because parallelism between phrases is strategically employed throughout the Hebrew Scriptures to emphasize a point). These "stars" are "angels" by virtue of the stated activity in the second phrase of this verse, i.e., "those who lead many to righteousness." In other words, the subject of each phrase in this verse receives its definition from the activity in that phrase, not from the literary use of parallelism in this instance. For example, the wisdom of the wise will cause them to radiate like the brightness of the (celestial) heavens (cf. Isa 58:8a, 10b). However, righteousness is something people are led into by proclamation, exhortation (teaching), and revelation knowledge. It is attested throughout Scripture that angels are the conveyors of all three of these avenues of God's Will and Word[45] and thus allows us to safely conclude that the term "stars" in this second phrase refers to angels, and not to celestial bodies, by virtue of the work of leading to righteousness.

The 'shining' of these stars, or angels, is also attested in Scripture by their appearance in "clothes that gleamed like lightning" (Luke 24:4) or "dressed in white" (Acts 1:10). Jesus also confirmed that those who inherit the resurrection unto eternal life will be in the form of angels (Luke 20:35-36). Finally, as the stars in the second phrase of Dan 12:3 will shine forever, we can safely conclude that those so characterized will live in the New Heaven and the New Earth, in which there will be no celestial bodies of light: "for the glory of God gives it light, and the Lamb is its lamp" (Rev 21:23b; 22:5).

Daniel 12:3 and its 2nd phrase, in particular, is a beautiful and symbolic characterization of John himself who, in the Spirit on the Lord's Day, was instructed to fulfill the angels' (stars') ministry of conveying revelation knowledge to God's people, the churches. In doing so, John is and will

---

45   Proclamation – Luke 2:8-14; Rev 14:6-11; Exhortation – Matt 1:20-21; Luke 1:26-37; Revelation Knowledge – Dan 7:15-16; 8:15-19; 9:20-23. These references are not exhaustive but representative.

be among the wise who will shine like the brightness of the heavens and who will lead many to righteousness through his proclamation, albeit in writing, to the seven churches. John is thereby brought into collegial relationship with the angels as a fellow servant (cf. Rev 19:9-10; 22:8-9).

When we consider, therefore, that angels are the higher life form (Ps 8:4-5), but that the saints, like John, will judge the angels (1 Cor 6:3); that in the resurrection the saints will be equal in form to the angels (Luke 20:34-36), and that the world to come will not be subject to angels, but to the Redeemer and to the redeemed of humanity, like John (Heb 2:5-9), then John's relationship to the angel of each church whom he is instructed to address is not only as their equal in his current ministry to the churches (Rev 19:9-10; 22:8-9), but also as their superior,[46] because of his redeemed relationship to Jesus, who is superior to the angels (Heb 1:4-7) and with whom he (John) will reign over the angels (along with all the redeemed) in the coming kingdom!

We have already noted the revelatory distinction of the Holy Spirit as Jesus' Angel (Rev. 1:1; 22:16). However, given the presence and participation of the angelic host as heavenly emissaries in the unfolding drama of *THE REVELATION*, it is proposed that the term "angel" here and elsewhere is a consistent reference to a heavenly being[47] and will be the interpretation of angels throughout this commentary on *THE REVELATION* text, unless otherwise noted.

---

46 This "superior" position of the redeemed in the coming kingdom manifests the divine principle that the first (angels) shall become last, and that the last (redeemed humans) shall become first (Matt 19:30; 20:16; Mark 10:31; Luke 13:30).

47 Beale, *THE BOOK OF REVELATION: A COMMENTARY ON THE GREEK TEXT*, 217. See footnotes number 133-137 on page 217 in Beale's text for authors who espouse other interpretations of these angels. Beale, however, asserts that since the Greek word for angel "refers without exception to heavenly beings in the visionary portion of Revelation (about 60 times) [then the term] points to the same identification here.

CHAPTER TWO

THE CHURCH IN EPHESUS
REVELATION 2:1-7

2:1 "To the angel of the church in Ephesus write: These are the words of him who holds the seven stars in his right hand and walks among the seven golden lampstands.

2 I know your deeds, your hard work and your perseverance. I know that you cannot tolerate wicked people, that you have tested those who claim to be apostles but are not, and have found them false.

3 You have persevered and have endured hardships for my name, and have not grown weary.

4 Yet I hold this against you: You have forsaken the love you had at first.

5 Consider how far you have fallen. Repent and do the things you did at first. If you do not repent, I will come to you and remove your lampstand from its place.

6 But you have this in your favor: You hate the practices of the Nicolaitans, which I also hate.

7 Whoever has ears, let them hear what the Spirit says to the churches. To the one who is victorious, I will give the right to eat from the tree of life, which is in the paradise of God."

VERSE 1

"To the angel of the church in Ephesus write: These are the words of him who holds the seven stars in his right hand and walks among the seven golden lampstands."

In Revelation 1:20, Jesus defined the seven stars in His right hand as the "angels of the seven churches," i.e., one for each church location, as indicated by the single angel being addressed in each letter (2:1, 8, 12, 18; 3:1, 7, 14). In addition to being characterized as "stars" by Jesus Himself, angels are also depicted in Scripture as God's "winds . . . messengers, flames of fire his servants" (Ps 104:4; Heb 1:7) and are affirmed as "ministering spirits sent to serve those who will inherit salvation" (Heb 1:14). The angel of the church in Ephesus, therefore, is an angelic messenger or spirit who has been assigned to the church in Ephesus for the purpose of communicating revelation knowledge concerning Jesus.

The church in Ephesus was founded by the Apostle Paul on his 3rd missionary journey (Acts 19:1-41), where he taught for three (3) years (Acts 20:31), and over which he left Timothy as Bishop (1 Tim 1:3). The church in Ephesus was a predominantly Gentile congregation (Eph 2:11-22), whose converts hailed from the city's Asiatic culture for which the main religion was the worship of Diana (also known as Artemis of the Ephesians), a multi-breasted goddess who represented an alleged power over conception and birth, among other attributes. Silversmiths in the city made their living by crafting small versions of her image (Acts 19:23-41); and her temple was ranked as one of the seven wonders of the ancient world.[48] The city's coastal location, however, made it the perfect gateway for the spread of the Gospel throughout Asia Minor (cf. Acts 19:8-10).

---

48   Unger, THE NEW UNGER'S BIBLE DICTIONARY, 366-367, 483-484.

In His 3rd command to John to write,[49] Jesus identified Himself to the "angel of the church in Ephesus" by two elements of the afore-mentioned Vision of His Resurrection Glory: "Him who holds the seven stars in His right hand" (Rev. 1:16) and "Him who walks among the seven golden lampstands" (Rev. 1:13). Since the angel being addressed is also one of the seven stars/angels that Jesus is holding in His right hand and who has been assigned to one of the lampstands, i.e., the church in Ephesus, among whom Jesus walks, then the angel's station of being held in Jesus' right hand re-affirms Jesus' authority over the angels who are sent to minister to the heirs of salvation, as "he became as much superior to the angels as the name he has inherited is superior to theirs" (Heb 1:4).

As the seven golden lampstands are indeed the seven churches,[50] then Jesus' "walk" in the midst of His Body as a whole (the number seven representing completeness), is first of all indicative of His ownership of the church, much as one can walk through one's own property at any time without being accused of trespassing. The Greek form of the verb for 'walks' suggests that Jesus is continually walking in the midst of His church.

As the seven golden lampstands, i.e., the churches, are channels of the Light of Jesus, then Jesus' walk in the midst of His Body, the churches, clearly indicates that He is both the source and the substance of the light of the Revelation concerning Himself (John 1:4, 9; 3:19-21; 8:12; 9:5; 12:35-36, 46; 1 John 1:5-7). Though John is told to write down the light of the Revelation of Jesus being dictated to him, and though the angel of the church is to receive and to communicate the light of the Revelation of Jesus to the church, and though the churches are to let their light shine by receiving, believing and obeying the proclaimed light of the Revelation

49   See discussion on Rev 1:11, 19

50   See discussion on Rev 1:20

of Jesus, each (John, angel and the churches) is totally dependent upon Jesus, who is the Light of the world.

For the individual believer, Jesus' 'walking' is equivalent to the indwelling presence and power of the Holy Spirit, who, in turn, empowers the believer to 'walk' with Jesus in the following ways:

- Walk in the good works that God has before ordained (Eph 2:10)

- Walk worthy of the vocation wherewith you are called (Eph 4:1; cf. Col 1:10; 2:6; 1 Thess 2:12)

- Walk not as other Gentiles walk (Eph 4:17-19), as we ourselves used to walk in times past (Eph 2:1-3)

- Walk in love, as Christ also has loved us (Eph 5:2)

- Walk as children of light (Eph 5:8, 11-14; cf. John 12:35; 1 Thess. 5:5)

- Walk circumspectly (Eph 5:15-17; cf. Col 4:5)

In a similar context of judgment, the question posed in Amos to the Nation of Israel, regarding their relationship to the LORD, applies to the church regarding her relationship to Jesus:

> *"Do two walk together unless they have agreed to do so?"*
> *(Amos 3:3).*

VERSE 2

I know your deeds, your hard work and your perseverance. I know that you cannot tolerate wicked people, that you have tested those who claim to be apostles but are not, and have found them false.

All of Jesus' credentials, as cited in verse one, i.e., holding the stars in His right hand, walking among the seven golden lampstands, and being the source and substance of light to His Body, the church, qualify Him to assert without equivocation, "I know your deeds." His assertion echoes the wisdom of Prov 5:21: "For a man's ways are in full view of the LORD, and he examines all his paths." The Father was the first to assert His Omniscience of the deeds of His people and of all the nations on the earth for the purpose of judging sin (Isa 37:28, 66:18a; Jer 16:17, 29:23c; Amos 5:12 – just to name a few). Jesus makes this same assertion of Omniscience concerning the deeds and faults of the church in Ephesus, as well as for five of the six remaining churches (Smyrna, Thyatira, Sardis, Philadelphia and Laodicea).[51]

Jesus' knowledge of the church's "hard work" is, in truth, His knowledge of their faith in Him, as defined in his answer to the question posed in John 6:27-29: "What must we do to do the works God requires?" Jesus answered them, "The **work of God** is this: to **believe in the one** he has sent" *[author's emphases]*. Maintaining one's faith in and faithfulness to Jesus is work, not only in response to persecutions from those outside the church, but especially in response to the apostasy of those within the church, as we will soon see.

The Greek word translated "perseverance," ὑπομονή (pronounced hū-pō-mō-nay´), actually bears the meaning of "patient endurance"

---

51   For the church in Pergamum, Jesus will state "I know where you are living, where Satan's throne is," which will be discussed at that point.

and expresses the believer's righteous response toward adverse situations, like trials, tribulations and persecutions.[52] The character of the church's patient endurance will be explained in verse 3 (see also discussion on Rev 1:9).

In the phrase "cannot tolerate / bear wicked people," the Greek verb translated tolerate or bear (βαστάζω – pronounced bâs-tâ´-dzo) is the same one used in John 10:31, where the Jews took up / picked up / bore up stones to stone Jesus for His claim, "I and the Father are One." As such, the use of the word here implies that the church could not tolerate or bear those who were persecuting the church through a rejection of Jesus as the church's Head. This implication is borne out by the church's activity in discerning and testing both the false apostles and the seditious doctrines that had crept into her midst.

Jesus commended the church for having followed the divine instruction regarding false teachers and false doctrines, i.e., to "not believe every spirit, but test the spirits to see whether they are from God . . . " (1 John 4:1). Jesus' commendation also indicated that the church in Ephesus had not become spiritual deserters of the Word, of which Paul forewarned Timothy in his second letter to him: "For the time will come when people will not put up with sound doctrine. Instead, to suit their own desires, they will gather around them a great number of teachers to say what their itching ears want to hear. They will turn their ears away from the truth and turn aside to myths" (2 Tim 4:3-4; cf. Isa 30:8-14).

---

52 Whereas ὑπομονή (hū-pō-mō-**nay**´) is the believer's response to adverse situations, another Greek word for patience, μακροθυμία (pronounced mă-krŏ-thū-mee´-â), is translated as one of the fruit of the Spirit (Gal 5:22) and is mainly the believer's response to persons. It is also used to depict the character of God's long-suffering towards those who are in sin.

It is worthy to note that there is ample Biblical testimony that false apostles, false teachers and false doctrines will infiltrate the church. In Matthew 7:15-20, for example, Jesus warned of false prophets in His Sermon on the Mount. In the apocalyptic passages of Matthew, Mark, and Luke (Matt 24:11, 24; Mark 13:21-23; Luke 21:8), Jesus also prophesied of the appearance of false Christs and false prophets as a clear sign of the coming judgment upon the world. The Apostle Paul characterized false teachers as those who would come preaching another Jesus, who would come with another spirit, and who would come presenting another gospel (2 Cor 11:4; Gal 1:9). These, he concluded, were/are the emissaries of Satan who, himself, "masquerades as an angel of light. It is not surprising, then, if his servants also masquerade as servants of righteousness. Their end will be what their actions deserve" (2 Cor 11:14-15). The Apostle Peter gives a more detailed and scathing description of the doctrine and behavior of false teachers (2 Peter 2:1-3, 12-22), and John, in the first of his pastoral Epistles, delivers the perennial command to

> "not believe every spirit, but test the spirits to see whether they are from God, because many false prophets have gone out into the world. This is how you can recognize the Spirit of God: Every spirit that acknowledges that Jesus Christ has come in the flesh is from God, but every spirit that does not acknowledge Jesus is not from God. This is the spirit of the antichrist, which you have heard is coming and even now is already in the world" (1 John 4:1-3).

VERSE 3

"You have persevered and have endured hardships for my name, and have not grown weary."

Jesus echoes His commendation of the church's perseverance, as introduced in verse 2, by coupling it with an on-going and untiring manifestation of patient endurance. The need for this quality of perseverance and endurance in the face of trials is also expressed in Luke 21:19, Revelation 13:10c, and Revelation 14:12, where some form of the same Greek word for patient endurance is used: ὑπομονή (pronounced hū-pō-mō-nay´).

In Jesus' commendation that the church had "endured hardships for my name," it is worthy to note that the Greek word for "endured" is the same one used in verse 2 for "tolerate" (βαστάζω – pronounced bâs-tâ´-dzo), but carries the affirmative dynamic of this word. In other words, Jesus commends the church for staying faithful to His name, or reputation, despite the opposition they have endured because of it. This same Greek word is used in John's Gospel account of Jesus carrying or bearing up under the weight of His Cross up Calvary's Hill (John 19:17). Not only does this word link between our current text and John's Gospel give us additional evidence that John is the recipient/scribe of THE REVELATION, but it also imparts the full force of this characteristic of the church's endurance for the sake of His name.

Jesus concludes this segment of His commendation of the church in Ephesus by noting their resilience, or steadfastness, in their patient endurance. This is expressed as having "not grown weary." Inasmuch as patient endurance is needed to wait for the Lord's return, then it becomes necessary for believers not to grow weary in doing the righteousness they know to do (Gal 6:9; 2 Thess 3:13), despite the opposition or persecutions they will incur along the way (cf. Matt 5:10-12).

VERSE 4

"Yet I hold this against you: You have forsaken the love you had at first."

Jesus highly commends the church for maintaining doctrinal purity as well as remaining faithful to His Name while suffering opposition. However, Jesus levies an indictment that is aimed behind the scenes at the motivational level, since it is an issue of the heart: the church has "forsaken the love you had at first."

Though the Greek root for "forsaken" is the word predominantly translated "forgiveness" (ἀφίημι – pronounced â-fee´-ay-mee), its current form in our current text carries the additional meaning of 'left' or 'forsaken' (ἀφῆκες - pronounced â-**fay´**-kĕs). This same meaning is appropriated a total of 32 times in the NT, ranging in significance from the leaving of a water pot by the Samaritan woman at the well (John 4:28), to the leaving of fishnets and all else by disciples to follow Jesus (Matt 4:22; Mark 1:20), to those who are left when others are taken during the coming judgment (Matt 24:40-41), to the judgment of Israel's house being left to them desolate (Luke 13:35), to Jesus' declaration that "The one who sent me is with me; he has not left me alone, for I always do what pleases him" (John 8:29).

Given that the church in Ephesus was primarily Gentile in composition (Eph 2:11-22), and that it was to her that the Apostle Paul first revealed the mystery of the church that entailed the inclusion of Gentiles as fellow heirs and partakers of God's promise in Christ (Eph 3:1-6), then the "first love," or "love that they had at first," which they had forsaken, was their humble gratitude for their salvation in Jesus Christ. In other words, the church had ceased to see others as they themselves had once been seen: as those who were once "separate from Christ, excluded from citizenship in Israel and foreigners to the covenants of promise, without hope, and without God in the world. But now in Christ Jesus you who once were far away have been brought near by the blood of Christ" (Eph 2:12-13).

In His indictment, Jesus is pointing out that though it is commendable to be doctrinally pure, it is of greater importance to be grateful for that purity. This gratitude of heart is characterized by the Apostle Paul in the Letter to the Ephesians as "being rooted and grounded in love . . . " and "to know the *love of Christ that surpasses knowledge* . . . " (Eph 3:16-19, *author's emphases*). The full character of the love of Christ is eloquently expressed in 1 Corinthians 13 and is the more excellent way (1 Cor 12:31) to minister the truth of Jesus Christ, both within the Body of Christ and to a world in which we all once walked. Jesus Himself brought both grace and truth (John 1:17). One without the other is a distortion of the love that God has already demonstrated toward us in Christ Jesus, and which we are commanded to extend to each other within the Body (John 13:34-35; 1 John 4:7-21). Otherwise, we will be prone to the pride that precedes destruction, and to the haughty spirit that precipitates our fall (Prov 16:18).

VERSE 5

> "Consider how far you have fallen. Repent and do the things you did at first. If you do not repent, I will come to you and remove your lampstand from its place."

The Greek verb translated "consider" is μνημόνευε (pronounced menay-**mŏ**´-noi-ĕ), from which we get the English word "mnemonics,"' is more accurately translated "remember" and is the same word used in Ephesians 2:11, where the Gentile believers in Ephesus are commanded to remember who and where they were before they were saved (Eph 2:11-12). It was from the position of being called "uncircumcised" that they had been lifted to the position of "fellow citizens" with the saints and of the household of God. Of special note is that the Greek word for 'remember' in the Ephesian text is rendered as a plural imperative, as if speaking to multiple individual believers. The Greek word for "remember" in our current text, however, is rendered as a singular imperative, implying that the church as a whole is to have a singleness of purpose — a unity of the Spirit (Eph 4:3) — in recalling their new estate in Christ Jesus!

The Greek verb translated "fallen" (πέπτωκας – pronounced **pep′-tō-kâs**) implies a fall from an exalted state or position to one of ruin or uselessness. The Hebrew word for "fall" or "calamity" in Proverbs 16:18 shares a similar meaning (כָּשְׁלוֹן pronounced kee-shăl-lōn′). Whereas the Gentile believers in Ephesus had been elevated to fellow citizenship in God's House through their conversion, they had now fallen from their elevation through ecclesiastical pride and a haughty spirit (see Lucifer's "I will" assertions in Isaiah 14:13-14).

The Greek verb translated "repent" (μετανόησον – pronounced mĕt-â-nŏ′-ay-sŏn) is from the root verb used throughout the NT for repent. It is the equivalent to the Hebrew word נֹהַם (pronounced nō-**hawm′**), which is used in the OT to denote sorrow or repentance (cf. Hosea 13:14). The above Greek word carries the meaning of changing one's mind, heart and behavior from sinfulness to righteousness. Romans 2:4 makes it clear that the purpose of remembering God's grace is to repent of having fallen short of it: "Or do you show contempt for the riches of his kindness, forbearance and patience, **not realizing that God's kindness is intended to lead you to repentance?**" (Rom 2:4, *author's emphases*)? For all that Jesus had done for the believers in the church in Ephesus (and every believer in every generation), He is calling them, really commanding them, to repent of their ecclesiastical arrogance and return to the humble mindset of being sinners saved by grace (Eph 2:1-10).

The first works that accompany the first love of those who are humbly grateful for salvation is to evangelize others with the same grace and truth with which one has been evangelized. Love for Christ is to be the guiding motivation for this work of evangelism, not one's rank and unwarranted sense of superiority over the lost sinner, as the church in Ephesus was evidently manifesting (cf. John 3:27; 1 Cor 4:7).

Jesus then pronounces that the church ("lampstand") will be "removed from its place" if she refuses to remember, to repent, and to do the first works. The Greek verb translated 'remove' is from the root verb κινέω (pronounced kǐ-nĕ´-ō) and generally means 'to set in motion' or 'to move.' However, in this verse and in Rev 6:14, the same word carries the connotation of removing something out of its place. "Removing the lampstand or church from its place" would entail removing the church in Ephesus from its position of favor and usefulness in Jesus' kingdom-building agenda or removing the church so that it no longer existed.

Though this judgment may sound harsh, we must remember that this is Jesus' Body for whom He died out of love for His Father and for us. When His Body accrues another reputation other than the love He has demonstrated toward us (John 13:34-35), then His Body is no longer acknowledging Him as Head and no longer carrying out His Great Commission to evangelize the lost (Matt 28:18-20; John 20:21). These two pillars of our definition as the body of Christ are the very pillars for which the church in Philadelphia will be praised, i.e., *kept my word* (which acknowledges Jesus as Head over all things in the church — Ephesians 1:22; Colossians 1:18 — and preaches Christ and Christ alone — 1 Corinthians 1:23-24), and *not denied my name* ("Everyone therefore who acknowledges Me before others, I also will acknowledge before My Father in heaven; but whoever denies Me before others, I also will deny before My Father in heaven" Matt 10:32-33).

When a church ceases to emit and exemplify the Gospel light of God's love in Christ Jesus, then other types of gospels creep in (Gal 1:6-9) and distract believers from their eternal inheritance for more earth-bound and flesh-satisfying pursuits. These pseudo-gospels and their accompanying works may have the appearance of righteous activity (cf. Matt 7:21-23) but will receive the same assessment as Jesus gave to the church in Sardis: i.e., *"you have a reputation of being alive, but you are dead"* (3:1c).[53]

VERSE 6

"But you have this in your favor: You hate the practices of the Nicolaitans, which I also hate."

Jesus then modulates back into the mode of commending the church for hating what He hates. Many of us struggle with the notion of Jesus hating anything, as it appears to be the antithesis of His loving character, as we understand love. However, God's Love includes His hatred of evil. In His Love, for example, God sent His Son to die for the forgiveness of the sin He hates.

The Greek word μισεῖς (pronounced mee-**sās**'), translated "hate," is similar in meaning to the Hebrew word used in Prov 6:16 (שָׂנֵא – pronounced sâh-**nay**'), which lists the seven things that God hates, among which are a proud look, a heart that devises wicked imaginations, and the person who sows discord among brothers. The same Hebrew word expresses the Psalmist's "perfect hatred" for those who hate the Lord and who rise up against Him (Ps 139:21-22). It is this same hate, expressed in the above Greek verb, which Jesus shares with the church in Ephesus towards the works of the Nicolaitans.

The origin of the sect called the Nicolaitans is uncertain. However, it is surmised, based on its additional mention in the Letter to the church in Pergamum and its apparent connection to the teachings of Balaam (2:14-15), that in addition to advocating the inclusion of idol worship with

---

53   The church in Sardis also receives similar injunctions to remember and to repent (Rev. 3:3).

the worship of Jesus (cf. Zeph 1:5; 1 Kgs 12:25ff - Jeroboam; 2 Kgs 21:1-18; 2 Chron 33:1-10 – Manasseh), the Nicolaitans supported a compromise with the surrounding pagan culture by advocating the eating of food sacrificed to idols and committing sexual immorality.[54] It was the decision of the Council of Jerusalem, however, that Gentile converts to Christianity abstain from both (Acts 15:19-20, 28-29). The church's hate for this sect was well-grounded and to their credit in Jesus' estimation.

VERSE 7

"Whoever has ears, let them hear what the Spirit says to the churches. To the one who is victorious, I will give the right to eat from the tree of life, which is in the paradise of God."

"Whoever has ears, let them hear" — In addition to the two identifying elements from the vision of Jesus' Resurrection Glory that are introduced at the beginning of this letter, this phrase also forms a characteristic "imprint" of Jesus' Authorship of this letter, not only because it is repeated in all seven letters, but because Jesus first used these same words in His delivery of four distinct teachings during His earthly ministry:

- Matthew 11:15 – Jesus' eulogy of John the Baptist, which includes His correlation of John's ministry as His forerunner with Malachi's prophecy regarding Elijah's coming (Mal 4:5)

- Matthew 13:9, 43; Mark 4:9, 23; Luke 8:8 – Jesus' Parable of the Sower

- Matthew 13:43 – Jesus' Explanation of the Parable of the Weeds Among the Wheat (13:24-30)

- Luke 14:35 – Jesus' Parable on Flavorless Salt

---

54 Unger, *THE NEW UNGER'S BIBLE DICTIONARY*, 921.

Though John did not record this saying of Jesus in his Gospel account, we can be sure that he was present and heard Jesus speak this injunction in each of the above-cited preaching and teaching events.

What is enjoined in both the above-cited instances and in our current text is that the listener have the kind of ear that possesses the ability to hear the Spirit. Consider the kind of ear that Scripture commends as possessing the ability to hear God's Word and God's Spirit:

- Inclined Ear
  Psalm 78:1; 119:112; Prov 2:1-2; 4:20; Isa 55:3

- Open Ear
  Job 33:14-17; 36:10-12, 15; Psalm 40:6; Isa 48:8; 50:4-5; Mark 7:34-35

- Attentive Ear
  Luke 19:48

- Bowed down Ear
  Prov 5:1-2

- Obedient Ear
  1 Sam 15:22-23; Prov 25:12

"Consider the opposite "ear"' conditions that have, unfortunately, characterized the "hearing" capacity of God's people in each generation:

1. Inclined vs Heavy (Isa 6:10)

2. Open vs Clogged (Mark 7:31-37)

3. Attentive vs Dull (Acts 28:27)

4. Bowed down vs Itching (2 Tim 4:3-4)

5. Obedient vs Rebellious (Jer 25:4, 35:15)

There are at least two occasions when the Word of God and/
or God's Spirit are hard to hear:

1.   When God's Word comes to our ears as **reproof**.
     Consider the following mnemonic definition of reproof:
     the **RE – PR**esentation of the **O**bvious **O**pportunities for
     Faith. As such, the sting of reproof is two-fold: it rehearses
     what we already know (or should know), and it rehearses it
     at a time when we have given evidence of having forgotten,
     neglected, and/or abandoned what we already know (or
     should know). However, the encouragement to hear God's
     reproofs as well as the consequences of refusing to hear
     God's reproofs are both aptly expressed in the Wisdom
     of Proverbs, where God's reproof is characterized as
     "wholesome admonition" and "instruction."

The ear that heeds wholesome admonition will lodge among
the wise. Those that ignore instruction despise themselves; but
those who heed admonition gain understanding. The fear of the
Lord is instruction in wisdom: and humility goes before honor
(Proverbs 15:31-33).

2.   When our current understanding of God's Word is
     challenged and/or updated with the presentation of new
     insights and revelations from God's Word. In His Sermon
     on the Mount, for example, Jesus introduced updates to the
     people's understanding of the Law with the phrase, "You
     have heard it said in times past . . . but I say unto you . . . "
     As was evidenced by the reaction of the religious leaders
     of Jesus' day, our human tendency is to resist the update

to our understanding, even to the point of betraying (Matt 26:14-16) or killing the messenger! Consider what Israel did to all of God's prophets (Matt 23:37; Luke 13:34)? Consider what the Jews attempted to do to Jesus (Matt 21:45-46; 26:59; Mark 11:18, 12:12, 14:1-2, Luke 4:28-30, 19:47-48, 20:19, 22:2; John 5:16-18, 7:30, 8:58-59, 10:30-31, 38-39)?

The command to 'hear' reverberates back to the Great 'Shema' (Hebrew word for 'hear') of Israel's covenantal relationship with the Lord and in which the clarion call of her "first love" is declared:

> *"Hear, O Israel: The LORD our God, the LORD is one. **Love the LORD your God** with all your heart and with all your soul and with all your strength . . . [and] your neighbor as yourself (Deut 6:4; Lev 19:18, **author's emphases**).*

The command to 'hear' also endorses the initial pathway of faith:

> *So faith comes from what is heard, and what is heard comes through the word of Christ (Rom 10:17 NRSV).*

Additionally, in His Parable of the Sower, Jesus declares that the ears that "hear the Word, and receive it, and bring forth fruit . . . " are considered good ground.

"The Spirit is saying to the churches" — Though the angel is the messenger of the message to the church, it is the Spirit of Christ who is speaking through the angel. This should not be hard to fathom, since angels are themselves ministering spirits (Heb 1:14). However, we should also remember that a significant part of the Spirit's ministry was defined by Jesus this way: "He will not speak on his own; he will speak only what he hears . . . He will glorify me [Jesus] because it is from me that he will

receive what he will make known to you" (John 16:13-14). And what the Spirit will declare to His church was identified by Jesus as falling into three categories of revelation knowledge: to "bring all things to your remembrance, whatsoever I have said to you" (John 14:26 KJV); to "guide you into all truth . . . and to show you things to come" (John 16:13 KJV). The church's letter, in particular, and THE REVELATION, as a whole, will reflect all three of these categories of revelation knowledge!

Finally, the exhortation is for "Whoever has ears, let them hear what the Spirit says to the *churches*" (plural, *author's emphases*). In contrast to the assumption that each of the seven churches only received the Letter addressed specifically to them, Jesus' recurring injunction to have an ear to hear is clearly addressed to His church in the plural, i.e., churches, as in this verse (Rev 2:11, 17, 29, 3:6, 13, 22).[55] What this means is that all the churches received each other's letter as well as the remainder of THE REVELATION, so that they could be edified and forewarned of slipping into any of the other levels of apostasy or encouraged to aspire to the faithfulness of the churches in Smyrna and Philadelphia. The truth of this is corroborated in the final chapter of THE REVELATION where Jesus again reveals His intent that the churches receive the entire *Revelation* that was given to John: "It is I, Jesus, who sent My Angel to you with this testimony for the *churches* . . . " (Rev 22:16a – *author's emphases*). Jesus' proclamation is followed by a response from both the Spirit and the bride — a clear reference to the collective church — who say "Come" (Rev 22:17a).

As the current age of grace — or church age — will conclude with the rapture of the true church, then the entire *Revelation*, as we have already mentioned, not only serves to exhort each church to heed Jesus' corrective for their specific, individual and congregational conditions,

---

55 Ben Witherington, III, *REVELATION* (Cambridge Bible Commentary) (New York: Cambridge University Press, 2003), 96; Steve Gregg, ed., Revelation - Four Views: A Parallel Commentary, 65.

but to both forewarn each church of slipping into any of the other levels of apostasy, as exemplified by the indictments against the other churches, and to inspire each church's faithfulness and readiness, as exemplified by the churches in Smyrna and in Philadelphia, for what will, in truth, be the first phase of Jesus' second coming, i.e., the rapture. Therefore, the churches here and in every generation are addressed first in *The Revelation* text, based upon the following principle: "For it is time for judgment to begin with God's household; and if it begins with us, what will the outcome be for those who do not obey the Gospel of God. And if it is hard for the righteous to be saved, what will become of the ungodly and the sinner?" (1 Peter 4:17-18).

Contrary to the world's view of victory and overcoming, our example resides in Jesus, who won the victory over Satan through sacrifice and death. It was while Jesus was occupying a weak posture, on a Cross, that He was securing victory over His enemy and ours. More importantly, it was while suffering the pain and humiliation of the Cross that Jesus remained faithful to His Father. Overcoming, therefore, means staying faithful while suffering for righteousness' sake – for the God of our faith has already won the battle on our behalf! It is our faith in Jesus, therefore, that overcomes the world and allows us to participate in the victory that has already been secured on our behalf through His Sacrificial Death and through His Triumphant Resurrection! *Our task is not to defeat a defeated foe, but to remain faithful to the Conqueror while suffering for His sake!*

The conjugated Greek verb νικάω (pronounced nĭ-**kâ**´-ō), translated "conquers," is the same Greek verb used in 1 John 5:4 to describe the believer's victory over the world: " . . . This is the victory that has overcome the world, even our faith." In fact, the noun 'victory' in the 1 John passage also comes from the same Greek root. Hence, victory and overcoming are integrally linked to our faith, i.e., our faith in and our faithfulness to Jesus Christ. The same Greek word is also used in 1 John 4:4 to describe our capacity for victory in Jesus:

> *You are of God, little children, and have overcome them, because greater is he that is within you than he that is in the world. (KJV)*

It is worthy to note that this same Greek word forms the first part of the name 'Nicolaitans,' as mentioned in verse 6. The play on words here suggests that overcoming by hearing what the Spirit is saying to the churches will be the only effective antidote to being overcome or conquered by the works and influence of the Nicolaitans.

The phrase "eat from the Tree of Life" is one of several allusions in *The Revelation* text to Genesis (Gen 2:9; 3:22, 24). The Genesis account reveals that the first humans actually had access to the Tree of Life; only the tree of the knowledge of good and evil was barred to them (Gen 2:16-17). After the fall, however, the Tree of Life became barred to the first humans, so that they would not eat of it and live forever. What this implies is that the fruit of the Tree of Life sustained eternal life, and that the first humans were originally created to live forever.

When we consider that the same Tree of Life is referenced three (3) times in the last chapter of *The Revelation* (Rev 22:2, 14, 19), in which the eternal Paradise of God is described, then we can safely conclude that what was once barred to a sinful humanity will then be made freely and forever accessible to a redeemed humanity. To eat of the Tree of Life is to live forever! The twelve manner of fruit produced by the Tree is symbolic of God's ample provision; and its healing leaves imply that there will be a complete absence of physical and spiritual want. The redeemed, in other words, will be completely satisfied!

The bridge between the Genesis "Tree" and *THE REVELATION* "Tree" is the "Tree" upon which Christ shed His blood for the forgiveness of sins and for the redemption of all who would believe in Him. That Tree was the Cross. It is the Cross that has now given the believer access to the Tree of Life!

"Paradise of God" — This is the Spirit's way of expressing the restoration of the perfect fellowship that humanity and all nature had with God in the Garden of Eden before the fall. The return to this Edenic state is articulated in many ways by the Spirit through the prophets of old. However, it receives its most beautiful expression in Revelation 21:3-4:

> *And I heard a loud voice from the throne saying, "Look! God's dwelling place is now among the people, and he will dwell with them. They will be his people, and God himself will be with them and be their God. He will wipe every tear from their eyes. There will be no more death or mourning or crying or pain, for the old order of things has passed away.*

THE CHURCH IN SMYRNA
REVELATION 2:8-11

8 "To the angel of the church in Smyrna write: These are the words of him who is the First and the Last, who died and came to life again:

9 'I know your afflictions and your poverty—yet you are rich! I know the slander of those who say they are Jews and are not, but are a synagogue of Satan.

10 Do not afraid of what you are about to suffer. I tell you, the devil will put some of you in prison to test you, and you will suffer persecution for ten days. Be faithful, even to the point of death, and I will give you life as your victor's crown.

11 *Whoever has ears, let them hear what the Spirit says to the churches. The one who is victorious will not be hurt at all by the second death.'"*

VERSE 8

"To the angel of the church in Smyrna write: These are the words of him who is the First and the Last, who died and came to life again:"

The angel of the church in Smyrna is an angelic messenger or spirit who has been assigned to the church in Smyrna for the purpose of communicating revelation knowledge concerning Jesus.[56]

Due to the Apostle Paul's extensive stay in Ephesus, during his 3rd missionary journey, Acts 19:10 states "that *all* the residents of Asia, both Jews and Greeks, heard the Word of the Lord" (*author's emphasis*). Though not explicitly identified in the Acts text, the spread of the Gospel would have included the city of Smyrna, since it was only forty miles north of Ephesus.[57]

The city's name, Smyrna, is the Greek word for myrrh, a costly spice that was not only presented to Jesus as one of three gifts from the Magi at the beginning of His Life (Matt 2:11), but was provided, along with aloes, in great quantity by Nicodemus for Jesus' burial (John 19:39-40). As John's Gospel notes, the wrapping of Jesus' body in strips of linen, with the myrrh and aloes interlaced, was a Jewish burial custom, and one scholar suggests that to the Jewish mind the myrrh in particular may have "represented the preservation of the body . . . as a prerequisite of resurrection."[58] The beauty of the city was often symbolized by a crown,

---

56   See discussions on Rev 1:20 and 2:1.

57   Unger, THE NEW UNGER'S BIBLE DICTIONARY, 1204.

58   Colin J. Hemer, THE LETTERS TO THE SEVEN CHURCHES IN ASIA IN THEIR LOCAL SETTING (Grand Rapids, MI: Eerdmans Publishing Company, 2001), 64.

which was derived from the architectural construction and arrangement of the city's buildings.[59] Combined with the use of myrrh as symbolizing preservation through death, this imagery of the crown will be elevated to the "victor's crown of life" that Jesus will confer on all who remain faithful until death as they suffer at the hands of those identified as "the synagogue of Satan."

It should be noted that Jesus identified Himself to John as "The First and The Last . . . the Living One [who] was dead . . . now alive for ever and ever" after John was shown the vision of Jesus' Resurrection Glory (1:17-18) to assure him that the One whose Glory he beheld was indeed his Lord and Savior Jesus Christ. Jesus now identified Himself to the church in Smyrna as "The First and The Last, who died and came to life again" not only to re-affirm His One-ness with the Eternal God and Father of all creation,[60] but to re-assert the reality of His resurrection from the dead. Both dynamics would be of great assurance to the church who is enjoined to not only retain her faith in Him who is Sovereign even over her affliction, her poverty and her persecutors, but who is promised that her faithfulness until death will be rewarded by Him who has already won the victory over death,[61] who holds the keys of Death and Hades,[62] and who is the Resurrection and the Life (John 11:25-26).

VERSE 9

'I know your afflictions and your poverty—yet you are rich! I know the slander of those who say they are Jews and are not, but are a synagogue of Satan.'

Affliction is the translation of the Greek word θλῖψις (pronounced

---

59   Ibid, 59.

60   See discussions on Revelation 1:8 and 17

61   See discussion on 1:5

62   See discussion on 1:18

thleeph´-sees) and includes the meanings of distress, hard circumstances and trouble. Given the church's opposition from the Jewish community in the city, coupled with the city's reputation as "an important centre of the imperial cult,"[63] i.e., emperor worship, the church in Smyrna represented a minority that was easy to target for persecution.

We can safely deduce that the "poverty" being referred to here is not spiritual but material, inasmuch as no word of reprimand is given to the church for any lack of spiritual stamina. The material definition of poverty in this verse is further endorsed by the use of the same Greek word πτωχεία (pronounced pe-tō-**kā´**-â) in 2 Corinthians 8:2 and 9, where its implications of material poverty are equally as clear. As the persecution of the church and its members could take the form of economic exclusion from the commercial advantages of the city, their material poverty would be a living reality. However, "has not God chosen those who are poor in the eyes of the world to be *rich in faith* and to inherit the kingdom he has promised those who love Him" (James 2:5, *author's emphasis*)? The same Greek word for rich πλούσιος (pronounced plū´-**sĭ**-ŏs) is used both here (Revelation text) and in James and carries the same connotation of spiritual wealth.

The word "slander" is the Greek word βλασφημία (pronounced blâs-phay-**mee´**-â), from which the English word blasphemy is derived. It is the prevalent word used in the NT to connote evil-speaking against God, Jesus, and the Holy Spirit (Matt 12:31-32; Mark 3:28-30; Luke 12:10; Rom 2:24). This same word is listed with twelve other abominations that proceed from within, out of the heart, and that defile us (Matt 15:18-20; Mark 7:20-22).

The slander that is being perpetrated against the church hails from "those who say that they are Jews and are not, but are a synagogue of

---

63   Hemer, *The Letters to the Seven Churches in Asia in Their Local Setting*, 69.

Satan." This same group will also be a source of persecution to the church in Philadelphia (Rev 3:9).

As the synagogue itself was the center of Jewish worship and of the teaching of the Law and the Prophets, then Jesus' use of the term synagogue highlights the Jewish influence in the persecution of the church in Smyrna. However, the source of their blasphemy, or evil-speaking, against the church in Smyrna comes from within the church through two potential groups, identified below as Synagogue of Satan (S.O.S.) Groups I and II, who are lying about who they really are:

- S.O.S. - Group I – Non-Jews who pretended to be Jews for whatever socio-economic and political benefits could be curried from the dominant culture and power brokers of the city. Participating in the persecution of the church probably won non-Jews favor among the Jews in the city. These non-Jews would have become members of the church under the pretense of conversion, in order to gain inside information to fuel Jewish persecution of the church.

- S.O.S. – Group II – These are former Jews, who converted to Christianity, but who under threat of persecution, revert to their old identity as Jews, in order to escape persecution as a Christian. These also would possess inside information to fuel Jewish persecution of the church.

The fact that both groups (pretenders and defectors) are lying about their true identity is what identifies them as "of Satan": for Satan is a liar and the father of it, and those who speak and perpetuate lies are Satan's children (John 8:38-45).

Again, note that both groups who are allied with the synagogue in the city are also in the church! Both groups typify that intimate level of betrayal that is characterized by the Psalmist and was exemplified by Judas' betrayal of Jesus:

> *It is not enemies who taunt me – I could bear that; it is not adversaries who deal insolently with me – I could hide from them. But it is you, my equal, my companion, my familiar friend, with whom I kept pleasant company; we walked in the house of God with the throng (Ps 55:12-13 NRSV).*

VERSE 10

"Do not afraid of what you are about to suffer. I tell you, the devil will put some of you in prison to test you, and you will suffer persecution for ten days. Be faithful, even to the point of death, and I will give you life as your victor's crown."

The injunction not to fear is critical, since fear is one of Satan's most subtle and seductive attacks against our faith — especially when suffering persecution. During His earthly ministry, Jesus counseled His disciples not to fear those who could only kill the body and not the soul; but to reserve their fear for the God who could destroy both body and soul in hell (Matt 10:28).

Contrary to the fatherhood of all liars, those who speak and perpetuate the truth of Jesus have God as their Father, who must accept the divine principle that "all [who] shall live godly in Christ Jesus will suffer persecution" (2 Tim 3:12 KJV). However, the principle of godly suffering is offset by the divine promise that God "has not given us a spirit of cowardice, but rather a spirit of power and of love and of self-discipline" (2 Tim 1:7-8 NRSV). Though there are many biblical passages of encouragement not to fear the deeds of evil-doers, some of the most poignant can be found in the following Psalms: Pss 27, 37, 56, 57, 64, 118.

Though the names Satan and the devil are used interchangeably to refer to the same fallen angel, known as Lucifer, the name Satan (σατανᾶ - pronounced sâ-tâ-nâ´) means adversary and appears in both Old and New Testaments. The name devil (διάβολος - pronounced dĭ-â´-bŏ-lŏs), however, means an accuser in the Greek and is used exclusively in the NT. The devil is characterized as "an accuser of the brethren" (Rev 12:10), whose works are manifest in the emergence of false witnesses against God's people. The false testimony against Jesus, for example, was the devil's handiwork (Matt 26:59-62; Mark 14:55-60; Luke 23:1-2).

However, the devil is permitted by God to occupy this role as an accuser of His people for the purposes of trying and refining the faith of believers (cf. Luke 22:31-32; James 1:2-3). The trial of Job is a classic example, and the crucifixion of Jesus at the hands of sinners is the ultimate example of the devil's expertise, albeit under God's control.

In the history of Christian martyrdom, prison was usually prologue to execution (cf. Matt 14:1-14; Mark 6:14-29) and death by some means of torture was certain (cf. Heb 11:35b-37a). Jesus said that prison would be the testing ground of the faith of some of the believers in the church in Smyrna. Some form of the Greek root πειράζω (pronounced pā-râ´-dzō) is used both here and in the following Scripture passages to convey the meaning of testing or trying of the faith.[64] It is also translated as 'trial' and 'temptation:'

- Matt 6:13; Luke 11:4 – The Lord's Prayer – "Lead us not into temptation (or testing);"

---

64   Though a different Greek word is used for 'testing' in 1 Peter 1:7 (δοκίμιον – dŏ-kĭ´-mee-ŏn), the doctrine of testing the faith is theologically similar: "That the trial (testing, genuineness) of your faith, being much more precious than of gold that perishes, though it be tried with fire, might be found unto praise and honor and glory at the appearing of Jesus Christ (KJV)."

- Luke 4:13 NRSV – Jesus' Wilderness of Temptation (Testing) experience: "When the devil had finished every test he departed from Him until an opportune time."

- 1 Peter 4:12-13 – Fiery trial (testing) signaling the believer's fellowship with Christ's suffering: "Dear friends, do not be surprised at the fiery ordeal that has come on you to test you, as though something strange were happening to you. But rejoice inasmuch as you participate in the sufferings of Christ, so that you may be overjoyed when his glory is revealed."

Jesus also stated that the suffering of some of the Smyrnean believers would last ten days. The number ten in biblical numerology symbolizes "the completeness of order" and the "entire round of anything."[65] With regard to the time span of the church's suffering, the number ten symbolizes that the devil will be allowed to execute a complete round of his persecuting tactics, including death. Because of the symbolic completeness of the number, the church's suffering will have a definite beginning and a definite end.

Jesus concludes His prediction of the church's season of suffering with an exhortation to follow His own example of faithfulness through it all; for He was indeed faithful until death (Phil 2:8) and had left an example as to how to suffer for righteousness' sake (1 Peter 2:21-23)

Though death looks like defeat, *faithfulness in death is the way to overcome and be victorious in Christ.* Just as Jesus was obedient unto death and is now highly exalted for His obedience, so we who are faithful unto death will be exalted to reign with Him (2 Tim 2:11-13). *Remember: Jesus has the keys to Death and Hades* (see discussion on Rev 1:18).

---

65 Bullinger, *NUMBER IN SCRIPTURE: ITS SUPERNATURAL DESIGN AND SPIRITUAL SIGNIFICANCE*, 243.

It is in James 1:12, where the "crown of life" is stipulated as the reward to those who exercise patient endurance while their faith is being tested. The same Greek roots for "patient endurance" (Rev 1:9; 2:2) and "tested," which have been engaged in previous verses within THE REVELATION text, are also employed in James' letter, as well, and thus forms a linguistic connection with our current verse:

> *Blessed is anyone who endures **temptation**. Such a one has stood the* > ***test** and will receive the **crown of life** that the Lord has promised to* > *those who love Him (NRSV, **author's emphases**)*

The Greek word στέφανον (pronounced **stě´-phâ-nŏn**), means crown, in the sense of a wreath or prize that is awarded upon winning a race or a game. It is the same Greek root from which the name Stephen is derived. Stephen was one of the first deacons of the early church (Acts 6:5) and her first martyr (Acts 8:54-60).

The life being referred to in the phrase "crown of life" is the eternal life that is the result of the first resurrection (Rev 20:4-6). This life will be lived in God's presence and favor for all eternity. With this understanding, the phrase might well read, " . . . I will give you that eternal life that is the victor's crown" (author's paraphrase)

As previously mentioned, the architectural structure of the city resembled the shape of a crown.[66] Jesus' promise of the crown of life was meant to set the believers' hopes and "affections on things above, not on things on the earth" (Col 3:2 KJV).

Please take note of the fact that Jesus has predicted the source (synagogue of Satan), the manner (prison), the purpose (to be tested), the duration (ten days), the condition of faithfulness (faithful until death), and the reward for faithfulness (the crown of life), regarding the

---

66   Hemer, *THE LETTERS TO THE SEVEN CHURCHES IN ASIA IN THEIR LOCAL*, 59.

persecution of which the church in Smyrna was not to be afraid! In other words, Jesus provides the church with Light on each one of the above dynamics, so that the church can walk in the Light of the Truth of what is going on and of how to respond to the glory of God!

VERSE 11

"Whoever has ears, let them hear what the Spirit says to the churches. The one who is victorious will not be hurt at all by the second death."

As in the first Letter and in the Letters to come, the invitation to have an ear to listen to what the Spirit is saying is an invitation to obey the counsel given for victory as well as to be forewarned of the consequences given for faithlessness. The fact that this invitation is extended to all seven churches, as indicated by the plural noun, i.e., churches, indicates that the message to each church also needs to be heeded lest the other churches become guilty of the same indictments and so that each church knows what victory in Jesus looks like as the reward for faithfulness. (See the initial discussion of this injunction to hear, as presented in the commentary on Revelation 2:7.)

Those who are victorious "will not be hurt at all by the second death." The second death is "second" to the first physical death that all must die (Heb 9:27). Revelation 20:14 acquaints us with the fact that "the second death" and "the lake of fire" are synonymous phrases denoting the final and eternal confinement of death and Hades (hell), as well as the eternal state and residence of the devil, the beast, the false prophet (Rev 20:10), fallen angels (Matt 25:41), and the wicked dead of all ages (Rev 20:15, 21:8).

Of this latter group, i.e., the wicked dead, Isaiah prophesies that "their worm does not die, and their fire is not quenched" (Isa 66:24b; cf. Mark 9:44, 46, 48). Thus, we can safely assert that the wicked dead will not only participate in the second resurrection that ends in the second death (cf. Dan 12:2; John 5:28-29; Rev. 20:11-15), but in that resurrection they will also receive a new body tailored to their eternal state of torment, which is the definition of the second death, i.e., a life of eternal torment. Consider, therefore, that if the wicked dead were destined to occupy the same flesh in which they died the first death, then the worm that does not die would cease to have something to feed on, and the fire that is not quenched would cease to have something to burn: for that flesh – the flesh in which we die the first death — would eventually be completely consumed by both elements, i.e., worm and fire. This internal witness allows us to safely assert that the condemned new body will continually and perpetually renew itself, in order to be available for the torment of both the undying worm and the unquenchable fire, and from which there will be no relief. Now, that's hell!

Additionally, Jesus' parable of the rich man and Lazarus (Luke 16:19-31) unmistakably reveals that, contrary to the notions that the second death is a state of oblivion or annihilation, those who inherit the second resurrection that leads to this eternal state of damnation will be alive enough to feel the pain! This brings us to the sterling realization that the second death is, in truth, a form of life that is lived outside of the favor of God and under the righteous wrath of God forever. And because the second death is a form of life, even in the second death, the Heavenly Father remains amazingly true to Himself as the God of all life!

Inasmuch as being dead in trespasses and sins in our present flesh is also a form of life that is lived outside of the favor of God and under God's righteous wrath (Eph 2:1-3), then the second death will not only be the inheritance of those who choose to remain "dead" in their trespasses and sins in this life, and who die the first death in that state, but the second death will be the ultimate and eternal reality of the life that will be lived under the wrath of God in a new flesh suited to its eternal and tormenting habitation.

Though Jesus' Resurrection is the gateway to both the First and Second Resurrections (cf. Dan 12:2; John 5:28-29; 1 Cor 15:20-26), those who are faithful to Jesus until death in this life will not be harmed by the second death: for they would have participated in the first resurrection unto eternal life – the crown of life (Rev 20:4-6)!

THE CHURCH IN PERGAMUM
REVELATION 2:12-17

12 "To the angel of the church in Pergamum write: These are the words of him who has the sharp, double-edged sword.

13 I know where you live—where Satan has his throne. Yet you remain true to my name. You did not renounce your faith in me, not even in the days of Antipas, my faithful witness, who was put to death in your city—where Satan lives.

14 Nevertheless, I have a few things against you: There are some among you who hold to the teaching of Balaam, who taught Balak to entice the Israelites to sin so that they ate food sacrificed to idols and committed sexual immorality.

15 Likewise, you also have those who hold to the teaching of the Nicolaitans.

16 Repent therefore! Otherwise, I will soon come to you and will fight against them with the sword of my mouth.

17 Whoever has ears, let them hear what the Spirit says to the churches. To the one who is victorious, I will give some of the hidden manna. I will also give that person a white stone with a new name written on it, known only to the one who receives it."

VERSE 12

"To the angel of the church in Pergamum write: These are the words of him who has the sharp, double-edged sword."

The angel of the church in Pergamum is an angelic messenger or spirit who has been assigned to the church in Pergamum for the purpose of communicating revelation knowledge concerning Jesus. (See discussions on Rev 1:20 and 2:1).

Due to the Apostle Paul's extensive stay in Ephesus, during his 3rd missionary journey, Acts 19:10 states "that all the residents of Asia, both Jews and Greeks, heard the Word of the Lord." Though not explicitly identified in the Acts text, the spread of the Gospel would have included the city of Pergamum, since it was located north of Smyrna and "20 miles inland from the Aegean Sea."[67] The city hosted a library of 200,000 volumes before it was "moved by Antony to Egypt and presented to Cleopatra. In this town was first discovered the art of making parchment, which was called pergamena"[68] (after the city's name).[69] In the Roman period, Pergamum became the religious capital of the province of Asia and was the focal point of emperor worship.[70] The city "was also a center of pagan cults of various deities. For example, the cult of Asclepius, the serpent god of healing, was prominent in Pergamum; the serpent symbol of Asclepius also became one of the emblems of the city and may have facilitated John's reference to 'the throne of Satan . . . ' Zeus, Athene, Demeter, and Dionysus were also gods receiving significant cultic attention. The reference to 'Satan's throne' may also have been brought

---

67   Unger, THE NEW UNGER'S BIBLE DICTIONARY, 986.

68   Ibid., 986

69   Hemer, THE LETTERS TO THE SEVEN CHURCHES OF ASIA IN THEIR LOCAL SETTING, 102.

70   Beale, THE BOOK OF REVELATION: A COMMENTARY ON THE GREEK TEXT, 246; Mounce, THE BOOK OF REVELATION REVISED, 78-79.

to mind because of the conical hill behind Pergamum which was the site of many temples, prominent among which was the throne-like altar of Zeus, which itself would have been sufficient to arouse the thought of the devil's throne."[71] In such a hotbed of idolatry, it is little wonder that steadfast allegiance to Christ and to the Christian faith resulted in the martyrdom of Antipas, whom Jesus lauded as "My faithful witness."

In Jesus' 5th command to John to write (see discussions on Revelation 1:11, 19), Jesus identifies Himself as the One "who has the sharp, double-edged sword." It is in the Vision of Jesus' Resurrection Glory that we discover that the "sharp, double-edged sword" comes out of His Mouth (Rev 1:16). This imagery is anticipated by similar references in Isaiah 11:4 and 49:2. For this reason, we can safely conclude that the "sharp, double-edged sword" is not a physical weapon that Jesus wields, but a metaphoric reference to the word of God, as is clearly indicated in the following Scriptures:

- Ephesians 6:17b – Part of the Whole Armor of God: "the **sword of the Spirit**, which is the **word of God**." (**author's emphases**)

- Hebrews 4:12 – Symbolic of the word of God that "is alive and active. **Sharper than any double-edged sword**, it penetrates even to dividing soul and spirit, joints and marrow; it judges the thoughts and attitudes of the heart." (**author's emphasis**)

- Revelation 19:15, 21; cf. Isaiah 11:4; 2 Thessalonians 2:8 – The divine weapon by which Jesus will strike

---

71   Ibid, 246.

down the nations of the earth: "Coming out of his mouth is a *sharp sword* with which to strike down the nations . . . The rest were killed with the *sword coming out of the mouth* of the rider on the horse . . . " (***author's emphases***)

- Psalm 149:6 – The weapon by which the faithful will judge the nations: "May the praise of God be in their mouths and a **double-edged sword**[72] in their hands."

- John 12:48 – Jesus clearly states that His Word will serve as judge on the last day, or the Day of Judgment: "There is a judge for the one who rejects me and does not accept my words; the **very words I have spoken will condemn them at the last day (author's emphasis)."**

---

72 The original Hebrew text of Psalm 149:6 reads "sword" in the singular and its edges or "mouths" in the plural. Thus, it is a single sword with two edges, not multiple swords. Several English translations (Holman CSB, KJV, NASB, Amplified Bible, Complete Jewish Bible) render "sword" in the singular and cross reference the term to Heb 4:12 and Rev 1:16. The NRSV and the NAB, however, render the term in the plural, which appears to imply that the miss-translated 'swords' are physical, not spiritual, weapons used to execute, punish and bind the enemies of God and of God's people, as expressed in the following verses of Psalm 149. However, this inaccurate plural rendition of the term and its implications contradict JESUS' own statement, regarding the use of a physical sword to execute judgment: "all who take up a sword will perish by a sword" (Matt 26:52 – Holman CSB).

READ Romans 1:18-32 – God's indictment is against those who suppress the truth (vs 18), who exchange the Glory of God for images resembling mortal man or creatures within the animal kingdom (vs 23), and who exchange the truth about God for a lie and worship and serve the creature over the Creator (vs 25). In three places in this passage, it is recorded that God "gave them up" to pursue their depravities (vss 24, 26, 28). Such was the spiritual condition of the majority of Pergamum's citizens among whom the believers in Pergamum lived.

VERSE 13

"I know where you live—where Satan has his throne. Yet you remain true to my name. You did not renounce your faith in me, not even in the days of Antipas, my faithful witness, who was put to death in your city—where Satan lives."

Whereas Jesus asserts in the other letters that "I know your works," He instead notes that He knows "where you [the church in Pergamum] are living," i.e., "where Satan's throne is."

The city's addiction to idolatry is what characterized it as "Satan's throne." As mentioned in the discussion on verse 12, the city of Pergamum not only hosted temples to a plethora of idols, some of whom were given the title of 'savior,'[73] but the city was also the seat of emperor worship in the Asiatic part of the Roman Empire. The construction of temples honoring an emperor became a litmus test of a city's civic and political loyalty to Rome, as exemplified by Pergamum's leadership in this area.[74]

---

73 Mounce, THE BOOK OF REVELATION REVISED, 78.

74 Ibid. 78-79. Mounce states that Pergamum "was the first city in Asia to receive permission to build a temple dedicated to the worship of a living ruler." See also Beale, 246.

The various temples to the gods of healing, especially the shrine to Asclepius, were also places of higher learning in the medical arts[75] and the symbol of the serpent was not only the symbol of this god of healing but also "became one of the emblems of the city."[76] The rampant idolatry of the city, therefore, characterized it as "Satan's throne" — the place where Satan and satanic devices had full sway over the lives of the people.

Jesus first commended the faithful believers in the church in Pergamum for "remaining true to My Name" as the spiritual tenacity needed to retain their Christian identity in the midst of an idolatrous culture. As pagan gods Zeus and Asclepius were regarded as savior in idol worship, so the church had to hold fast to Jesus as their Savior.

The Greek word κρατέω (pronounced krâ-**tĕ´**-ō), meaning to hold fast, or remain true for the purpose of not letting go, is used both in Jesus' commendation of the faithful in the church in Pergamum as well as in the indictment against those who are holding fast to false teachings and doctrines within the same congregation. From the use of this same Greek word to characterize opposing postures in relationship to God's Word, it is critical that we understand that it is not our adamant hold on a doctrine that makes it right, but the rightness of the doctrine itself that validates our adamancy or faithfulness to it. Jesus alone is worthy of our faith and of our faithfulness.

When Jesus refers to "My Name" as the object of the church's faithful tenacity, He is referring to His Identity as The Only Begotten Son of the One True and Living God, to His Sacrificial Work as Savior, to His Pre-eminence as the Firstborn of the dead, and to His Eternal Reign as King of kings and Lord of lords. Each of these dynamics of His Name stood in stark contrast to any claims made by the false deities of the city, placing

---

75   Ibid., 78.

76   Beale, *The Book of Revelation*, 246.

the faithful in the church in direct opposition to the dominant culture of idolatry. The power of Jesus' Name is stated best in Peter's bold declaration to the Sanhedrin as to the cause for the healing of the man who had been lame from birth:

> Salvation is found in no one else, for there is **no other Name** under heaven given to mankind by which we must be saved (Acts 4:12, author's emphasis).

In the NRSV, NIV, NAB and the Holman CSB, this phrase "did not denounce *your faith* in Me" is rendered to convey that the church did not deny *their faith* in Jesus. However, the Greek construction of this phrase suggests that the faith that is not denounced is Jesus' Faith, i.e., "did not denounce *My Faith*," which not only serves as a parallel to the church holding fast to *My Name* in the previous phrase, but is so rendered in the NASB, KJV, and the Amplified translations.[77]

The Greek construction throws a whole new light on what Jesus is actually saying here to the church: that their spiritual tenacity has been a credit, not to their faith in Him, but to His Faith in His Father to keep those whom the Father has given to Him as gifts. In other words, faith is a three-way transaction in the divine economy of our relationship with Jesus: for the faith that Jesus has in His Father is the same faith the Father has in Jesus and is the same faith that the Father has given to us to believe in Jesus! Ephesians 2:8 clearly affirms that the faith we have in Jesus is God's gift to us to empower us to believe in Jesus. This gift of faith from God makes all believers gifts to Jesus from His Father (cf. John 17:6, 9-10). So, Jesus' Faith, i.e., "My Faith," in His Father is that no one whom the Father has given Him (believers) will be snatched from His Father's Hands (John 10:27-29). So, the phrase could read "you did not

---

77 Both the NRSV and the Holman CSB do provide a footnote that cites "My Faith" as an alternate translation.

deny My Faith in My Father to keep you, who are gifts to Me from My Father" (author's paraphrase). This understanding gives new meaning to the truth that "if we are faithless, He [Jesus] remains faithful – for He cannot deny Himself" (2 Tim 2:13, *author's clarifying insertion*), since He and the Father are One (John 10:30).

The church's faithfulness in remaining true to Jesus' Name and their steadfastness to Jesus' Faith in His Father to keep those given to Him as gifts was outstandingly manifested "in the days of Antipas, my faithful witness, who was put to death in your city – where Satan lives." Antipas was executed by the priests of the temple of Asclepius, the god of healing,[78] whose emblem was the serpent. Though his death at their hands may have signaled victory for the surrounding idolatrous culture, it did not produce a falling away from the faith by the church. Instead, the martyrdom of Antipas was met with the church's steadfastness to Jesus' Faith in His Father, which meant victory for them!

Antipas is mentioned only here in all of Scripture, but with the highest accolade a believer could receive from our Lord: "My faithful witness." His name in the Greek language could be translated "instead of" (anti) "all" (pas), thus giving his death the tonality of a substitutionary sacrifice as one out of many who was chosen to suffer for the faith, much as Jesus was chosen by Caiaphas, the high priest, to be the one to die for the nation:

> You do not understand that it is better for you to have one man die
> for the people than to have the whole nation destroyed. He did not
> say this on his own, but being high priest that year he prophesied that
> Jesus was about to die for the nation, and not for the nation only, but
> to gather into one the dispersed children of God (John 11:50-52 NRSV).

---

78   Unger, THE NEW UNGER'S BIBLE DICTIONARY, 83.

Inasmuch as witnessing to Jesus and remaining faithful to Him even unto death are the high call of all believers, Antipas exemplified both virtues in his martyrdom[79] for the faith, for it closely resembled Jesus' own sacrifice for us all as He retained His Faith in His Father through it all.

VERSE 14

"Nevertheless, I have a few things against you: There are some among you who hold to the teaching of Balaam, who taught Balak to entice the Israelites to sin so that they ate food sacrificed to idols and committed sexual immorality."

The "teaching of Balaam" had apparently invaded the church through some who thought it more expedient to be in complicity with the dominant culture of idolatry in order to avoid persecution. As a result, this teaching encouraged believers to abandon the godly separation and the pilgrim character of their faith walk in favor of conformity to the world.

Complicity with or conformity to the world is the essence of the teaching of Balaam. In Numbers 25:1-18 and 31:16, it is recorded that the hireling prophet, Balaam, who was a Midianite priest, advised the women of Moab to entice God's people, who were on the threshold of entering the Promised Land, to commit fornication with the daughters of Moab and to join themselves to the worship of Baal-peor, the god of Peor, Balaam's home town. Balaam offered this advice after failing to curse God's people at Balak's request (Num 22:1 - 24:25). Those who yielded to this temptation were killed at the Lord's command (Num 25:4-5). One Israelite in particular, named Zimri, of the tribe of Simeon, brazenly brought his Midianite wife, named Cozbi, into the camp. It was Phinehas, the grandson of Aaron, who avenged the Lord's holiness by killing them both with his sword (Num 25:6-18). It is worthy to note

---

79 Greek word μάρτυς (pronounced **mar´**-tūs) means both 'witness' and 'martyr.'

that Jesus will also use the "sword of His Mouth" to deal with this same brazen tendency in the church in Pergamum, of which Phinehas' sword was but a foreshadowing (see verse 16).

VERSE 15

"Likewise, you also have those who hold to the teaching of the Nicolaitans."

The "teaching of the Nicolaitans" was the same false teaching that plagued the church in Ephesus (Rev 2:6). As our previous discussion revealed, there were at least two postures of worldly compromise espoused by the Nicolaitans, both of which constituted insidious add-ons to the teaching of Balaam. These two Nicolaitan postures of worldly compromise are repeated here from the Revelation 2:6 discussion to emphasize this point:

- This was a faction within the church that supported a compromise with the surrounding pagan culture by advocating the eating of food sacrificed to idols and committing sexual immorality. It was the decision of the Council of Jerusalem, however, that Gentile converts to Christianity were required to abstain from both (Acts 15:19-20, 28-29).

- In addition to the above-mentioned violations to doctrinal and practical purity, the Nicolaitans also advocated the inclusion of idol worship with the worship of Jesus (cf. Zeph 1:5; 1 Kgs 12:25ff - Jeroboam; 2 Kgs 21:1-18; 2 Chron 33:1-10 – Manasseh).

It is apparent by Jesus' indictment that some (not all) in the church in Pergamum subscribed to both sets of false teaching and were guilty of sexual immorality, eating meat sacrificed to idols, and co-mingling idol worship with the worship of Jesus. Both teachings would have had great appeal to those wishing to escape the scrutiny and the persecution of the idolatrous culture of the city.

VERSE 16

"Repent therefore! Otherwise, I will soon come to you and will fight against them with the sword of my mouth."

In every NT occurrence of the Greek word translated "repent," i.e., μετανοέω (pronounced mĕ-tâ-**nū**´-ō),[80] the meaning of changing one's mind, heart and behavior from sinfulness to righteousness is intended. It is worthy to note that the Greek word for "repent" is rendered in its second person singular form, as if addressing as a collective singular unit those who were following the false teachings of Balaam and of the Nicolaitans within the congregation.

Romans 12:2 issues the clear command that believers "not be conformed to this world, but be transformed by the renewing of [their] minds, so that [they] may discern what is the Will of God – what is good and acceptable and perfect (NRSV)." Inasmuch as the renewal of the mind is made possible only by the word of God, then any other doctrine corrupts this process and places the believer in a state of compromise and complicity with the world. James makes a searing indictment against those who fall into this state of compromise and complicity, when he says "Adulterers! Do you not know that friendship with the world is enmity with God? Therefore whoever wishes to be a friend of the world becomes an enemy of God" (James 4:4 NRSV; cf. 2 Cor 6:17-18; 1 John 2:15-17).

Consequently, a decisive change of mind, i.e., "repent," is the only remedy Jesus extends to those in the church who have been seduced by

---

80   For definition of the contraction of "oe" to "ou," see William D. Mounce, *Basics of Biblical Greek Grammar* (Grand Rapids, MI: Zondervan, 1993), 10, 135-143.

the idolatrous culture of the city. Jesus seals His command to repent with the Greek word translated "therefore" to indicate that repenting is the only option open to them with no room for negotiation.

Jesus then articulates the consequences for failing to repent: "Otherwise, I will soon come to you and will fight against them with the sword of my mouth." The pronoun "you" is rendered in the 2nd person singular, mirroring the same form of the command to repent and thus pointing again to the same singular collective unit that is composed of those who were following the false teachings of Balaam and of the Nicolaitans within the congregation. It is to these that Jesus will come "soon," a Greek word, i.e., ταχύ (pronounced tâ-kū´), translated 'soon' here and "quickly" in other translations. It is used twelve times in the NT, six of which occur in THE REVELATION text in contexts of judgment (Rev 2:16, 3:11, 11:14, 22:7, 12, 20).[81] The theology of Jesus' swift movement in judgment is symbolically articulated as His coming as a "thief in the night" (Matt 24:43; Luke 12:39; 1 Thess 5:2; 2 Peter 3:10; Rev 3:3, 16:15).

Jesus' agenda in coming soon to those subscribing to the false teachings of Balaam and the Nicolaitans is to "fight against them with the sword of my mouth." As mentioned in the discussion on verse 12, the "sword" is symbolic of the word of God and is a part of the whole armor of God. As this double-edged sword constitutes the only offensive weapon of warfare in the vision of Jesus' Resurrection Glory, then it will be the very word of God that proceeds out of Jesus' mouth that will serve as the weapon of judgment to lance, or to purge, those holding to and endorsing the contaminant doctrines and practices within His Body. If the offenders repent, this same sword will serve as Jesus' instrument of surgery to circumcise their hearts and minds of the false doctrines with which they have become infected.

---

81 Another word that hails from the same root, ταχει (pronounced tâ-kay´), and carries the meanings of 'shortly' or 'swiftly,' is employed in Rev 1:1.

In a city where gods of healing were venerated, the Church's healing can only come from the Word of God, which is not only able to judge the thoughts and intents of the heart, but also possesses the surgical capacity to divide soul from spirit and joints from marrow (Heb 4:12).

VERSE 17

"Whoever has ears, let them hear what the Spirit says to the churches. To the one who is victorious, I will give some of the hidden manna. I will also give that person a white stone with a new name written on it, known only to the one who receives it."

As in the first two Letters and in the Letters to come, the invitation to have an ear to listen to what the Spirit is saying is an invitation to obey the counsel given for victory as well as to be forewarned of the consequences given for faithlessness. The fact that this invitation is extended to all seven churches, as indicated by the plural noun, i.e., churches, indicates that the message to each church also needs to be heeded lest the other churches become guilty of the same indictments, and so that each church knows what victory in Jesus looks like as the reward for faithfulness (See the initial discussion of this injunction to hear, presented in the commentary on Revelation 2:7).

In defining "hidden manna," we must first acknowledge that manna is a direct reference to the supernaturally-provided bread that fell from heaven every day during Israel's 40-year wilderness trek to the Promised Land (Exod 16:4-35). As such, manna is symbolic of Jesus who is the Bread of God, the Bread of Life, and the Living Bread who came down from heaven as God's ample provision of salvation (John 6:33-35, 48-51, 58). Secondly, Colossians 2:3 declares that all the treasures of wisdom and knowledge are hidden in Jesus. When we place the above-cited truths side by side, then hidden manna is the wisdom and knowledge of Jesus that eclipses the so-called wisdom and knowledge of false deities. The hidden nature of the wisdom and knowledge of Jesus is that it can only be known by direct revelation from God through the agency of the Holy Spirit (cf. Matt 16:17), and not through human learning or sophistries (READ 1 Cor 2:1-16). Hidden manna, therefore, is revelation knowledge upon which overcomers will feast for all eternity (cf. 1 Cor 13:12)!

The symbolism of the "white stone" receives various interpretations among biblical scholars. This variation in interpretation is presented in Colin J. Hemer's THE LETTERS TO THE SEVEN CHURCHES OF ASIA IN THEIR LOCAL SETTING,[82] where he and others characterize the white stone as possibly holding one of the following contextual meanings:

- The white stone of acquittal used in the Greek courts

- The lot cast in elections in Greek politics

- A stone given to victors in the Greek games

- Its economic value provided its possessor with carte blanche or free access to favors or services within the community.

However, Scripture refers to believers as "living stones" (1 Peter 2:5) who are in the likeness of Jesus, the "Living Stone," who was "rejected indeed of men, but chosen of God, and precious" (1 Peter 2:4). The stone, therefore, would be symbolic of steadfast faith, and the color white would be symbolic of the victory secured through that faith (1 John 5:4). Together, the white stone symbolizes the victory of the life of faith in Jesus, which only Jesus, the Faithful One (Rev 1:5) is qualified to bestow.

Let us note at this point that the connection between the "hidden manna" and the "white stone" metaphors are beautifully blended in the account of the revelation knowledge Peter received on the identity of

---

82 Hemer, THE LETTERS TO THE SEVEN CHURCHES OF ASIA IN THEIR LOCAL SETTING, 96-102.

Jesus, when he said, "You are the Christ, the Son of the living God" (Matt 16:16). Jesus, in turn, affirmed that Peter had not received this truth from flesh and blood but that it was revealed to him by the Father — making the truth of Jesus' identity "revelation knowledge" (Matt 16:17). And it is this revelation knowledge of who He is that Jesus characterized and defined as the rock upon which He would build His church and against which the gates of Hell would not prevail (Matt 16:18). As our previous discussion on Revelation 1:11 revealed, the rock upon which Jesus would build His church is presented as the feminine Greek noun "petra," which corresponds to the feminine Greek noun for "revealed," i.e., apokalupsis. Peter, whose Greek name is "Petros" and masculine in gender, knew immediately that Jesus was not planning to build His church on him, as so many have erroneously concluded! The rock imagery forms the perfect complement to the white stone imagery that will be part of the victorious believer's reward from Jesus: for the white stone imagery of faith is deposited into the rock of the revelation of who Jesus is!

As the "new name" written on the white stone will only be known by those to whom it is given, the mystery of the new name must stand (cf. Prov 25:2a). Even Jesus will have "a Name inscribed that no one knows but Himself" (Rev 19:12) when He returns in conquering glory!

When we survey the Scriptures, however, there are several significant occasions when a new name was appropriated to the heirs of God's covenant promises:

- Abram (high father) was changed to Abraham (father of a multitude) (Gen 17:4-5)

- Sarai (dominating) was changed to Sarah (princess) (Gen 17:15-16)

- Jacob (heel-catcher) was changed to Israel (he will rule as God) (Gen 32:28; 35:10)

- Simon (hearing) was changed to Peter (stone) (Matt 16:18)

- Saul (asked) was changed to Paul (little) (Acts 13:9)

The only characteristic we can safely give to the "new name" is that it will be eternal! In summary, the full reward of the conquering believers will be the full knowledge (1 Cor 13:9, 12), the full victory (1 John 5:4-5), and the new name that will be given to each in glory!

THE CHURCH IN THYATIRA
REVELATION 2:18-29

18 "To the angel of the church in Thyatira write: These are the words of the Son of God, whose eyes are like blazing fire and whose feet are like burnished bronze:

19 I know your deeds, your love and faith, your service and perseverance, and that you are now doing more than you did at first.

20 Nevertheless, I have this against you: You tolerate that woman Jezebel, who calls herself a prophet. By her teaching she misleads my servants into sexual immorality and the eating of food sacrificed to idols.

21 I have given her time to repent of her immorality, but she is unwilling.

22 So I will cast her on a bed of suffering, and I will make those who commit adultery with her suffer intensely, unless they repent of her ways.

23 I will strike her children dead. Then all the churches will know that I am he who searches hearts and minds, and I will repay each of you according to your deeds.

24 Now I say to the rest of you in Thyatira, to you who do not hold to her teaching and have not learned Satan's so-called deep secrets, 'I will not impose any other burden on you,

25 Except to hold on to what you have until I come.'

26 To the one who is victorious and does my will to the end, I will give authority over the nations—

27 That one 'will rule them with an iron scepter and will dash them to pieces like pottery'—just as I have received authority from my Father.

28 I will also give that one the morning star.

29 Whoever has ears, let them hear what the Spirit says to the churches."

VERSE 18

"To the angel of the church in Thyatira write: These are the words of the Son of God, whose eyes are like blazing fire and whose feet are like burnished bronze:"

The angel of the church in Thyatira is an angelic messenger or spirit who has been assigned to the church in Thyatira for the purpose of communicating revelation knowledge concerning Jesus. (See discussions on Rev 1:20 and 2:1).

Due to the Apostle Paul's extensive stay in Ephesus, during his 3rd missionary journey, Acts 19:10 states "that all the residents of Asia, both Jews and Greeks, heard the Word of the Lord." Paul's ministry would have included Thyatira, since it is located SE of Pergamum. The only other reference to the city itself occurs in the Acts text in relationship to Paul's first convert in Europe, named Lydia, who was then living in Philippi, but who hailed from Thyatira as a seller of purple (Acts 16:14) for which the city of Thyatira was well known. "An outstanding characteristic of Thyatira was the large number of trade guilds that flourished there.

Since the trade guilds were inseparably intertwined with local religious observances, they posed a special problem for the economic well-being of Christians. The divine guardian of the city was the god Tyrimnos (identified with the Greek sun-god Apollo), who would be conceived of as the patron of the guilds and therefore honored in their festivities."[83]

Participation in the guild on this level was apparently key to commercial and financial security. In other words, a craftsman had to belong to a trade guild or union, and participate in the pagan feasts, in order to thrive in business, or go bankrupt. The twin gods of the city were Apollo and Artemis (Diana). Both were considered to be the children of the god Zeus. However, Apollo and the emperor "were referred to as sons of the god Zeus," posing a contest of allegiance to the true Son of the true God to whom the church was to "give their exclusive adoration . . . and trust . . . for their economic welfare."[84]

In Jesus' 6th command to John to write, He identifies Himself by the title "Son of God." Though the full title Son of God is used approximately 49 times throughout the NT, it appears only once, in this verse, in the entire book of *The Revelation*. It is worthy to note that though aspects of the vision of Jesus' Resurrection Glory are included in the letter's introduction, as in the previous and upcoming letters, the "Son of God" title is not mentioned in the vision shown to John. Though "Son of Man" (Rev 1:13) is a testimony of Jesus' humanity, the title "Son of God" is a clear testimony of His Deity. The question, therefore, is why this title for Jesus, "Son of God," is mentioned only here in *The Revelation* and in this particular letter? Based on the pagan context of the city of Thyatira, the following four reasons provide needed correctives in the church's understanding of who Jesus is by this title:

---

83 Mounce, *The Book of the Revelation Revised*, 84-85.

84 Beale, *The Book of the Revelation*, 259.

1. Jesus wanted the church to know that despite the claims of the adherents of Apollo – that Apollo was a 'son of god' – He, Jesus was/is *the True Son of the One True and Living God*. He was not only the true Son of God *in His humanity*, but also the true Son of God *in His divinity*. He is above all that calls itself a god or 'a son of god' (cf. Eph 1:20-21; Phil 2:10-11)

2. Jesus wanted the church to know that *He alone reigns in the exalted position to rule, to judge, to punish, and to forgive or grant mercy* – claims that the adherents of Apollo made of their god, as well.

3. Jesus wanted His Body to know it was *He who died and was raised from the dead for their salvation* – something Apollo had not and could not do because he was 'a son of no god' and only the work of men's hands and imaginations (cf. Pss 96:5; 97:7; 115:1-8; 135:15-18; Isa 42:17-18; 44:6-20; 46:5-7).

4. Jesus wanted His church to know that, despite the claim of Apollo as a 'sun-god', He alone is the *Light* of the world (Ps 36:9; 119:105, 130; Isa 60:19-20; Rev 21:23; 22:5; John 1:4-5; 8:12; 9:5; 12:35-36, 46), and that it is in His Face that "the *light* of the knowledge of the Glory of God" (2 Cor 4:6, *author's emphasis*) *resides*, and that "His Face is *like the sun shining in full force*" (Rev 1:16, *author's emphasis*).

Jesus then continues to identify Himself by another aspect of the vision of His Resurrection Glory: "who has eyes like a flame of fire." This description constitutes an echo of Daniel's vision (Dan 10:6) and of His return in conquering glory (Rev 19:12).

Fire is biblically symbolic of God's Holiness, Presence and Power. The 'fire' of God's Holiness, for example, is able to purify, sanctify and refine God's people (Zech 13:9; Mal 3:2-3; Matt 3:11-12; 1 Cor 3:12-15; 1 Peter 1:7). The 'fire' of God's Presence commissions (Exod 3:2), protects (Exod 13:21), equips (Acts 2:1-4) and reveals (Deut 5:4). And the 'fire' of God's Power judges, consumes and destroys (Gen 19:24; 1 Kings 18:38; Deut 4:24; Heb 12:29; 2 Peter 3:7; Rev 20:10, 14-15). Fire also produces light, making it a revealer and an instrument of search. However, it also denotes God's anger against sin (Gen 19:24; Jer 4:4; 2 Peter 3:3-7).

With all the above attributes, Jesus' "eyes like a flame of fire" have the penetrating power to reveal our motives, to make manifest our deeds, to search our hearts, to try our minds, to purify our souls, and to refine our spirits. Such will be His work in the church of Thyatira and in all the churches (Rev 2:23b).

Jesus concludes His Self-Identification with another dynamic of the vision of His Resurrection Glory (Rev 1:15a), which is also reflected in Daniel's vision (Dan 10:6): "whose feet are like burnished bronze." In both Daniel and *THE REVELATION*, this particular attribute is keyed to Jesus' role as Judge in executing His Father's wrath against sin and unrepentant sinners. In the ultimate scene of judgment, Jesus will *"tread* (with His burnished bronze Feet) the winepress of the fury of the wrath of God Almighty"* (Rev 19:15c, *author's emphasis and clarifying insertion*).

Bronze, or brass, is considered a symbol of physical strength, power, durability, and steadfastness. In the refining of metals, brass can withstand the highest degrees of heat, thereby making it stronger than any of its contributing metals. Brass is refined in grades. For example, low-grade brass is an alloy of copper and tin; medium grade brass is an alloy of copper and gold, and fine or burnished brass is an alloy of gold and silver. It is with feet of the highest grade of brass, symbolically speaking, that Jesus is not only able to withstand the heat of any opposition to His unique Sonship, but is also able to break, trample, and shatter in pieces anyone and anything of lesser quality.

VERSE 19

"I know your deeds, your love and faith, your service and perseverance, and that you are now doing more than you did at first."

In asserting once again that He "knows" the Church's works, Jesus proceeds to itemize an impressive list of works that fall into two categories: motive works = love and faith; and word works = service and patient endurance. The two categories of works are related as follows: love leads to service (John 14:15, 21), and service is to be ministered in love (1 Cor 12:29 – 14:1). Faith leads to perseverance (Rom 4:18-22), and perseverance is to be premised upon faith (Heb 11:11). In other words, it is a sign that we love God and God's people when we are willing to serve or to minister (cf. 1 Cor 12:31 – 13:13); and if we have the Faith of Jesus operating in us (Heb 12:1-4), then we will persevere, or exercise patient endurance, knowing that God is in control and will work out all things according to His purpose in our life (Rom 8:28-39).

The Greek word for 'love' is αγάπη (pronounced â-**gâ**´-pay), which denotes the unconditional love of God for His people and the love that His people are to have for one another (John 3:16; 13:34-35; 1 John 3:1, 11, 14, 16-18, 23-24; 4:7-13, 19-21). This same Greek word also carries the meaning of the Holy Communion meal that was shared in the early church and in every church since then, as the celebration of Jesus' Sacrificial Death on Calvary.

The Greek word πίστις (pronounced **pees**´-tees) is the primary word used for 'faith' in the NT. It is succinctly defined in Hebrews 11:1 and abundantly illustrated in the remaining verses of that Chapter, known as the 'Hall of Faith:'

> *"Now faith is the assurance of things hoped for, the conviction of things not seen" (Heb 11:1 NRSV)*

The Greek word for 'service' is διακονία (pronounced dĭ-â-kŏ-**nĭ'**-â) and carries the meanings of service, contribution, help, support, and mission. It is also the word from which we derive the English word 'deacon.'

We have already discussed the Greek word ὑπομονῇ (pronounced hū-pŏ-mŏ-**nay'**), translated "perseverance,'" as it relates to the believer's response to trials, tribulations and persecutions while remaining faithful to God through it all (see discussion on Rev 2:2).

Whereas the church in Ephesus was indicted for having abandoned her first works (Rev 2:4-5), the church in Thyatira had, in fact, increased her first works since her inception as a church: "that you are doing more than you did at first." This liberal commendation from the Lord serves as prologue to the coming *nevertheless* of His indictment against them. What will be revealed is that our faith walk is more than just doing the good we know to do: it is also about confronting the evil that is within our midst.

VERSE 20

"Nevertheless, I have this against you: You tolerate that woman Jezebel, who calls herself a prophet. By her teaching she misleads my servants into sexual immorality and the eating of food sacrificed to idols."

In contrast to the previously stated commendations, "nevertheless" not only introduces Jesus' following indictment but indicates that He is aware of the division in the church between those who are heirs to His commendations and those who are not.[85] The Greek word ἀφεῖς (pronounced â-**fās'**), which is rendered "tolerate," is derived from a root

---

85 The Churches in Smyrna and Philadelphia receive no contrasting conjunction, based on their uniform allegiance to JESUS. The Church in Laodicea receives no contrasting conjunction based on their uniform 'lukewarm-ness' toward JESUS.

verb that carries several meanings in addition to the current one: let, let be, let go, leave behind, cancel, forgive, remit, dismiss, divorce. Coupled with other words, it also connotes death and the giving off a loud cry. Only here does it bear the meaning to "tolerate" in the sense of allowing and indulging an abomination.

The church is tolerating "that woman Jezebel, who calls herself a prophet . . . " The name Jezebel is first introduced in the OT as the dominating and manipulating wife of Ahab, king of the 10 northern tribes of Israel (1 Kings 16:30-32; 18:4, 19; 21:5-16, 25). She was the daughter of the king of Sidon, (Ethbaal – whose name means either 'with Baal' or 'man of Baal'); and her marriage to Ahab was a political alliance that allowed Ahab to use the excellent sea ports of Tyre and Sidon as trade routes for his nation's exports. Her most insidious influence upon him and upon the northern tribes of Israel was her active and insistent propagation of the worship of Baal and Asherah, which included both the eating of meat sacrificed to idols and sexual immorality. Her two most heinous crimes were the extermination of the Lord's prophets, except for the 100 prophets whom Obadiah hid in caves to save them from her wrath, and the killing of Naboth, the Jezreelite, to secure his vineyard for her husband, King Ahab. (Read 1 Kings 16:30-32, 18:4, 19, 21:5-16, 25; 2 Kings 9:7-10, 30-37; Prov 2:16-19, 5:3-14, 7:1-27).

Jezebel's fate was pronounced by the prophet Elisha (1 Kings 21:23) and was, in turn, articulated through one of Elisha's prophetic students to Jehu (2 Kings 9:1-10), who succeeded Ahab's son, Joram, as king of Israel. Jehu carried out the execution of Jezebel, and her death was in keeping with the prophecy through Elisha (2 Kings 9:30-37).

As such, Jezebel of the OT is characterized by the proverbial description of the 'loose woman' (Prov 2:16-19, 5:3-14, 7:1-27): for though she was not an adulteress physically, she was one spiritually in leading God's people away from the worship of the One True and Living God through the propagation of idol worship. According to Elisha's prophecy, cited above, her end was indeed as "bitter as gall, sharp as a double-edged sword." Both in the above-cited Old Testament texts as well as in our current text, Jezebel is the personification of the proverbial 'loose woman'.

It has not been settled whether the female false prophet in the church in Thyatira was actually named Jezebel, or whether the Lord gave her that name to symbolize her influence in the church as reminiscent of the idolatry of her Old Testament namesake. However, the similarities between the past and present Jezebels are striking, beginning with their name:

- First, the name 'Jezebel' is the Greek translation of Ἰεζάβελ (pronounced ee-**zâ´**-bĕl) and the Hebrew name אִיזֶבֶל (pronounced ee-zĕh-**bĕl´**). The name was originally attached to that of Baal to indicate Baal's married status.[86] However, when the name Jezebel appeared alone, it connoted an unmarried or chaste virgin. Neither the Old Testament nor New Testament Jezebels lived up to their name in this regard!

- Secondly, both Jezebels introduced idolatry, or a severe compromise of the true faith, on political and economic grounds. The Old Testament Jezebel gave Ahab access to her father's seaports for trade, as previously mentioned. In return, Jezebel was given free rein to set up Baal and Asherah altars throughout the Northern Kingdom, and to recruit

---

86 Francis Brown, *THE NEW BROWN-DRIVE-BRIGGS-GESENIUS HEBREW AND ENGLISH LEXICON*, (Peabody, MA: Henrickson Publishers, 1979), Number 348, 33b.

prophets for each god. The New Testament Jezebel encouraged participation in the licentious feasts of the trade guilds, in order for Christian craftsmen to stay in business. The latter is evident by the content of Jezebel's teaching in the church in Thyatira, "to commit fornication and to eat food sacrificed to idols," since such was the nature of guild activities.[87] Such a teaching would have sounded reasonable since 'business is business' and 'one has to eat.'

- Thirdly, both Jezebels were advocates for their brand of idolatry. The Old Testament Jezebel supported the prophets of Baal and Asherah by regularly hosting them at her table, while zealously persecuting and killing the prophets of the Lord, whom she viewed as competition to her religious views. The New Testament Jezebel advocated for a syncretistic approach that compromised and combined the worship of Jesus with participation in the idolatrous guilds.

- Fourthly, both Jezebels occupied high and influential positions among God's people. The Old Testament Jezebel was the wife of Ahab, king of the northern kingdom of Israel. This made her queen with access to her husband's power, which she abused in favor of her idolatry. The New Testament Jezebel was a self-proclaimed prophet, implying that she was not called, anointed, and ordained by Jesus to this office, but took it upon herself. Since the office of prophet is one of the spiritual gifts to the church

---

87 Mounce, THE BOOK OF THE REVELATION REVISED, 84-85.

(1 Cor 14), then we may safely conclude that Jezebel was able to occupy this high and influential position because she was a member of the church, and not some outside fortune-teller who could have been easily repudiated by the church. This conclusion is further confirmed by the invitation from Jesus for her to repent as one who had gone astray and had caused others to do the same.

The beguiling or deceiving nature of Jezebel's teaching may have included the following implied and/or stated compromises of the truth in favor of the dominant culture of idolatry:

- "Since Jesus has set us free from all things and paid the price for all things, then believers must be free to participate in whatever they desire with no fear of harm."

  - Truths compromised by this rationale: Romans 6:11-23; 1 Corinthians 6:12-13; Galatians 5:1, 13;

- "That God would understand their need to make a living and overlook their participation in the licentious activities of the guilds; for the Scriptures say 'anyone unwilling to work should not eat'" (2 Thessalonians 3:10)

  - Truth compromised by this rationale: Matthew 6:24-34

- "That participation in the guilds would give believers an opportunity to witness to their unbelieving guild associates."

- Truth compromised by this rationale:
  1 Corinthians 8:8-13

- "That separation from the guilds and their activities would mean financial suicide and render believers unable to support the church."

  - Truths compromised by this rationale: 2 Corinthians 6:14-18; Philippians 4:11-13, 19; 1 Timothy 6:6-8; Hebrews 13:5-6

- "That if a believer is to "render unto Caesar the things that are Caesar's, and unto God the things that are God's" (Matt 22:21), then participation in the idolatrous trade guild feasts is one's Christian duty."

  - Truth compromised by this rationale: Romans 13:8

Since Jezebel is a woman who occupies both a prophetic and a teaching posture within the church, we are compelled at this juncture to examine the Scriptures that both forbid and commend women to occupy these postures in the church. First, both 1 Corinthians 14:34-38; 1 Timothy 2:11-15 address specific problems within the churches in Corinth and in Ephesus that prohibited women from teaching or prophesying in church. As both Corinth and Ephesus were centers of idolatrous worship, many of the female Gentile converts to Christianity may have been ex-temple prostitutes. Their new-found freedom as whole persons in Christ was probably expressed with the flamboyance that characterized their former life. The opportunity to be included in the same worship experience with men, which was not the Jewish or Greek religious practice, most likely gave rise to a misuse of the freedom of speech in articulating questions or offering their insights, as an attempt to confirm their equal status in the Body of Christ. Confusion was the result. Thus, Paul's prohibitions would be contextually applicable to the church in Thyatira, or to any church, in which the above situations abounded. Such a response would aptly apply to Jezebel and her false prophetic and teaching posture.

Secondly, Joel 2:28-29, Acts 2:16-18, Acts 21:8-9, 1 Corinthians 1:26-31, and Galatians 3:26-29 each affirm God's inclusion of women in the prophetic role. Whereas the truths stated by Paul in his prohibitions were and are contextual in nature and in their application, both then and now, the above-cited texts are universally applicable to the body of Christ in all ages. God's promise to pour out His Spirit upon all flesh, so that sons and daughters would prophesy, was initially fulfilled on the Day of Pentecost. Those tarrying for the Spirit in an upper room included not only the male disciples and Jesus' brothers (Acts 1:12-13, 14d), but also included the women who had supported Jesus' ministry as well as Jesus' mother (Acts 1:14abc). When the Holy Spirit arrived, the text says that *"All* of them were filled with the Holy Spirit, and began to speak with other tongues, as the Spirit enabled them" (Acts 2:4, *author's emphasis*). The women's inclusion in the outpouring of the Holy Spirit was further corroborated by Peter's quote of the Joel prophecy (Joel 2:28-29).

Evidence of the continuous inclusion of women in the Spirit's outpouring was manifested in the four daughters of Philip, who were anointed with the spiritual gift of prophecy (Acts 21:8-9). Given the cultural response to women in biblical times, their position of low regard perfectly fulfilled the profile of those whom God chooses to use in His service. According to the world's definition of women, they were considered not wise, not mighty, not noble, foolish, weak, base, despised, and are not (in terms of not being regarded as a person, but only as property) (1 Cor 1:26-31). Though women were/are none of these things, it was nevertheless how they were viewed in their cultural settings. God, however, takes the world's view of women and uses it to bring Him glory by anointing them into His service.

The capstone truth, which was articulated by the same Paul who wrote the previously-cited prohibitions against women, is that gender is a mute issue in the body of Christ: for "as many of you as were baptized into Christ have clothed yourselves with Christ. There is no longer Jew or Greek, there is no longer slave or free, there is *no longer male and female*; for all of you are one in Christ Jesus. And if you belong to Christ, then you are Abraham's offspring, heirs according to the promise" (Gal 2:27-29 NRSV, *author's emphasis*).

Both the practice of fornication and the eating of food sacrificed to idols have already been cited as the defining activities of Nicolaitanism and Balaamism (see discussion on Rev 2:14-15 – church in Pergamum), as well as in the worship of Apollo (see discussion on vs 18). Both practices have also been cited as the prohibitions that were placed upon Gentile converts to Christianity by the Council of Jerusalem (Acts 15).

Though these licentious activities suggest physical activities, they are also indicative of spiritual apostasy. Worshipping other gods, for example, has consistently been described as spiritual harlotry or whoredom (Jer 2:20; 3:2, 6; Ezek 16:15-26, 28-43; 23:1-49; Hosea 1:2; 2:1-13). Following false doctrine or teaching has consistently denoted the eating of food sacrificed to idols and is succinctly summarized and prohibited in 1 Cor 10:21 NRSV:

> *You cannot drink the cup of the Lord and the cup of demons. You cannot partake of the table of the Lord and the table of demons.*

However, the Jezebel in our current text was an advocate for the co-mingling of these practices with the worship of Jesus. The only result of this co-mingling of the world's way with the way of Christ is apostasy: for "no one can serve two masters . . . " (Matt 6:24; Luke 16:13). Elijah's question in the contest against the Baal prophets on Mt Carmel takes on timeless relevance for the church in Thyatira and for the church in every generation:

How long will you go limping with two different opinions? If the LORD is God, follow Him; but if Baal, then follow him. The people did not answer him a word (1 Kings 18:21 NRSV).

VERSE 21

"I have given her time to repent of her immorality, but she is unwilling."

In 2 Peter 3:8-9, the Spirit reminds us through Peter that "with the Lord one day is like a thousand years, and a thousand years are like one day." The generosity of time is a gift of God's grace to the sinner who needs to repent. This gift is given because our God is "not wanting anyone to perish, but everyone to come to repentance" and because He has "no pleasure in the death of the wicked, but rather that they turn from their ways and live . . ." (Ezek 33:11; cf. 18:23). Both aforementioned principles constitute the foundation of Jesus' generosity of grace in granting Jezebel time to repent.

Jezebel's refusal to repent is the result of the deceitfulness of sin (Heb 3:13), which produces a hardness of heart that refuses the grace and the gracious opportunities to repent. Jezebel's hardness of heart points in two directions. It points back to the hardness of Pharaoh's heart (Exod 7:3, 13, 14, 22; 8:15, 19, 32; 9:7, 12, 34-35; 10:1, 20, 27; 11:10; 14:4, 8); and it points forward to the unrepentant response from those suffering under the 6th Trumpet (Rev 9:20-21) and the 5th Bowl of Wrath (Rev 16:10-11) judgments.

VERSE 22

"So I will cast her on a bed of suffering, and I will make those who commit adultery with her suffer intensely, unless they repent of her ways."

Several linguistic features and their meanings are worthy to note in this verse. For example, the Greek verb here translated "cast" (Βάλλω – pronounced **bá´-lō**) which is used to articulate Jesus' judgment against

Jezebel, will be the same Greek word preceded by a negative particle in verse 24, translated "not impose" (οὐ Βάλλω – pronounced oo **bâ´**-lō) that Jesus will engage to offer encouragement to the faithful remnant to "not impose" any additional burden to their charge to hold fast to their faith in Him until He comes.

It is also worthy to note that the Greek word for 'bed' in Jesus' judgment against Jezebel (κλίνη – pronounced **klĭ´**-nay) is the same word Jesus used when He commanded the man sick with palsy to "Arise, take up your bed and go to your house" (Matt 9:6 NKJV). We can safely conclude, therefore, that the bed on to which Jezebel will be thrown is a bed of physical affliction. Inasmuch as the controversy that surrounded Jesus' healing of the man with palsy was His authority to forgive sins, it becomes clear in the current context that the judgment Jesus decrees is Jezebel's just dessert for her unrepentant response to Jesus' indictment of her sins.

Whereas the Greek word for "sexual immorality" (verse 20) is πορνεύω (pronounced por-**nū´**-ō), from which we get the word "pornography", the Greek word for "adultery" is μοιχεύω (pronounced moi-**chū´**-ō - ch=k sound), and represents a more specific brand of sexual immorality. Regarding its spiritual significance, adultery denotes an unholy alliance with all that is opposed to the knowledge of God. Those in the church in Thyatira who followed Jezebel's teaching are characterized as being in an adulterous relationship with her.

Though the Greek word for "distress" (θλίψις – pronounced **thleep´**-sees) is also used elsewhere to denote the suffering and afflictions of the righteous, it here reflects Peter's caution not to suffer "as a murderer, a thief, or wtih any other kind of criminal, or even as a meddler" (1 Peter 4:15). The same Greek word is also translated "tribulation" in the rendition of this verse in the KJV, NASB, Holman CSB, and others, and thus foreshadows the great tribulation that will come upon the whole world (cf. Rev 4.20).

The gracious opportunity of time to repent that was extended to Jezebel is the same gracious opportunity extended to those who have been deceived by her teaching. Though repentance is usually from one's own sins, Jesus surprisingly requires that the deceived repent of *her works*. Those who followed Jezebel had allowed themselves to be seduced and deceived by the persuasive compromise of her teachings. Jesus' exhortation to repent of her seductive and deceptive doctrines would require the deliberate effort of testing the spirit of her false doctrine by the Word of God (1 John 4:1-6). In doing so, the deceived, yet repentant, believers would then see her doctrine for what it was and turn from it. With God's Word being the Light, their repentance would be the equivalent of the blind recovering their sight.

VERSE 23

"I will strike her children dead. Then all the churches will know that I am he who searches hearts and minds, and I will repay each of you according to your deeds."

Those within the church in Thyatira who agree with and who propagate Jezebel's doctrine are referred to as "her children" whom Jesus "will strike dead" unless they repent. Jesus' judgment here also points in two directions. In pointing back to the Old Testament, God's triad of affliction included the sword, famine, and pestilence as the instruments of death (2 Chron 20:9; Jer 21:7, 9; 24:10; 27:8, 13; 29:17-19; 38:2). The death resulting from any of these three was usually a physical death. Any one (or all three) of these instruments could be implied as the instrument Jesus will use to strike dead those who follow and support Jezebel's teachings. In pointing forward, the death of Jezebel's unrepentant followers signals the ultimate condemnation of the second death (Rev 20:14; 21:8), which is also a physical death to which the cited categories of sinners will be consigned for all eternity. In other words, the second death, also known as the lake that burns with fire and sulfur, is a form of life lived in perpetual torment (Rev 20:10, 15), and those who inherit this death will be alive enough to feel the pain (cf. Isa 66:24; Mark 9:47-48)! It should be noted that Jezebel and her children, if unrepentant, fall into every cited category of those whose end will be the second death:

> But the cowardly, the unbelieving, the vile, the murderers, the sexually immoral, those who practice magic arts, the idolators and all liars - they will be consigned to the fiery lake of burning sulfur. This is the **second death** (Rev 21:8, **author's emphasis**).

The phrase "all the churches will know . . ." is one of the clearest indications that all seven of the churches will receive each other's letter as well as the complete content of THE REVELATION OF JESUS CHRIST. This truth is ultimately endorsed in Revelation 22:16a:

> I, Jesus, have sent My Angel to give you this testimony for the **churches (author's emphasis)**

The two-fold benefit of receiving each other's letters is the forewarning each letter will provide to every other church not to fall into the same stage of apostasy, as well as the promise of the prize that will be accorded to overcomers in each instance!

What Jesus declares that all the churches will know is that "I am he who searches hearts and minds, and I will repay each of you according to your deeds." This is the second "I Am" assertion made by Jesus in

THE REVELATION text.[88] As previously discussed, the "I Am" assertion is the English translation of the Greek ἐγώ εἰμι (pronounced ě-**gō´** ā-**mee´**), which identifies Jesus with His Father's Eternal Name, i.e., "I Am that I Am" (Exod 6:3; see also discussion on Rev 1:8). It is worthy to note that only in John's Gospel are all 15 of Jesus' "I Am" assertions recorded (John 6:35, 41, 48, 51; 8:12, 18, 58; 9:5; 10:7, 9, 11, 14; 11:25; 14:6; 15:1), lending further credence to John's identity as the recipient of the entire *Revelation* text.

Jesus' ability to search minds and hearts is not only reflected in the attribute of having "Eyes like a flame of fire" (see notes on vs 18), but also constitutes an allusion[89] to a similar declaration made by His Father through the prophet Jeremiah that—

> *I the LORD test the mind and search the heart, to give to all according to their ways, according to the fruit of their doings (Jer 17:10 NRSV)*

Jesus' "I Am" assertion also includes His Divine Prerogative to render judgment according to our works. John's Gospel also records Jesus' inheritance of the office of Judge from His Father:

> *Moreover the Father judges no one, but has entrusted all judgment to the Son . . . and He has given Him authority to judge because He is the Son of Man (John 5:22, 27).*

---

88   The first "I Am" statement occurs in Rev 1:17b. However, the 'I Am' statement recorded in 1:11 in the KJV, the Living Bible and the Amplified Bible, i.e., "I Am Alpha and Omega, the First and the Last . . . " is a textual addition in the ancient manuscript, called the Byzantine Majority MSS with commentary by Andreas of Caesarea (MA), that does not appear in the Greek text (though noted in the critical apparatus for this verse) nor in most other English translations, e.g. Complete Jewish Bible, Holman Christian Standard Bible, NAB, NASB, NIV, NRSV).

89   See footnote #4 in Overview.

VERSE 24

"Now I say to the rest of you in Thyatira, to you who do not hold to her teaching and have not learned Satan's so-called deep secrets, 'I will not impose any other burden on you,"

The phrase " to the rest of you in Thyatira" is indicative of a division within the church and a distinction between those who have followed Jezebel and those who have not followed her compromising teachings. The phrase refers to the latter group to whom the rest of this letter pertains, and who are characterized by the following three key phrases:

1.   Do not hold to her teaching

The Greek word ἔχω (pronounced ĕ'-chō) is translated "'hold" and is pronounced like the English word 'echo.' In a play on words, the "rest in Thyatira" are those who do not echo, hold to, parrot, or subscribe to the compromising teachings of Jezebel. As Jesus is able to search the mind and the heart, then He knows that the faithfulness of the rest in Thyatira is not just "lip" loyalty but heart loyalty, as well (cf. Luke 6:45).

2.   Not learned . . . Satan's so-called deep secrets

Biblical scholar, Robert H. Mounce, suggests that the "deep things of Satan'" carried with it the false notion that "in order to appreciate fully the grace of God one must first plumb the depths of evil. Later Gnosticism boasted that it was precisely by entering into the stronghold of Satan that believers could learn the limits of his power and emerge victorious."[90]

As the bedrock of her seductive doctrine, this slogan most likely served as the byline of Jezebel's false teaching. The slogan actually represented a perversion of the Christian doctrine to know the "deep things of God", as revealed by the Spirit (1 Cor 2:10), and based its rationale on a gross yet

---

90 Mounce, *THE BOOK OF THE REVELATION REVISED EDITION*, 89.

subtle misapplication of the Word of God (see discussion on vs 20, pp. 145-6). G. K. Beale gives a good rehearsal of the biblical passages that were possibly being used to endorse Jezebel's false teaching on the legitimacy of knowing the 'deep things of Satan':

"Possibly the false teachers were misapplying Paul's statement in 1 Cor. 8:4 by saying that if, indeed, "an idol has no real existence in the world," then participation at a feast honoring an idol could not harm one spiritually. They might have also appealed, in support of this teaching, to a misunderstanding of Jesus' words in the Gospels ("render to Caesar the things that are Caesar's, and to God the things that are God's," Matt.22:21; Mark 12:17) or of Paul's admonition that "every person be in subjection to the governing authorities" (Rom 13:1) . . . Perhaps also the errant teaching was based on a misreading of Paul's exhortations in 1 Cor.5:9-11 about not associating with idolaters or in 1 Corinthians 8–10 that a degree of participation in the idolatrous demonic realm by the "strong" was permissible as long as it did not make the "weaker" brother stumble . . . Perhaps the false teachers reasoned that God's grace could be appreciated most fully by learning the real nature of sin by experiencing it in the midst of Satan's stronghold."[91]

3.   Will not impose any other burden on you

This phrase must be connected to the beginning of the next verse (vs 25) in order to make sense. However, we can note at this point that the Greek word Βάλλω (pronounced **bâ´-lō** meaning "throwing,") which was used in vs 22 in connection with Jezebel's judgment, is the same Greek word used here, preceded by a negative particle, translated "not impose" (οὐ Βάλλω – pronounced oo **bâ´-lō**) to convey the consolation and the encouragement that Jesus will not impose upon the faithful any additional burden.

---

91   Beale, *The Book of Revelation*, 265-6.

It is also worthy to note that this is the last time the Greek word βάρος (pronounced **bâ´-rŏs**), translated "burden,'" appears in the Scriptures. Consider the significance of this by reading Jer 23:33-40.

VERSE 25

"Except to hold on to what you have until I come."

The "burden'" of the faithful remnant within the church to which Jesus will not add any additional requirements is the burden to "hold on" not only to sound teaching but also to that which was placed upon all Gentile converts at the Council of Jerusalem, both of which would keep them undefiled by Jezebel's false teachings:

> Hold to the standard of sound teaching that you have heard from me, in the faith and love that are in Christ Jesus (2 Tim 1:13 NRSV)

> For it seemed good to the Holy Spirit and to us to impose on you no further burden than these essentials: that you abstain from what has been sacrificed to idols and from blood and from what is strangled and from fornication (Acts 15:28-29 NRSV).

It is worthy to note that though the church is divided between the deceived and the faithful, the faithful are not enjoined to leave the church, or to persecute the deceived, or to oust the Pastor. They are instead instructed to take a stand by holding fast to sound doctrine. Holding fast takes more spiritual tenacity than running from the problem and brings with it the patient endurance that is necessary to "wait on the Lord." Sound doctrine would also include the certainty of Jesus' return, i.e., "until I come," and in His conclusion to the Parable of the Wheat and the Tares, Jesus commends His own ability and authority to separate the deceived from the faithful at that time:

Let both grow together until the harvest. At that time I will tell the harvesters: First collect the weeds and tie them in bundles to be burned; then gather the wheat and bring it into my barn (Matt 13:30).

VERSES 26-27

"To the one who is victorious and does my will to the end, I will give authority over the nations—That one 'will rule them with an iron scepter and will dash them to pieces like pottery'—just as I have received authority from my Father."

As previously discussed, the conjugated Greek verb νικάω (pronounced nĭ-kâ´-ō), translated "is victorious," is the same Greek verb used in 1 John 5:4 to describe the believer's victory over the world: " . . . This is the victory that has overcome the world, even our faith" (see discussion on Rev 2:7). The reference "to the one who is victorious" not only imply the faithful who had not been deceived by Jezebel's false teachings, but also includes the repentant from among her adherents (verse 22).

The original list of commendations in verse 19 is characterized here as "My will," or Jesus' will. Included in His will, i.e., "love, faith, service, and patient endurance," would be the critical work of holding fast to sound doctrine. Continuing in Jesus' will "to the end" is not only the condition that must be met in order for the faithful and the repentant to receive what will be promised to the victorious, but it is equally applied to two events of which we know not the day nor the hour: our own death and the rapture of the church, whichever occurs first.

In the concluding phrase of this verse and all of verse 27 Jesus' promise to both the faithful and the repentant is an allusion to Psalm 2:8-9 in which Jesus is promised by the Father an inheritance of all nations over which He (Jesus) will rule:

Ask me, and I will make the nations your inheritance, the ends of the earth your possession. You will break them with a rod of iron; you will dash them to pieces like pottery.

The other clue that Psalm 2:8-9 is being referenced is that Jesus is referred to as the "Son" of God in verse 18 of this Letter and in verses 7 and 12 of Psalm 2:

I will proclaim the LORD's decree: He said to me, 'You are my son; today I have become your father (Psalm 2:7).

Kiss his Son, or he will be angry . . . (Psalm 2:12).[92]

Other references are embedded in the quote from Psalm 2:8-9. For example, there is also an allusion to Isa 11:1 where Jesus is referred to as "a rod out of the stem of Jesse . . ." The word "rule" is the Greek word ποιμαίνω (pronounced poi-**mī´**-nō), which carries the meaning "to shepherd" or "to keep sheep." When coupled with the instrument of "an iron rod," it conveys the shepherd's role in warding off ravaging beasts with a staff or club capped with iron. The intent, in this case, is to kill or destroy the beast. Both Revelation 12:5 and 19:15 confirm the character of Jesus' Rulership as with "a rod of iron" and also pick up the imagery of Psalm 2:8-9, as well. It is the second of these two references (Rev. 19:15), that combines this imagery with the effect of Jesus' Feet being "burnished bronze" (Rev 1:15), in order to "tread the winepress of the fury of the wrath of God Almighty," His Father.

The reference to "dash them to pieces like pottery" conveys the absolute power of Christ in His Returning Glory and of those who will reign with Him. The imagery is also an allusion to Nebuchadnezzar's dream of the great statue composed of various metals representing

---

92   The pronoun "son" does not occur in the NRSV but is present in the original Hebrew text and in most translations of Psalm 2:12.

the succession of Gentile kingdoms (Dan 2:31-45). The last kingdom, symbolized by feet of clay and iron (which don't mix), was struck by "a stone cut out without hands" and shattered the entire statue into pieces. Though the imagery varies, the result and the meaning are the same.

Regarding His promise to those who are victorious, Jesus, in the context of His answer to Peter concerning the reward for following Him, promised the apostles that they will sit on twelve thrones judging the twelve tribes of Israel during His millennial kingdom (Matt 19:27-30). Jesus also promises all believers that those who suffer with Him in this life will reign with Him in His coming kingdom and forever (Rom 8:17; 2 Tim 2:12; Rev 20:4, 6, 22:5c). Hence, Jesus' gift to believers, "I will give authority . . . ," will be joint-heirship with Him over the nations "even as I also received authority from my Father."

As previously discussed, Jesus' right to rule has been bestowed upon Him by His Father (John 5:22, 27). Even His right to the Davidic throne is by divine design, as His Father ordained His Incarnation through the seed of David (Luke 1:32; 3:23, 31; Rom 1:3; cf. 2 Sam 7:12-14a). The prophecies of Jesus' ultimate rulership over the nations are abundant. The one given to Daniel firmly establishes the 'end-time' context of His authority and serves as prologue to the *key verse* of the entire *Revelation* text:

> *To Him was given dominion and glory and kingship, that all peoples, nations, and languages should serve Him. His dominion is an everlasting dominion that shall not pass away, and His kingship is one that shall never be destroyed (Dan 7:14 NRSV).*

> *The seventh angel sounded his trumpet, and there were loud voices in heaven, which said, 'The kingdom of the world has become the kingdom of our Lord and of His Messiah, and He will reign forever and ever (Rev 11:15).*

VERSE 28

"I will also give that one the morning star."

What appears to be an additional gift from Jesus to those who conquer is a further confirmation of their reign with Him in Glory. The imagery of the "morning star" is most likely derived from Num 24:14-20 where the future ruler of Israel is described as "a star . . . out of Jacob" and as a "scepter . . . out of Israel" (24:17) who will crush Gentile nations. The two images in the Numbers text echo the same context of judgment as that of Psalm 2:8-9. The connection between the current text and the two images in Numbers 24 becomes even stronger when we consider that the above prophecy was issued by Balaam, whose doctrine had invaded the church in Pergamum (Rev 2:14), and whose enticements were the same as the false teaching of Jezebel (see notes on verse 20).

> The name "Esther" is derived from the above Greek word for 'star' and bears the same meaning. What more fitting connection could be made to intone that ALL (men and women) who hold fast and remain faithful will rule with authority with Christ in His Coming Kingdom!

Given the above reference in Numbers 24, the "morning star" takes on the significance of Jesus' Messianic rule during the millennial kingdom, in fulfillment of the Davidic covenant. It is worthy to note, that Lucifer's name in the Hebrew language (הֵלֵל – pronounced hĕ-**lel**′) also means "morning star" and, as such, gives clear evidence of the primordial tension between him and Jesus who is called the "Bright Morning Star" (Rev 22:16). However, Lucifer lost this name in his fall (Isa 14:12-17; Ezek 28:11-19; Rev 12:7-9) and is not referred to by it in the remainder of the Old Testament nor in the New Testament.

The Greek word πρωϊνός (pronounced prō-ee-**nŏs´**), translated 'morning', suggests the inauguration of Jesus' reign.[93] The Greek word ἀστήρ (pronounced **ăs´**-tare) is translated 'star,' and is symbolic of a king or rulership. As Jesus is here promising the victorious a "co-star" role in His coming kingdom, we are reminded of Daniel's prophecy of those who will inherit everlasting life: they will be the "wise [who] shall shine like the brightness of the sky . . . like the stars forever and ever" (Dan 12:3 NRSV). Inasmuch as our initial discussion on "stars" concluded that they are the angels whom Jesus is holding in His right hand (see discussion on Rev. 1:20), then believers who inherit eternal life will be "like the angels," according to Jesus' account of the resurrection from the dead (Matt 22:30; Mar 12:25; Luke 20:36)!

VERSE 29

"Whoever has ears, let them hear what the Spirit says to the churches."[94]

See the initial discussion of this injunction to hear as presented in the commentary on Rev 2:7.

---

93 Beale, *THE BOOK OF REVELATION*, 269.

94 Whereas the injunction to have "an ear [to] listen to what the Spirit is saying to the Churches" preceded the promises to overcomers in the first three letters, it is postured after the promises in this letter and in the remaining three letters. The change in position is a matter of scholarly debate, but in no way alters the meaning nor the significance of the injunction.

CHAPTER THREE

THE CHURCH IN SARDIS
REVELATION 3:1-6

3:1 "To the angel of the church in Sardis write: These are the words of him who holds the seven spirits of God and the seven stars. I know your deeds; you have a reputation of being alive, but you are dead.

2 Wake up! Strengthen what remains and is about to die, for I have found your deeds unfinished in the sight of my God.

3 Remember, therefore, what you have received and heard; hold it fast, and repent. But if you do not wake up, I will come like a thief, and you will not know at what time I will come to you.

4 Yet you have a few people in Sardis who have not soiled their clothes. They will walk with me, dressed in white, for they are worthy.

5 The one who is victorious will, like them, be dressed in white. I will never blot out the name of that person from the book of life, but will acknowledge that name before my Father and his angels.

6 Whoever has ears, let them hear what the Spirit says to the churches."

VERSE 1

"To the angel of the church in Sardis write: These are the words of him who holds the seven spirits of God and the seven stars. I know your deeds; you have a reputation of being alive, but you are dead."

As mentioned in the previous discussions on Revelation 1:20 and 2:1, the angel of the church in Sardis is an angelic messenger or spirit who has been assigned to the church in Sardis for the purpose of communicating revelation knowledge concerning Jesus. More insight on angels will be presented in the discussion on the seven stars that are also referenced in this verse.

The church in Sardis would have been included in the Apostle Paul's extensive stay and ministry in Ephesus during his third missionary journey, since the city of Sardis was located "some fifty miles east of Ephesus on a northern spur of Mt. Tmolus overlooking the broad and fertile plain of the Hermus."[95] Acts 19:10 records that during Paul's 3rd missionary journey to Ephesus "all the residents of Asia, both Jews and Greeks, heard the word of the Lord."

The city's high and fortified position on Mt. Tmolus not only made it impregnable to military attack, but as the city grew, "it became necessary to develop a lower city to the north and west . . . on the banks of the Pactolus River."[96] Along with a Roman theatre and stadium, the lower city also hosted "an exceptionally large temple dedicated . . . to a local Asiatic goddess usually referred to as Cybele (identified with the Greek Artemis), who was believed to possess the special power of restoring the dead to life."[97] The city's history credits it with being the birthplace of coined money (both silver and gold), and "the first [place] to discover the art of

---

95   Mounce, THE BOOK OF THE REVELATION REVISED, 91.

96   Ibid., 92.

97   Ibid., 92.

dyeing wool."[98] The Jewish synagogue within the city was not only of exceptional size, but occupied a prominent place within the gymnasium-complex,[99] thus reflecting not only its affluence and acceptance but also its assimilation into the Asiatic culture of the city.

In this 7th command to John to write (see discussions on Rev 1:11, 19), Jesus first identifies Himself as the One who possesses the seven Spirits that are before His Father's throne. As discussed in the previous commentary on Revelation 1:4, the seven Spirits of God are the seven-fold fullness of the One Holy Spirit, the Third Person of the Trinity. As such, the seven Spirits are the manifold agents of the revelation of God and of His Will. Isaiah 11:2 lists the seven Spirits as the Spirit of the Lord, wisdom, understanding, counsel, might, knowledge, and fear of the Lord, by whose power Jesus will reign.

The seven Spirits of God are also identified elsewhere in *THE REVELATION* by different imageries and functions. In Revelation 4:5, the seven Spirits of God are depicted as the seven flaming torches before the Throne; and in Revelation 5:6, the seven spirits are portrayed as the seven eyes of the Lamb slain. Both depictions are related to throne scenes in heaven.

The One Holy Spirit, who is the consummate expression of the seven Spirits of God, is personified in the following passages as the Divine Agent by whom all believers are baptized into the body of Christ and by whom believers are indwelt, instructed, and empowered to do God's will (John 14:26; 15:26; 16:12-15; Rom 8:9-10; 1 Cor 12:13; Gal 5:22).

Most importantly, the Holy Spirit is the divine agent of Jesus' Resurrection from the dead and the divine agent by whom all believers will be resurrected, as well (Rom 8:11; 1 Cor 15:22-23). The significance of

---

98   Ibid., 92.

99   Hemer, *LETTERS TO THE SEVEN CHURCHES IN THEIR LOCAL SETTING*, 137.

the seven-fold fullness of the Holy Spirit will be discussed more fully in relationship to the indictment against the church.

The seven stars were identified in Revelation 1:20 as the angels of the seven churches and are also referenced in Revelation 2:1 in the letter to the church in Ephesus. Given the aforementioned identification of the seven Spirits of God and the aforementioned discussion on the seven stars, the answers to at least two questions are critical to our understanding of the rest of the letter to the church in Sardis.

The first of these two critical questions is this: What is the relational significance between the seven stars and the seven Spirits of God for the church in Sardis? The answer resides in the fact that since the seven stars or seven angels are the emissaries of Jesus' message to each church, then Jesus' possession of all seven stars or angels strongly suggests that the church in Sardis is in dire need of heeding not only its own letter but the letters to the other six churches, as well — seven in total. In other words, Jesus' indictment of their dead state makes them guilty of each letter's indictment: 1.) of abandoning their first love (Ephesus); 2.) of being fearful of persecution (Smyrna); 3.) of subscribing to false doctrine and complicity with the dominant culture (Pergamum); 4.) of tolerating false teachers (Thyatira); 5.) of not keeping God's Word and of denying His Name (the opposite of Jesus' perfect commendation of the church in Philadelphia); and 6.) of becoming lukewarm (Laodicea). For this reason, the seven-fold or complete fullness of the Holy Spirit is needed to reverse the church's dead state to a living state in Jesus. In other words, the church in Sardis was in need of a resurrection experience in their relationship with Christ!

The second of these two critical questions is this: Why does Jesus find it necessary to identify Himself to the church in Sardis as possessing all seven Spirits of God and all seven stars? The answer points to the fact that, given their respective functions in relationship to His Body, the seven stars and the seven Spirits of God unmistakably establish Jesus' total Authority (seven stars) and Power (seven spirits of God) over the church. In other words, Jesus' possession of the seven stars establishes Him as the Author and the Authority of each letter, as well as the Commander-in Chief over the heavenly emissaries through whom His message is transmitted. His possession of the seven-fold fullness of the Holy Spirit, on the other hand, establishes Him as the Omniscient or All-Knowing Head, the Sole Judge, and the Eternal Life Principle of the church's existence as His Body. Since the seven stars or angels come from the ranks of the myriad of angels that surround the Father's throne (Dan 7:10; Rev 5:11), and since the seven Spirits of God reside before the Father's throne (Rev 1:4; 4:5; 5:6), then Jesus' possession of both, coupled with the authority and power that emit from both, comes from His Father, by whom He (Jesus) has been made heir of all things (Heb 1:1-2; cf. John 5:21-23, 26-27; 16:15a) and into whose hands His Father has committed all power and all judgment (Matt 28:18; John 5:26-27).

In rehearsing His Omniscient perspective on the church in Sardis, i.e., "I know your works . . . " (see discussion on Rev 2:2), Jesus articulates His indictment against the church: "You have a name of being alive, but you are dead." The Greek word ὄνομα (pronounced ŏ′-nŏ-mâ), is translated people or name three other times in this letter (verses 4 and 5), but only here does it carry the meaning of "reputation." It carries this same meaning in Mark 6:14, where it states that Herod had heard of the reputation of Jesus and had erroneously concluded that Jesus was John the Baptist raised from the dead. It is from Mark's use of the word in relationship to Herod, an unbeliever, that we can initially conclude that the Greek word in our current context connotes the church's reputation as perceived by those outside the faith. Additionally, the above-cited Mark text reveals that Herod drew his conclusion concerning the reputation of Jesus based on the works that Jesus and His disciples were doing, e.g. preaching, casting out demons, anointing the sick with oil and healing them. What these works have in common is that they are performed on a tangible, observable, and measurable level of reality.

Let us be clear: though the work of preaching, casting out demons and healing the sick (among others) are good works, their tangibility and their ability to be observed with the naked eye also render them easy to be imitated and easy to be pursued for the wrong reasons (Matt 6:1, 5, 16; Phil 1:15-18). As a result, what may look like a living, thriving church to outsiders, based on these works, is, in truth, a dead church producing fruitless works if these works do not emit from faith in Jesus (cf. Rom 14:23) and if they are not purposed to glorify God (Matt 5:16). Jesus makes this very clear in His Sermon on the Mount:

> Not everyone who says to Me, 'Lord, Lord,' will enter the kingdom of heaven, but only the one who does the Will of My Father in heaven. On that day many will say to Me, 'Lord, Lord, did we not **prophesy in Your Name, and cast out demons in Your Name, and do many deeds of power in Your Name?'** Then I will declare to them, 'I never knew you; go away from Me, you evildoers' (Matt 7:21-23 NRSV; cf. Luke 13:24-28, **author's emphasis**).

What the above-cited text indicates is that many good works can be done in the Lord's Name without a relationship with the Lord by faith. A faith relationship with the Lord would entail receiving His instructions to do one or more of the above-cited works, to which a faithful response would constitute an act of obedience. If Jesus did not tell the person to do the above-cited works, then these same works become acts of presumption. Jesus, in other words, received His Father's instructions and did everything His Father told Him to do and said everything His Father told Him to say (John 5:19; 7:16-18; 8:28; 12:49-50; 14:10, 24; 17:8). Jesus did not design His own ministry but came to fulfill His Father's Will. By example, therefore, Jesus demonstrates that true ministry is nothing less than an act of obedience to His instructions, not just a self-appointed agenda of good works!

When Jesus declared that the church was dead, He was indicting the church for having a level of busyness that was being pursued to impress those outside the faith[100] and which did not emit from faith in Him. Just as James says that "faith without works is dead" (James 2:17, 20, 26), then it stands to reason that works that do not emit from faith are dead works (cf. Rom 14:23).

Jesus' indictment, therefore, is double-edged: their dying faith is producing dead works (busyness); and their dead works are the result of their dying faith (notice that Jesus does not commend them for a single work).

In summary, the church is Sardis is physically alive, but spiritually dead. This is the state that the Scriptures declare we were all in when it says that we were "dead in trespasses and sins" (Eph 2:1, 5). It is from this dead state that we were quickened by the hearing of the word of God through which faith comes (Rom 10:17). This quickening is also known as being born again and can aptly be characterized as the initial stage of our resurrection experience in the Lord.

VERSE 2

"Wake up! Strengthen what remains and is about to die, for I have found your deeds unfinished in the sight of my God."

In stark contrast to their dead state, Jesus issues the command to "Wake up!" The Greek phrase γίνου γρηγορέω (pronounced **gee´-nū grā-gŏ-**

---

100   One such likely group outside the faith could have been the influential and thriving Jewish population who had a prominent synagogue in the center of the city. See Hemer, *LETTERS TO THE SEVEN CHURCHES IN THEIR LOCAL SETTING*, 137.

rĕ′-ō) is properly, yet awkwardly, translated "Be awakening," combining the present tense imperative (Be) with a continuous action participle (awakening). Jesus' command, therefore, is the church's wake-up call to reverse her current, sleep-walking trek toward total spiritual death to a quickened and energetic press toward spiritual life. The present tense imperative (Be) implies that this action is to be taken immediately — right now — as the beginning of this reversal process. Then, just as the trek toward spiritual death had been a process, so the reversal toward spiritual life would also be a continuous and sustainable process, as indicated by the continuous action participle (awakening), and by the action required by the four remaining imperatives within this letter, i.e., "strengthen," "remember," "hold fast," and "repent" — each of which will be discussed below.

> Jesus' initial command to "Wake up" or "Be awakening" is like God's Word in creation when He said, "Let there be . . . " God's spoken Word in creation brought something out of nothing. And since Jesus is God's Word by Whom He created all things (John 1:1-3), then Jesus' spoken Word has this same creating and resurrecting power. The Record clearly shows that during His earthly ministry, Jesus' spoken Word brought the dead to life (Mark 5:35, 39-42; Luke 7:11-15; John 11:43-44), and that at His spoken command all dead will be brought to life, both in the first and second resurrections (cf. Isa 26:19; Dan 12:2; John 5:25, 28-29; 1 Thess 4:16).

The first of the four imperatives involved in the church's awakening is Jesus' command to "strengthen what remains and is about to die." What is quizzical here is that Jesus' indictment states that the church is dead, but His admonition addresses that which remains that is *about to die*. It is critical to identify what remains that is about to die but is evidently not yet dead. What we can safely deduce from Jesus' indictment is that the church's works are dead because they do not proceed from a living faith in Him but rather from a dying faith in Him. What we can conclude, therefore, is that what remains that is about to die is the church's faith in Christ.

The Greek imperative στήρισον (pronounced **stā´-rĭ-sŏn**), translated 'strengthen', is used in only one other place in the New Testament. As prologue to telling Peter that he would deny Him three times, Jesus declared to Peter that He had prayed that his faith would not fail, since Satan desired to sift him as wheat; and "when you are turned about, *strengthen* your brothers" (Luke 22:31-32, *author's emphasis*). Since it is the Sardian church's faith that needs to be strengthened, then 2 Peter 1:5-11 is most instructive as to what needs to be added to faith in order to strengthen it:

> *For this very reason, you must make every effort to support your faith with goodness, and goodness with knowledge, and knowledge with self-control, and self-control with endurance, and endurance with godliness, and godliness with mutual affection, and mutual affection with love. For if these things are yours and are increasing among you, they keep you from being ineffective and unfruitful in the knowledge of our Lord Jesus Christ . . . For in this way, entry into the eternal kingdom of our Lord and Savior Jesus Christ will be richly provided for you (NRSV).*

Because a living faith in Jesus is validated by "works" of obedience (James 2:17, 20, 26), and not presumptive busy-works (Matt 7:21-23), then Jesus' assessment of the church's works, as being unfinished, also suggests that the quality of their faith is a dying one. When answering the people's question, "What must we do to perform the works of God?" Jesus answered: "This is the work of God, that you believe in Him whom He has sent" (John 6:28-29). Hebrews 11:6 also endorses that " . . . without faith it is impossible to please God . . . " On the contrary, the church's presumptive busyness is not pleasing "in the sight of My God" because they are without a faith foundation in God's Son. Jesus' assessment, therefore, is a judgment He shares with His Father, who has committed all judgment into His Son's hands (John 5:22, 27, 30; 7:24; 8:16).

VERSE 3

"Remember, therefore, what you have received and heard; hold it fast, and repent. But if you do not wake up, I will come like a thief, and you will not know at what time I will come to you."

The remaining three of the four imperatives involved in the church's awakening are Jesus' commands to "remember . . . hold it fast . . . and repent." Jesus first commands that the Sardian church "remember . . . what you have received and heard." The Greek word μνημόνευε (pronounced mě-nay-**mŏ´**-nū-ě), from which our English word mnemonics is derived, carries the meaning of assisting the memory or of engaging devices to aid one's memory. This same Greek word was used in Ephesians 2:11 and in Revelation 2:5, where the Gentile believers in Ephesus were commanded to remember who and where they were before they were saved (Eph 2:11-12) and to remember from what they had fallen (Rev 2:5). As both texts involve a resurrection or restoration experience, remembering appears to be the first step toward that end!

It is worthy to note that the Greek word translated "remember" in Ephesian 2:11 is rendered as a plural imperative, as if speaking to individual believers within the church in Ephesus. However, the same word in our current text to the church in Sardis is rendered as a singular imperative, implying that the church as a whole is to have a singleness of purpose and a unity of the Spirit (Eph 4:3) in engaging their individual and collective memory.

Though the NRSV and other translations record Jesus' command that the church remember "what you received and heard,"[101] the Greek text uses the particle πῶς (pronounced pōs), meaning how, so that the command actually reads "Remember then how you received and heard . . . " The translation that beautifully combines the "how" and the "what" is the New American Bible/Catholic Edition: "Call to mind *how* you accepted *what* you heard; keep to it, and repent (*author's emphasis*)."[102]

Before we examine the *how* of Jesus' command, let us identify *what* was received and heard. Though not explicitly stated, what the church in Sardis received and heard was the Gospel of Jesus Christ. The Gospel itself is characterized in several ways in Scripture that should inform the church's recall. The Gospel of Jesus Christ is:

- "The Good News of the Kingdom" – Matthew 4:23; 9:35; 24:14

- "The Good News of God's Grace" – Acts 20:24

- "The Power of God for salvation to everyone who has faith, to the Jew first and also to the Greek" – Romans 1:16

- "The Gospel of Peace" – Ephesians 6:15

- "The Gospel of God" – Romans 1:1; 15:16; 1 Thessalonians 2:2, 9

- "The Glorious Gospel of the Blessed God" – 1 Timothy 1:11

- "The Implanted (Engrafted – KJV) Word that has the power to save your souls" – James 1:21b

---

101 The other translations that echo the NRSV include, but are limited to, the NIV, NASB, Holman CSB, and the Complete Jewish Bible.

102 http://www.usccb.org/bible/permissions

- "Pure, Spiritual Milk, so that by it you may grow into salvation" – 1 Peter 2:2

Now that we have established *what* was received and heard, the recall of *how* the Gospel was received and heard (cf. Luke 8:18) becomes the necessary next step of the church's resurrection in faith. Scripture commends at least five ways that answer *how* the Sardian believers (and all believers) first received and heard the Gospel:

- "By Grace" – Ephesians 2:8-9

- "Through Faith" – Romans 10:17; Ephesians 2:8-9

- "With Meekness" – James 1:21b

- "With Gladness" – Acts 13:46-48

- "As A Little Child" – Matthew 18:3-4; 19:13-15; Mark 10:15; Luke 18:17

Thus, Jesus is commanding the Sardian believers to remember both their attitudinal posture of humility when they received the Gospel (how) as well as the doctrinal tenets of the Gospel (what).

"Remembering" on both levels serves as prologue to the final two imperatives of the church's awakening. Jesus' command to "hold it fast, and repent" are commands that are inseparably linked throughout Scripture. Both obedience, which is implied by the phrase "hold it fast," and repentance constitute the indispensable responses to receiving and hearing the Gospel. In the anatomy of our faith, we first hear, then believe, then repent, then obey. However, obedience, or holding fast, is the sum of this entire process and is, therefore, listed first in this phrase.

Repentance has its own fruit (Matt 3:8; Luke 3:8), the character of which is seven-fold, suggesting a complete turnaround in heart, mind and action. As succinctly outlined by Paul to the church in Corinth (2 Cor 7:9-11), the fruits of repentance are, as follows:

- Earnestness of effort

- Eagerness to prove your innocence

- Indignation over sin

- Fear of God

- Longing for God

- Zeal for God

- Rendering of God's Justice

Again, obedience and repentance are the works that need to be resurrected in the church in Sardis as evidence of a living faith in Jesus Christ.

As in all the Letters, Jesus clearly outlines the consequences of disobedience. In His ultimatum to the church in Sardis, Jesus states: "If you do not wake up, I will come like a thief, and you will not know at what time I will come to you."

Several Scriptures characterize Jesus' second coming as a "thief in the night" (Matt 24:42-44; Luke 12:39-40; 1 Thess 5:2-11; 2 Peter 3:10-14; Rev 16:15). Unreadiness (Matt 25:1-13), incomplete works (Matt 25:24-30), or states of spiritual lethargy or spiritual sleepwalking (Matt 25:41-46) are the spiritual conditions that Jesus will "break into" as a thief upon His return. In any of these states, the church is evidently not awake, or alive, or alert, or watchful, as Jesus has commanded.

The above-cited Scriptures also declare that those in the above-cited states will not know at what hour the Son of Man will come (cf. Matt 25:13; Mark 13:35-37). In our current text, this same warning is rendered in the Greek with a double negative (οὐ μή – pronounced 'oo may' – translated 'not not' or 'never'), implying no possible way of perceiving or knowing the hour of His return. Though Jesus had already declared that not even He knows the day nor the hour of His return, but only His Father (Mark 13:32; cf. Matt 24:36), Jesus' not knowing is an act of faith in His Father, whereas the Church's not knowing would be an act of faithlessness on their part.

VERSE 4

"Yet you have a few people in Sardis who have not soiled their clothes. They will walk with me, dressed in white, for they are worthy."

Not everyone in the Church in Sardis needs the prescriptive awakening. Jesus identifies the faithful as "a few people in Sardis . . ." The Greek word translated "people" literally means "names" (ὀνόματα – pronounced ŏ-nŏ´-mâ-tâ), so that some translations read "you have a few names in Sardis . . . " (KJV, ASV, Amplified). As such, at least two biblical passages are alluded to by this phrase:

> *For the gate is narrow and the road is hard that leads to life, and there are **few** who find it (Matt 7:14 NRSV; cf. Luke 13:23-24, **author's emphasis**).*
>
> *He calls His own sheep **by name** and leads them out (John 10:3b, **author's emphasis**).*

Both above-cited Scriptures denote that there are a few in the church in Sardis whom Jesus knows by name. The significance here is not that He doesn't know the names of the others, but that the faithful few are a remnant in the church who are following Him, doing His Will, and are counted worthy to be His sheep (cf. John 10:14, 27).

Inasmuch as the rest in the church have manifested dead works emanating from a dying faith, then the "few people" have distinguished themselves by works of righteousness that are the fruit of a living faith. Righteousness is often depicted in Scripture as a garment, and the righteousness that comes from faith in Jesus (Rom 10:6) is characterized as "fine linen, bright and pure" (Rev 19:8). It is this garment that will adorn the bride of Christ, the church, at the Marriage Supper of the Lamb, and will characterize her as "not having spot, or wrinkle, or any such thing . . . holy and without blemish" (Eph 5:27). Scripture is also clear that the righteousness of Jesus is imputed to believers by the seven-fold fullness of the Holy Spirit (Rom 4:13, 21-24; 10:4; 2 Cor 5:21; Phil 3:9; James 2:23).

On the other hand, the busyness of the majority in the church is considered a soiled garment because the church's busyness consists of works of self-righteousness that are like filthy rags (Isa 64:6; cf. Rom 10:1-3), or like the dyed wool that was the city's main export.[103]

NOTE: In the Divine reality, the garments of God's righteousness are made white in the Blood of the Lamb (Rev 7:14)!

NOTE: In Ezekiel's prophecy of the millennial Temple and its priesthood, the priests of Zadok, who will minister the holy things of God, will wear linen, and are instructed not to wear wool or anything that makes them sweat (Ezek 44:15-18).

NOTE: READ James 1:27 for the definition of an undefiled religion. This, too, must proceed from a living faith in Jesus.

White is the color of victory in biblical imagery. This victory implies purity, holiness and righteousness, which are also symbolized by the color white. The Greek word translated "white" (λευκοῖς – pronounced loo-**koyce**') also means "shining" and "brilliant." The fact that the faithful few will walk with Jesus in victory denotes that through their faith in Him they have overcome the world (1 John 5:4).

The secondary meanings of the color white, i.e., shining, brilliant, reflect Daniel's prophecy of those who will participate in the first

103 Mounce, *The Book of the Revelation Revised*, 92

resurrection to eternal life:

> *Those who are wise shall shine like the brightness of the heavens, and*
> *those who lead many to righteousness, like the stars forever and ever*
> *(Dan 12:3)*

From a Divine perspective, therefore, the color white is used only as a metaphor here, and is, in truth, a color we have never seen or imagined, since it refers to a reality we have yet to experience!

It is of special note that the Greek word translated "worthy"' is the same word attributed to Jesus by the myriad of angels in heaven before the opening of the scroll in Revelation 5:12:

> *Worthy is the Lamb who was slain to receive power, and wealth, and*
> *wisdom, and strength, and honor, and glory, and praise.*

In addition to "Well done" (Matt 25:21, 23), the title "Worthy" accords to the faithful the full inheritance of our Lord!

VERSE 5

> *"The one who is victorious will, like them, be dressed in white. I will*
> *never blot out the name of that person from the book of life, but will*
> *acknowledge that name before my Father and his angels."*

Jesus now redirects His encouragement to those who need to wake up, strengthen, remember, hold fast and repent. Those who satisfy all the imperatives will be considered victors. As such, Jesus makes a three-fold promise to those who do submit to and obey His commands: "The one who is victorious will, like them, be dressed in white. I will never blot out the name of that person from the book of life, but will acknowledge that name before my Father and his angels."

As in the previous letters, the Greek word νικάω (pronounced nǐ-kâ´-ō), translated "victorious," is the same word used in 1 John 4:4 and

5:4 to describe the believer's conquering and overcoming victory in Jesus and over the world:

> *Little children, you are of God, and have conquered them, for the One who is in you is greater than the one who is in the world (1 John 4:4 NRSV)*
>
> *This is the victory that has overcome the world, even our faith (1 John 5:4)*

In fact, the noun victory in this latter passage comes from the same root. Conquering, overcoming, and victory, therefore, are integrally and synonymously linked to a living faith in Jesus, as will be true for the Sardian believers and for believers in every age.

The Book of Life is first referenced in Moses' petition to God that if He would not forgive the people for constructing the golden calf (in the wilderness), that God would blot his name out of the "Book that You have written." God's answer to Moses was "Whoever has sinned against Me I will blot out of My Book" (Exod 32:32-33; cf. Ps 69:28).

The Book of Life, as the heavenly record in which the names of the faithful are written, is cited and/or implied in Daniel 12:1, Luke 10:20, and Philippians 4:3. However, The Book of Life is mentioned six times in The Revelation, including its first occurrence in the current text: Revelation 3:5; 13:8; 17:8; 20:12, 15; 21:27.

In addition to being victorious, those who obey the five imperatives of Jesus' commands to wake up, remember, strengthen, hold fast and repent will inherit the first of Jesus' three-fold promise: to be clothed in white like the faithful few. The parenthetical phrase "like them," which translates the single Greek word οὕτως (pronounced **hū´-tōs**), could have been placed in relationship to the preceding clause, i.e., "The one who is victorious *like them*," and would have been equally as valid in its import. The meaning would have stressed that the overcomer's victory would resemble the victory that already belonged to the faithful few. However, this meaning is not lost but is included in the fact that the overcomer will walk with the same Lord and wear the same garment as the faithful few, thus sealing the fact that their victory will be complete!

The second of Jesus' three-fold promise to overcomers is that He "will not blot [their] name out of the book of Life." This promise raises several observations we should not miss. Jesus did not say that their names would not be entered into the book of Life because their names were indeed entered at the time of their initial faith in Jesus. It stands to reason, therefore, that one cannot blot out what isn't already written. However, by saying that their names will not be blotted out, Jesus is telling the unfaithful Sardian believers that their names would be in danger of being blotted out if they do not obey.

It is clear from Jesus' current statement that the unfaithful, i.e., those who were once saved but refused to hear and heed His word of rebuke and instruction and who persist in their sin (cf. Rev 22:11), can have their names blotted out of the book of Life. If this were not true, Jesus would not have proposed it as a potential consequence of their rebellion.

This is probably the most controversial statement in all the letters, in that it contests the popular notion that "once saved, always saved," which comes with the presumption that a life of sin can still be pursued without consequences. The notion appears to come from Jesus' declaration that "My Father, who has given them (the disciples) to Me, is greater than all; no one can snatch them (the disciples) out of My Father's Hand" (John 10:29). However, the interpretation must allow that though no one can snatch a saint from the Father's Hand, this truth does not prevent God Himself from removing a habitual sinner from His hand and from His heavenly record.

Jesus' authority to blot out names is derived from the truth that the book belongs to Him, i.e., " . . . the Lamb's book of life, the Lamb who was slain from the creation of the world" (Rev 13:8), and is articulated as a precedent in Exodus 32:33 and Psalm 69:28. Daniel 7:10 also refers to opened books of judgment that anticipate the open books at the ultimate judgment of the Great White Throne (Rev 20:12). The fairness of Jesus' judgment to blot out names is clearly articulated in Ezek 18:1-32; 33:1-20; cf. Jer 18:7-10 – Please Read!

Those who are victorious will not have to fear being expunged from the heavenly record. However, the exhortation to "work out [our] own salvation with fear and trembling . . . " (Phil 2:12) should be re-visited by all believers with a heightened level of seriousness and gratitude!

The third of Jesus' three-fold promise, i.e., "I will acknowledge that name before my Father and before His angels," is an allusion to three recorded statements made by Jesus in the Gospels: Matthew 10:32-33; Mark 8:38; Luke 12:8-9:

> *Whoever acknowledges me before others, I will also acknowledge before my Father in heaven. But whoever disowns me before others, I will disown before my Father in heaven. (Matt 10:32-33)*

> *If anyone is ashamed of me and my words in this adulterous and sinful generation, the Son of Man will be ashamed of them when he comes in his Father's glory with the holy angels. (Mark 8:38)*

> *I tell you, whoever publicly acknowledges me before others, the Son of Man will also acknowledge before the angels of God. But whoever*

disowns me before others will be disowned before the angels of God.
(Luke 12:8-9)

Taken together, the above declarations ensure that Jesus will acknowledge the faithful before His Father and before the angels! Not only the faithful few but whoever in Sardis responds in submission to Jesus' imperatives in this letter will have the joy of having Jesus confess their names before His Father and before His angels. Confessing Jesus' Name is the way to keep our own name in the book of Life!

VERSE 6

"Whoever has ears, let them hear what the Spirit says to the churches."

Inasmuch as the first of the five imperatives instructed the Sardian believers to remember not only how they heard but what they heard at the beginning of their salvation, this rehearsal to have an ear to hear what the Spirit is saying carries the same injunctions of attentiveness to Jesus' instructions in their current context of a dying faith.

Whereas this cyclical exhortation to hear preceded the promises to overcomers in the first three letters, it is postured after the promises in this letter, in the letter to Thyatira, and in the remaining two letters. The change in format is a matter of scholarly debate, but in no way alters the meaning nor the significance of the exhortation.

THE CHURCH IN PHILADELPHIA
REVELATION 3:7-13

7 *"To the angel of the church in Philadelphia write: These are the words of him who is holy and true, who holds the key of David. What he opens no one can shut, and what he shuts no one can open.*

8 *"I know your deeds. See, I have placed before you an open door that no one can shut. I know that you have little strength, yet you have kept my word and have not denied my name.*

9 *I will make those who are of the synagogue of Satan, who claim to be Jews though they are not, but are liars—I will make them come and fall down at your feet and acknowledge that I have loved you.*

10 *Since you have kept my command to endure patiently, I will also keep you from the hour of trial that is going to come on the whole world to test the inhabitants of the earth.*

11 *I am coming soon. Hold on to what you have, so that no one will take your crown.*

12 *The one who is victorious I will make a pillar in the temple of my God. Never again will they leave it. I will write on them the name of my God and the name of the city of my God, the new Jerusalem, which is coming down out of heaven from my God; and I will also write on them my new name.*

13 *Whoever has ears, let them hear what the Spirit says to the churches."*

VERSE 7

"To the angel of the church in Philadelphia write: These are the words of him who is holy and true, who holds the key of David. What he opens no one can shut, and what he shuts no one can open."

As mentioned in the previous discussions on Revelation 1:20 and 2:1, the angel of the church in Philadelphia is an angelic messenger or spirit who has been assigned to the church in Philadelphia for the purpose of communicating revelation knowledge concerning Jesus.

Due to the Apostle Paul's extensive stay in Ephesus, during his 3rd missionary journey, Acts 19:10 states "that all the residents of Asia, both Jews and Greeks, heard the word of the Lord." Paul's ministry in Asia would have included Philadelphia, since it was located "twenty-eight miles SW of Sardis and 100 miles W of Smyrna."[104] Though the city was named after, and possibly founded by, Attalus II, who won the title "Philadelphus," meaning "brotherly love," for his loyalty to his brother Eumenes,[105] the re-named city was actually the ancient city of Rabbah,[106] capital of the ancient peoples of Ammon.[107] Located in the valley below Mt. Tmolus, the soil was suited to growing vines; as a result, wine production was the major crop and export of the city.[108] The city hosted not only the church, but also a synagogue of Hellenized Jews,[109] and a

---

104   Unger, *THE NEW UNGER'S BIBLE DICTIONARY,* 999.

105   Mounce, *THE BOOK OF THE REVELATION REVISED,* 98.

106   Joseph L. Gardner, *READER'S DIGEST ATLAS OF THE BIBLE* (Pleasantville, NY: The Reader's Digest Association, Inc., 1981), 154; Hemer, *THE LETTERS TO THE SEVEN CHURCHES OF ASIA IN THEIR LOCAL SETTING,* 154; Mounce, The Book of the Revelation, 98-99

107   The Ammonites were descendants of Ammon, son of Lot, who was sired in an incestuous relationship between Lot and the younger of his two daughters in a cave following the destruction of Sodom and Gomorrah The ancient Rabbah was also one of the cities not conquered during Joshua's military entrance into the Promised Land (Josh 13:25), but remained undisturbed on the border of the land allotted to Gad. However, the city was eventually conquered by Joab and King David (2 Sam 11:1; 12:26-29; 1 Chron 20:1).

108   Mounce, The Book of the Revelation Revised, 98 – Wine was a major part of Philadelphia's agricultural and commercial importance.

109   Hemer, *THE LETTERS TO THE SEVEN CHURCHES OF ASIA IN THEIR LOCAL SETTING,* 160 – Though Hemer could "find no external evidence for the existence of a Jewish community in Philadelphia during this period . . . the presence of Judaistic influence is however attested by the reference to the 'synagogue of Satan' (Rev. 3:9) . . . and the parallel with Smyrna (Rev 2:9)."

temple to Dionysius, the Greek god of wine and ecstasy and the chief deity,[110] among many others.[111] Philadelphia suffered several devastating earthquakes, the most severe of which occurred in 17 AD. The city was re-built by Emperor Tiberius, who changed the name of the city for a short period to Neo-Caeserea, meaning "New Caesar." It was later re-named "Flavia" under Vespasian's rule (69-79 AD).[112] However, it never lost the name Philadelphia, through it all.

In His 8th command to John to write (see discussions on Rev 1:11, 19), Jesus identifies Himself as "holy." The title is an abbreviated allusion to His Father's Name in relationship to the Nation of Israel, i.e., "The Holy One of Israel," which appears repeatedly throughout the Psalms and the Prophets.[113] Additionally, both the abbreviated and fuller titles are also attributed to the Christ in Isa 49:7, as the "The Holy One" and as "The Holy One of Israel," in speaking of Jesus as the Messiah of both Jew and Gentile.

Jesus' title "holy" takes on additional significance in Heb 7:26 where His current office as the Ascended High Priest affirms Him as "holy, blameless, pure, set apart from sinners, and exalted above the heavens."

Based upon the above-cited references, Jesus' title "holy" identifies Him as One with the Father (cf. John 6:69; 10:30), as occupying His exalted position at the right hand of His Father's throne, where He reigns as the church's Great and Eternal High Priest, after the order of Melchizedek (Heb 6:20; 7:16-17, 21-22), and as the Mediator of the New

---

110   Gen 19:30-38 records that wine was used by Lot's daughters to seduce their father Lot into incestuous relations, from which both Moab and Ammon were born – see Note 64.

111   Mounce, *THE BOOK OF THE REVELATION REVISED*, 99

112   Mounce, *THE BOOK OF THE REVELATION REVISED*, 99

113   Cf. Lev 20:26; 1 Sam 6:20; 2 Kings 19:22; Pss 16:10; 71:22; 78:41; 89:18; Isa 1:4; 5:24; 10:20; 12:6; 17:7; 29:19, 23; 30:11-12, 15; 37:23; 41:14; 43:3, 14-15; 45:11; 47:4; 48:17; 54:5; 55:5; 57:15; 60:9, 14; Jer 50:29; 51:5; Ezek 39:7; Hos 11:9; Hab 1:12

Covenant (Heb 8:6). In all three roles, i.e., Exalted at the Right Hand of His Father, Great High Priest, and Mediator of the New Covenant, holiness is the chief requirement.

Jesus' title "true" alludes to His singular declaration as "The Way, the Truth, and the Life" (John 14:6). The title also alludes to His singular obedience to His Father's Will, even to His death on the Cross (Phil 2:8), and to His faithful witness to the Father throughout His earthly ministry (John 5:19, 30; 6:38; 12:49-50; 17:4; Rev 1:5).

It is in Revelation 6:10 that the two titles come together again in the prayer of those who will have been martyred for the word of God:

> They called out in a loud voice, 'How long, Sovereign Lord, **holy and true**, until you judge the inhabitants of the earth and avenge our blood?' **(author's emphasis)**

We can safely conclude, therefore, that the use of the two titles together, both in Revelation 6:10 and in our current text, imply the character of Jesus' office as the sole Judge of His Body, the church, and of the world, an office bestowed upon Him by His Father "because He is the **Son of Man** (John 5:27, **author's emphasis**).

Whereas the two titles are not explicitly employed in the Vision of Jesus' Resurrection Glory (Rev 1:12-16), they are, in truth, characteristically implied by Jesus' Messianic title "the Son of Man," which is articulated by John in the Patmos Vision (Rev 1:13).

The "key of David" is the 3rd key in JESUS' possession: the first two are the keys of Hell and of Death (Rev 1:18).

Jesus further identifies Himself as He "who holds the key of David.

What he opens no one can shut, and what he shuts no one can open." This entire phrase is an allusion[114] to Isaiah 22:20-25, where Eliakim, the son of Hilkiah, prefigures the kingship and the kingdom of Christ. It is upon the shoulders of Eliakim that the "key of David" is laid, pointing towards the inheritance of the kingship of the ultimate Davidic heir, i.e., Jesus. The content of the Davidic covenant, in which David is promised a perpetual kingship and a perpetual kingdom, is found in 2 Sam 7:1-29 and in 1 Chron 17:3-27. Though the immediate contexts of these passages refer to Solomon, David's son by Bathsheba, these passages ultimately refer to Jesus in fulfillment of God's promise to David: that "You shall never fail to have a successor to sit before me on the throne of Israel . . . " (1 Kings 8:25; cf. 2:4; 9:5; 2 Chron 6:16; Ps 89:4; Jer 33: 17). In His Incarnation, Jesus was born of the lineage of David, and in His Resurrection, Jesus became the King of kings who lives forever to reign upon the throne of His ancestor David (Luke 1:32-33).

The phrase "What he opens no one can shut, and what he shuts no one can open" denotes both here and in Isaiah 22:20-25 the absolute power of Jesus' reign as King of kings and Lord of lords. What Jesus has the power to open and shut that no one will be able to reverse will become clear in the following discussion on His gift to the church of an opened door.

VERSE 8

"I know your deeds. See, I have placed before you an open door that no one can shut. I know that you have little strength, yet you have kept my word and have not denied my name."

As in His previous and upcoming letters, Jesus announced His

114   Remember: an allusion is an indirect quote without a formulaic introduction, e.g., "for it is written," etc.)

Omniscience regarding the church's works: "I know your works."[115] It is what Jesus knows of the church's works that substantiates His following commendation of the church's witness.

Before commending the church for her two dynamics of faithfulness, Jesus first utters the invitation to "See" as translated from the Greek word ἰδοὺ (pronounced ĭ-**du'**). This invitation to "See" is present in the Greek text and in the NIV rendition but is omitted from several other translations.[116] However, its presence is critical to understanding what follows: for what follows is not something that can be seen or beheld with the naked eye. Jesus says "See, I have placed before you an open door that no one can shut." This open door is not a physical structure but a spiritual reality, which Jesus gives as a gift to the church, as indicated by the Greek verb δέδωκα (pronounced **dĕ'**-dō-kâ) meaning 'to give' but translated "I have placed . . . " Hence, Jesus is inviting the church to behold the spiritual reality of His gift of an open door with the eyes of faith (cp. Acts 14:27). One of the spiritual realities that is beheld with the eyes of faith is hope:

> . . . Now hope that is seen is not hope. For who hopes for what he sees? But if we hope for what we do not see, we wait for it with patience. (Rom 8:24 NRSV)

Hence, the open door which no one can shut is the door of hope that the church in Philadelphia must claim by faith as the spiritual reality with which Jesus has gifted them.

Most Bible versions (Amp, Holman CSB, KJV, NASB, NIV, NRSV) translate Jesus' gift as "an open door" as if there is no agent involved in opening it. However, the Greek syntax reveals that the word "open" is a

---

115 See discussions on Rev 2:2 and 3:1

116 Other English versions that do include the translation of the Greek word ἰδοὺ in this verse include the Complete Jewish Bible, Holman CSB, KJV, NASB, and the NRSV.

Remember that JESUS declared that "I Am the Door . . ." (John 10:7) The Greek word for "door" there is the same Greek word for "door" here (θύρα – pronounced **thū´-rah**).

perfect passive participle, which should be properly translated "opened," indicating that the door has been "opened" by Someone. Given Jesus' assertion that He is the author of the gift in this verse, i.e., "I have placed before you . . . ," we can safely conclude that Jesus is the Someone who has "opened" a door for the church that no one can shut. This is plainly articulated in the Living Bible translation: " . . . Therefore I have **opened** a door to you that no one can shut" (**author's emphasis**).

The "opened door" forms a parallel to Jesus' possession of the "key of David," mentioned in verse 7, as His authority to open a door that no one can shut. As previously mentioned, this language forms an allusion[117] to the symbolic inauguration of Eliakim, as recorded in the prophecy through Isaiah:

> I will place on his shoulder the key to the house of David; what he opens no one can shut, and what he shuts no one can open (Isa 22:22).

In addressing the church in Philadelphia as both David's Heir and as the Head of His Body, the church, we need to connect these two Messianic roles to the "opened door" with which Jesus has gifted the church. As the ultimate Son of David, Jesus possesses the "key to the house of David," thus making Him "the door" into the Davidic or millennial kingdom. As "the Way, the Truth, and the Life . . . " (John 14:6) back into His Father's presence, Jesus is "the door" into His Father's eternal kingdom. Taken together, Jesus' two messianic roles give Him complete control over the entrance into both the millennial and eternal kingdoms. We can safely

---

117 Remember: an allusion is a direct quote without a formulaic introduction, e.g., "for it is written", etc.)

conclude, therefore, that the "opened door" that no one is able to shut is Jesus' gift to the church in Philadelphia of the sure hope of access into both the Davidic (millennial) and eternal kingdoms.[118]

The above conclusion is corroborated by the fact that Jesus promised the apostles that He would "confer on [them] a kingdom, just as [His] Father conferred on [Him]" and that they would "sit on thrones, judging the twelve tribes of Israel" (Luke 22:28-29; cf. Matt 19:27-28). We can safely conclude that this activity will take place during the millennial kingdom when Jesus reigns on the throne of David in fulfillment of the Davidic covenant.

The above conclusion is also validated by the following promises made to those who share in Jesus' sufferings:

> *Now if we are children, then we are heirs – heirs of God and co-heirs with Christ – if indeed we share in His sufferings in order that we may also share in His glory (Rom 8:17).*
>
> *If we endure, we will also reign with Him (2 Tim 2:12).*

The church's entrance into the millennial kingdom will be facilitated by the "opened door" of the rapture, as anticipated by the revelation given to the Apostle Paul in 1 Thess 4:16-17, as corroborated by Jesus' promise to the Philadelphian church to keep, or provide a way of escape, "from the hour of trial that is coming on the whole world to test the inhabitants of the earth" (Rev 3:10b), and as represented by the door that is opened in Heaven when Jesus commands John to "Come up here, and I will show you what must take place after this" (Rev 4:1), typifying the translated posture of the true church before the Tribulation Period commences. By way of the "opened door" of the rapture, which is the church's immediate

---

118   See Mounce, *The Book of the Revelation Revised*, 101, for a clear affirmation that Jesus has placed before the Church an open door into the eternal kingdom~!

hope, the church will escape (an opened door is a way of escape) the Tribulation Period on the earth, will reside with Jesus in the air, and will return and reign with Him during the millennial kingdom, as the following Scriptures attest: Matthew 19:27-28; Luke 22:28-29; 2 Timothy 2:12; Revelation 5:9-10; 20:4-6.

The church's entrance into the eternal kingdom will be conducted through the "gates" of the New Jerusalem (Isa 26:2; Rev 21:27; 22:14-15), the entrance to which is prophetically anticipated in Psalm 118:19-20 and divinely reserved for the righteous to enter:

> *Open to me the gates of righteousness, that I may enter through them and give thanks to the LORD. This is the gate of the LORD; the righteous shall enter through it (NRSV).*

The Church's entrance into the eternal kingdom is further substantiated by the character of the rewards promised to overcomers in the Church (3:12), which closely resemble the character of those who will inhabit the New Paradise in the New Heaven and the New Earth of the Eternal Kingdom (Rev 21:22; 22:3-4).

When we consider, therefore, that Jesus possesses the key to both the millennial and eternal Kingdoms, and that upon the conclusion of His one-thousand-year reign He will surrender the millennial kingdom to His Father (1 Cor 15:24-28), so that in the eternal Kingdom "God may be all in all," then we can safely conclude that Jesus Himself is the "Opened Door" and the "Gate of the LORD" through which the righteous will enter (John 10:1-10)!

As noted by Robert Mounce, "the more common interpretation [of the open door] is that it denotes a great opportunity for missionary activity."[119] Mounce goes on to quote Paul's use of the metaphor in his

---

119   Mounce, *The Book of the Revelation Revised*, 100. See also Hemer, The Letters to the Seven Churches of Asia in Their Local Setting, 162.

Letter to the Corinthian church where he cites his plans to stay in Ephesus until Pentecost "because a *great door* for effective work *has opened* to me, and there are many who oppose me" (1 Cor 16:9, *author's emphasis*; cf. 2 Cor 2:12; Col 4:3). However, the messianic implications in our current text, and the rewards to overcomers that are cited in the upcoming verses, endorse the kingdom interpretation as the more feasible one to embrace.

The phrase "that no one will be able to shut" also echoes Isaiah 22:22 and is acknowledged by G. K. Beale as a metaphoric contrast to the prevalent practice of excommunicating converted Jews from the local

> Though the fulfillment of the Davidic covenant was the major hope of all Jews (Acts 1:6-7), their right to the Davidic kingdom was temporarily suspended (not annulled) due to their rejection of Christ as their King during His first advent (John 19:15; cf. Rom 11:1-36). Their rights under the Davidic covenant will only be restored through their faith in the Davidic Messiah, i.e., Jesus Christ, who holds the key to their entrance into that kingdom. Their ultimate faith is prophetically implied by Jesus' declaration to the unbelieving Jews of His generation: "Look, your house is left to you desolate. For I tell you, you will not see me again until you say, 'Blessed is he who comes in the name of the Lord" (Matt 23:38-39; Luke 13:35; cf. Rom 10:9). The singular problem with the Jews in Philadelphia, however, is that they are not Jews and are lying. This is what makes them a "synagogue of Satan," who is the father of lies. More about this in verse 9.

synagogue in the city.[120] In other words, the doors to the local synagogue were shut to believing Jews because of their conversion to the Christian

---

120   Beale, *THE BOOK OF THE REVELATION*, 284.

faith. Whereas the unbelieving Jews of the synagogue would have claimed to be the chosen people of God, converted Jews would have also acknowledged that they, too, were chosen of God (1 Peter 2:9). Such a claim would not have been tolerated by the Jewish synagogue. Such a claim from converted Gentiles would also have been reprehensible to unbelieving Jews, thus making the church, as a whole, the object of Jewish persecution. Though the unbelieving Jews could shut the door of the local synagogue on converted Jews and believing Gentiles, they could not shut the door that had been opened by Jesus to both Jews and Gentiles who believe in Him!

To the church to whom Jesus levied no indictment or reproach, the phrase "little strength" constitutes the summary portrayal of the following two commendations, which Jesus extends to the church in Philadelphia. In the church's "little strength" we discover that her reputation as the Perfect church is based, not on the absence of trouble or trial, nor on a complex line-up of multiple programs and projects, but is based on her allegiance to a very small and simple agenda of faith: for Jesus states that the church in Philadelphia has "kept My Word" and has "not denied My Name." To better understand this stellar commendation and its components, we need to answer at least two questions: What is so significant about this agenda of faith? And why does Jesus refer to it as the church's "little strength?"

First, the significance of this agenda of faith — of keeping Jesus' Word and of not denying His Name — is that it reflects as in a mirror the very same agenda by which the Father, the Son, and the Holy Spirit achieved our salvation. Consider the following evidence that supports this assertion:

- The Father kept His own prophetic Word to send His
  only begotten Son to pay the price for our sins and
  He brought glory to His own Name when He raised

Him from the dead! (Isa 53:5-6; John 3:16; Heb 1:1-2)

- Jesus, the Son, kept His Father's Word to lay down His life for the sheep and He brought glory to His Father's Name by saying and doing everything His Father told Him to say and do, and by completing His mission, even to His death on the Cross. (John 10:14-18; 12:49; 17:4; Phil 2:5-8)

- The Holy Spirit keeps Jesus' Word by declaring only what He hears Jesus say (John 16:13-15), and the Spirit empowers our witness to the glory of Jesus' Name: for no one can call Jesus Lord, except by the power of the Holy Spirit (1 Cor 12:3)

We can safely assert, therefore, that if the fullness of the Godhead was able to accomplish our salvation on this very small and simple agenda, we must know that Jesus is most pleased to see this same divine agenda reflected in the faith posture of the church who were bought by His blood, endowed by His Spirit, and called by His name!

And because the church's agenda of faith is a direct reflection of God's own agenda of faithfulness, the term "little strength" is not a demeaning or diminutive term nor a put-down, but rather a term of endearment, denoting that the Almighty and All-Powerful God sees a little of the God-Self in that church, much as a parent sees a little of the good of him or herself in their child. Hence, the church in Philadelphia is commended and applauded because her agenda of faith — of keeping Jesus' Word and of not denying Jesus' Name —- made her look more like Jesus than all the other churches put together! Remember, the church is His Body!

What Jesus called "little strength" was probably seen as weakness by others, considering the dominant and opposing ideology of the city. Some scholars attribute the church's "little strength" to what may have been the small size of the congregation.[121] Both positions have merit and, when combined, remind us of a couple of Scriptures that speak to what God can do with what the world deems small, weak, or insignificant:

> *Consider your own call, brothers and sisters: not many of you were wise by human standards, not many were powerful, not many were of noble birth. But God chose what is foolish in the world to shame the wise; God chose what is weak in the world to shame the strong; God chose what is low and despised, things that are not, to reduce to nothing things that are, so that no one might boast in the presence of God (1 Cor 1:26-29 NRSV)*

> *My Grace is sufficient for you, for [My] power is made perfect in weakness . . . Therefore I am content with weaknesses, insults, hardships, persecutions, and calamities for the sake of Christ; for whenever I am weak, then I am strong (2 Cor 12:9a, 10 NRSV)*

As inseparable attributes of the church's faithfulness to Jesus, i.e., "kept My Word and not denied My Name," it is worthy to note that the past tense translation of the verbs in this phrase, i.e., "kept" and "not denied", implies a reputation of faithfulness that was earned in the past but was still an active part of their present testimony. This reputation of faithfulness would most likely have been earned during a past or present season of persecution or trial in which the church had remained faithful in these two ways, i.e., kept His Word and not denied His Name. The possibly small size of their congregation had not determined the size nor the steadfastness of their faith and their faithfulness! Remember Jesus' Parable of the Mustard Seed (Matt 17:20). Consider what their stellar faithfulness may have looked like under persecution:

- To keep Jesus' Word under persecution is to maintain

---

faith in His Deity and in His Humanity as God in the Flesh, despite competing theologies and ideologies (cf. 1 John 4:1-3)

- To not deny His Name under persecution is to maintain faith in the truth that "Salvation is found in no on else, for there is no other name under heaven given to mankind by which we must be saved" (Acts 4:12), despite inducements to recant or to assimilate to the idolatry of the dominant culture.

As both dynamics of faithfulness constituted the church's "little strength," then Jesus found no fault with the sum total of their works! As such, the church in Philadelphia would be heir to the promise cited by the Apostle James:

> *Blessed is anyone who endures temptation (testing, trial). Such a one has stood the test and will receive the crown of life that the Lord has promised to those who love Him (James 1:12 NRSV).*

VERSE 9

"I will make those who are of the synagogue of Satan, who claim to be Jews though they are not, but are liars—I will make them come and fall down at your feet and acknowledge that I have loved you."

Like verse 8, this verse in the Greek text also contains and actually begins with the interjection ἰδού (pronounced ĭ-**du´**), meaning "See" or "Behold," but is omitted from the NIV rendering of this verse.[122] However, it's presence in the Greek text forms a parallel to verse 8, coupled with the use of same root verb (δίδωμι - pronounced **dĭ´**-dō-mĭ), meaning "to give," to describe the action that follows. For example, in verse 8, the

---

122 Other English versions that do include the translation of the Greek word ἰδού in this verse include the Complete Jewish Bible, Holman CSB, KJV, NASB, and the NRSV.

verb is translated, "See, I have placed . . . [have given]" (δέδωκα - pronounced **dĕ´**-dō-kâ), and in verse 9, the verb is translated "Look, I will give . . . " (διδῶ - pronounced dĭ-**dō´**).

Coupled with this linguistic parallelism in the structure of verses 8 and 9 is the parallelism in meanings. Just as the verb "to give" defined the opened door as a gift from Jesus, so this same verb is now defining Jesus' gift of those who will submit to the church, as later articulated in this same verse. Again, the invitation to "See" or "Behold," also carries the import of needing spiritual sight or discernment to perceive those who claim to be what they are not.

Thus, the first phrase of this verse identifies who the church's enemies are: "those who are of the synagogue of Satan, who claim to be Jews though they are not, but are liars." In our first discussion on the "synagogue of Satan" in the church in Smyrna (Rev 2:9), this persecuting element appeared to be operating in the church with connections to the Jewish synagogue in the city. In Philadelphia, this same persecuting faction appears to occupy the same posture. Also, the fact that the members of the synagogue of Satan are claiming to be Jews, "and are not, but are liars," not only rehearses their character as pretenders and defectors of the Christian faith, as already discussed in Rev 2:9, but also causes us to reflect on Paul's definition of a true Jew:

> *A person is not a Jew who is one only outwardly, nor is circumcision merely outward and physical. No, a person is a Jew who is one inwardly, and circumcision is circumcision of the heart, by the Spirit, not by the written code. Such a person's praise is not from other people, but from God (Rom 2:28-29)*

Hence, the believing Jews and Gentiles who compose the church in Philadelphia, and in every succeeding generation, are the spiritual descendants of Abraham by faith (Gal 3:6-9; Rom 4:9-12) and are thereby the true Jews[123] who are heir to the Davidic Covenant and joint-heirs with Christ in His Davidic kingdom — a truth that unbelieving Jews would have disdained.

Jesus goes on to declare in kingdom terms what the synagogue of Satan's relationship will be to the church: "I will make them come and bow down before your feet, and acknowledge that I have loved you." This is the third instance in this Letter in which the interjection ἰδοὺ (pronounced ĭ-**du´**), meaning "See" or "Behold," is again omitted from the NIV,[124] but whose meaning projects toward an unseen yet prophesied kingdom reality: that the persecutors of God's people will come and fall down and worship at their feet. This truth is initially articulated in the following passages as the inheritance of a regathered and restored Israel from the Gentile nations during the kingdom age:

> This is what the LORD says: The products of Egypt and the merchandise of Cush, and those tall Sabeans - they will come over to you and will be yours; they will trudge behind you, coming over to you in chains. They will bow down before you and plead with you, saying, 'Surely God is with you, and there is no other; there is no other god (Isa 45:14).

> Kings will be your foster fathers, and their queens your nursing mothers...I will contend with those who contend with you...Then all mankind will know that I, the LORD, am your Savior, your Redeemer, the Mighty One of Jacob (Isa 49: 23a, 25b, 26b).

> The children of your oppressors will come bowing before you; all who despise you will bow down at your feet and will call you the City of the LORD, Zion of the Holy One of Israel (Isa 60:14).

---

123   Hemer, THE LETTERS TO THE SEVEN CHURCHES OF ASIA, 67.

124   Other English versions that do include the translation of the Greek word ἰδοὺ in this verse include the Complete Jewish Bible, Holman CSB, KJV, NASB, and the NRSV.

In the NT, this inheritance has been consummated in Jesus, at whose Name "every knee should bow . . . and every tongue acknowledge that Jesus Christ is Lord, to the glory of God, the Father" (Phil 2:10-11).

Hence, as the seed of Abraham by faith in Jesus Christ, believers within the body of Christ — both Jew and Gentile — will be joint-heirs with Christ in this inheritance of exaltation during His Davidic reign (cf. Rom 8:17; 2 Tim 2:12a). Robert H. Mounce quotes James Moffatt in calling this reversal of roles a "grim irony of providence, [for] what the Jews fondly expected from the Gentiles, they themselves will be forced to render to Christians. They will play the role of the heathen and acknowledge that the church is the true Israel of God.[125] In other words, what the unbelieving Jews of the synagogue believed would be their due from Gentiles would now be their posture before Christians, i.e., submission and adoration!

> The Greek word for "perseverance"' in Hebrews 12:1 is the same word translated "patient endurance" in Revelation 3:10.

In the final phrase of Isaiah 49:26b, as previously quoted, it was and is God's intention in judgment that all flesh know who He is in relationship to His people: "Then all mankind will know that I, the LORD, am your Saviour, your Redeemer, the Mighty One of Jacob." It is in these three roles that Jesus has loved His Body, the church: as her Savior by shedding His Blood for her; as her Redeemer by paying the price for her sins; and as her Deliverer (the meaning of 'the Mighty One of Jacob') by delivering her from the penalty of sin and from an eternal hell.

Jesus, in other words, is the Personification of God's Love for all who believe in Him. In addition to John 3:16, which is familiar to us all,

---

125   Mounce, *THE BOOK OF REVELATION: REVISED EDITION*, 102.

God's love is also succinctly stated in the first of John's Pastoral Epistles, as follows:

> *God's love was revealed among us in this way: God sent His only Son into the world so that we might live through Him. In this is love, not that we loved God but that He loved us and sent His Son to be the atoning sacrifice for our sins (1 John 4:9-10 NRSV).*

VERSE 10

> *"Since you have kept my command to endure patiently, I will also keep you from the hour of trial that is going to come on the whole world to test the inhabitants of the earth."*

Again, the past tense "kept" implies a previous season of persecution or trial during which the church remained faithful. What the church had kept and was continuing to keep was Jesus' word of patient endurance. We know from our previous discussion that the Greek word ὑπομονῆ (pronounced hū-pŏ-mŏ-**nay´**) invokes the meaning of patient endurance in situations like trials, tribulations and persecutions. What is significant here is that it is "Jesus' (My) command of patient endurance." What this means is that the church suffered their season of trial after the example of Jesus. This commendation is not a new one but a summary of the two previously itemized dynamics of their faithfulness, recorded in verse 8b: "You have **kept My Word** and **not denied My Name**" (**author's emphases**).

First Peter 2:21-23 articulates the Suffering Servant character of Jesus through the lens of Isaiah's prophecy (Isa 53:1-12), which the saints in the church in Philadelphia apparently emulated:

> *To this you were called, because Christ suffered for you, leaving you an example, that you should follow in his steps. He committed no sin, and no deceit was found in his mouth. When they hurled their insults*

at him, he did not retaliate; when he suffered, he made no threats. Instead, he entrusted himself to him who judges justly.

As the church had proved, and was continuing to prove, faithful in keeping Jesus' Word of patient endurance, so Jesus promised to respond in like faithfulness to keep the church from the hour of trial that was due to come upon the whole world. "The hour of trial" is a direct reference to the upcoming Great Tribulation Period and fully satisfies the definition of "coming upon the whole world," as the text states.

Most scholars[126] base their interpretation of Jesus' promise in this verse on His petition in His High Priestly Prayer:

My prayer is not that you take them out of the world but that you protect them from the evil one (John 17:15).

Scholars conclude that Jesus' petition indicates that the church would not have to be physically removed from the world, as in the rapture, to be kept from the hour of trial but would instead be spiritually and physically preserved through the hour of trial while still present on the earth.

Though Jesus is more than capable of preserving His own, both spiritually and physically, through fiery trials (remember the three Hebrew boys in the fiery furnace were preserved both physically and spiritually), it seems questionable that Jesus would allow the church in Philadelphia to go through the most intense season of global suffering, albeit preserved, if they had indeed already proved faithful during previous seasons of persecution. Since it is because of their previous faithfulness that Jesus is making His promise to the church, i.e., "Since you have kept my command to endure patiently . . . ," then it only makes sense that the church would be completely removed from the earth during the coming hour of trial as their reward for faithfulness.

---

126   Beale, *THE BOOK OF THE REVELATION*, 290-2; Mounce, The Book of the Revelation, Revised Edition, 103. Both authors refer to other scholars who agree with their interpretation.

Though believers will suffer through a degree of persecution during the church age (John 16:33; 2 Tim 3:12), it will not come close to the intensity that is prophetically predicted for the hour of trial that is to come upon the whole world (cf. Dan 12:1; Matt 24:21; Mark 13:19). Hence, Jesus' high priestly petition (John 17:15), which is prayed on behalf of those who will minister during the church age, can initially be interpreted as a contextual reference to the church age until Jesus comes back to claim His faithful ones in the rapture, involving their physical removal from the earth.

It should nevertheless be remembered that the objects of persecution during the upcoming hour of trial will be believing Jews (Rev. 7:3-8; cf. Ezek 9:3-6) and believing Gentiles (Rev. 7:9-10, 13-17) who will come to faith in the Messiah during the hour of trial or Great Tribulation Period (Jer 30:7; Dan 9:20-27; 12:1) and will be persecuted by the anti-Christ for doing so (Rev 6:9-11; 11:1-13). The reason why some may think that the church will still be present during the Great Tribulation Period is because God is consistent in saving both believing Jews and believing Gentiles during both dispensations, as the previously cited Scriptures declare. However, the similarity in composition of those saved during the church Age and during the Great Tribulation Period, i.e., believing Jews and believing Gentiles, in no way aborts or blurs the distinction between these two dispensations in God's Plan of Salvation, but serves to affirm the consistency of God's Amazing Grace in both dispensations.

The parallelism in God's dealing with believing Jews and believing Gentiles in both the church age and the Great Tribulation Period is unmistakable: both will endure or go through a degree of suffering but will be ultimately and physically delivered from the worst suffering decreed. The Tribulation saints will also inherit the benefit of Jesus' high priestly petition. They, too, will suffer through the appointed first half of the prophetic week, i.e., 3½ years, but then be physically taken out of the world for the remaining half of the seven-year hour of trial (cf. Matt 24:22; Mark 13:20).

This truth is beautifully typified by the raising up and the rapture, if you will, of the two witnesses after 3½ days during which their physical dead bodies lay in the street (Rev. 11:7-12). Their physical resurrection at the end of 3½ days, which is symbolic of the half-way point of the hour of trial, will be their reward for faith in and faithfulness to Jesus the Messiah, much as the physical rapture of the church will be their reward before the hour of trial commences! In each case, believers of both the church Age and of the Great Tribulation Period (the hour of trial) will be physically and spiritually preserved through and then physically brought out of and removed from their seasons of persecution!

If a physical deliverance has not been the character of any of the promises made to overcomers in the previously-addressed Letters or in the one to come, then physical deliverance stands as the singular reward of the church in whom Jesus found no fault (cf. Eph 5:25-27; Rev 19:6-8) and serves as the paradigm for any church and any individual believer who seeks to be ready for the rapture, which will include the physical redemption of our bodies (cf. Rom. 8:22-23; Phil 3:20-21)!

As such, this is the first indication of the rapture of the church (1 Thess 4:16-17) in THE REVELATION text, as a whole, and in the letters to the churches, in particular. In the theology of pre-tribulationism (which this author espouses), the rapture of the true church will occur before the world undergoes the Great Tribulation Period that was prophesied by Daniel and others and which defines all of the judgment activity in THE REVELATION from Chapters 6 – 20. In other words, the true church will not be present on the earth to experience the horrific events of the Great Tribulation Period but will be raptured up out of the world before these events commence. The truth of the rapture of the true church is also typified by Jesus' command to John, as a representative of the true church, to "Come up here, and I will show you what must take place after this" (Rev 4:1). "Up here" is defined in 4:2 as "in heaven" (cf. Rev. 11:12) where John beholds a throne and the One seated on it. Since this command to "Come up here" will occur after the communication to all seven churches has ended, then Jesus' promise to the church in Philadelphia, i.e., to keep them from the hour of trial that is coming on the whole world, strongly suggests that this will be the sequence of events for them, as well.

Regarding this same command in Revelation 4:1, it should not be missed that John first saw an opened door in heaven through which the Spirit would transport him to behold the things that would occur "after this." This opened door correlates beautifully to the "opened door" that Jesus has given to the church in Philadelphia as the door through which they, too, will be transported into heaven in the rapture.

The hour of trial will be a time of testing. The Greek word πειρασμός (pronounced pā-râs-**mŏs′**), translated "test," is the same word used in 1 Peter 4:12 in describing the fiery trial that is used as a period of testing. The object of this testing is to dross and refine the faith. The grace in the use of this word in relationship to the Great Tribulation period is that it implies that some will pass the test and come to faith in Christ during this time of great trial. The truth of this is borne out by the 144,000 Jews who will be sealed during this horrific season of distress, as well as the salvation of an innumerable host of Gentiles who will hail from every nation, kindred, peoples, and tongues (Rev 7:4-10, 13-17).

Equally as true is that many will fail the test of this most severe period of testing by refusing to come to faith in Christ (Rev 9:20-21; 16:10-11, 21). Persistent unbelievers will suffer the second death along with Satan, the false prophet, the beast, death, Hell, and the wicked dead of all ages (Rev 20:11-15; 21:8).

VERSE 11

"I am coming soon. Hold on to what you have, so that no one will take your crown."

The Greek adverb ταχύς (pronounced tâ-**chūs´** - ch=k sound) is translated "quickly" or "soon" in several passages in *The Revelation* text, four of which occur in the letters to the churches, including this one. However, Jesus' coming quickly to the churches in Ephesus (Rev 2:5), Pergamum (Rev 2:16), and Sardis (Rev 3:3 – as a thief), poses a threat of judgment to each of these churches.

In the current text, however, His coming quickly to the church in Philadelphia, in whom He has found no fault, implies His reward for their faithfulness. The validity of this interpretation is corroborated not only by what follows in the current text concerning a crown and the rewards of verse 12, but also by its connection to the use of the same Greek adverb in Revelation 22:12 to describe Jesus' return with rewards, as well:

> *Look, I am coming soon! My reward is with me, and I will give to each person according to what they have done.*

In reviewing the commendations that Jesus has made to the church in Philadelphia, it is self-evident that His injunction "to hold on to what you have" is directed toward the church's steadfastness, i.e., keeping His Word, not denying His Name, and keeping His Word of patient endurance.

The Greek root κρατέω (pronounced krâ-**tĕ´**-ō), which means to "hold on," is the same root used in the injunction to the church in Thyatira to "hold on" to what they have until Jesus comes (Rev 2:25). The implication of the word is that the church in both instances is to "keep holding on," as a continuation of their present faithfulness.

As was discussed in the letter to the church in Smyrna, the Greek word στέφανον (pronounced **stĕ´**-phâ-nŏn), which is translated "crown," is the same root word from which the name Stephen is derived. Stephen was one of the first deacons of the early church (Acts 6:5) and her first martyr (Acts 8:54-60). The Greek word denotes a wreath or prize that is awarded upon winning a race or game. The race for which this crown is the prize is expressed in Heb 12:1-2:

> *Therefore, since we are surrounded by so great a cloud of witnesses, let us also lay aside every weight and the sin that clings so closely, and let us run with perseverance the race that is set before us, looking to Jesus the pioneer and perfecter of our faith, who for the sake of the joy that was set before Him endured the cross, disregarding its shame, and has taken His seat at the right hand of the throne of God (NRSV).*

VERSE 12

"The one who is victorious I will make a pillar in the temple of my God. Never again will they leave it. I will write on them the name of my God and the name of the city of my God, the new Jerusalem, which is coming down out of heaven from my God; and I will also write on them my new name."

One might ask, "What is there to conquer or overcome if there is no fault within the church?" The answer resides in Jesus' injunction that the church keep holding on to what they have, i.e., their little strength, as composed of their faithfulness in keeping His Word, in not denying His Name, and in keeping His Word of patient endurance.

The implied dangers are those of pride, arrogance and a haughty spirit — all which precede a fall from grace (cf. Prov 16:18). Even a perfect church needs to stay humble in their relationship with the Lord! It is for this reason that the persecutions from the synagogue of Satan are permitted against the church, much as Paul's thorn in the flesh was permitted in order to keep him humble, due to the abundance of revelations entrusted to him (2 Cor 12:7-10).

Whereas the church is initially characterized as having "a little strength," part of their reward from Jesus will be "pillar" strength.

Though pillars of stone were erected throughout Israel's history as places of worship (cf. Gen 28:18-22; 31:13; 35:14-15), the most poignant connection is made to the two pillars in Solomon's temple (1 Kings 7:21; 2 Chron 3:17). It is noteworthy that the names of these two pillars were יָכִין (pronounced yah-**keen´**), meaning "He shall establish" and בֹּעַז (pronounced bō-**ahz´**), meaning "in strength." Together, they form the sentence, "He shall establish (it) in strength" — a fitting tribute to a Church that has remained faithful with a little strength.

In light of Revelation 21:22, we can deduce that the pillar imagery does not refer to a physical structure:

> I did not see a temple in the city, because the Lord God Almighty and the Lamb are its temple.

In such a temple, as described above, the pillar imagery more likely suggests stability and permanency within God's House. The Psalmist articulates this permanency in the 27th Psalm:

> One thing I asked of the LORD, that will I seek after: to live in the house of the LORD all the days of my life, to behold the beauty of the LORD, and to inquire in His temple" (Ps 27:4 NRSV).

The three-fold inscription upon the faithful. i.e., "I will write on you the name of my God, and the name of the city of my God . . . and my new name" denotes their full citizenship in the Kingdom of God, to which Jesus holds the key (see discussion on verse 7).

"The name of my God" implies that the faithful belong to God and are born of His Spirit. The fact that Jesus refers to His Father as "My God" implies that believers are His Father's gift to Him and ultimately belong to the Father (cf. John 17:6). Jesus, therefore, returns to His Father what belongs to Him, signaling His submission to His Father's Sovereignty over all (1 Cor 15:28).[127]

"The name of the city of my God" is defined in the text as "the New Jerusalem that comes down from My God out of heaven" and is meticulously described in Revelation 21:10-27. This is the city that Paul characterizes as from "above . . . free, which is the mother of us all" (Gal 4:26), in speaking about the difference between the earthly Jerusalem that now is and the heavenly one to come. This is the city for which Abraham looked, "that has foundations, whose Architect and Builder is God" (Heb 11:10). And this is the city in which all believers will reside, "the city of the living God, the heavenly Jerusalem" (Heb 12:22).

"My new name" implies the ultimate summation of all the Names by which Jesus is already known (cf. Rev. 19:11, 13, 16). This ultimate summation of Jesus' Names will constitute a new name denoting the complete revelation of His Glory!

VERSE 13

"Whoever has ears, let them hear what the Spirit says to the churches."

See the initial discussion of this injunction to hear as presented in the commentary on Revelation 2:7. Note that the word "churches," in the plural, reminds us again that not only did all seven churches receive each other's letters, but that the message to each church is the message to all churches in every generation! The requirement is the same: to have an ear to hear what the Spirit is saying to the churches!

---

127 Note that Jesus also called His Father "My God, My God" in His 4th Word from Calvary, where He paid the price for our sins in submission to His Father's Will (Matt 27:46).

THE CHURCH IN LAODICEA
REVELATION 3:14-22

14 "To the angel of the church in Laodicea write: These are the words of the Amen, the faithful and true witness, the ruler of God's creation.

15 "I know your deeds, that you are neither cold nor hot. I wish you were either one or the other!

16 So, because you are lukewarm—neither hot nor cold—I am about to spit you out of my mouth.

17 You say, 'I am rich; I have acquired wealth and do not need a thing.' But you do not realize that you are wretched, pitiful, poor, blind, and naked.

18 I counsel you to buy from me gold refined in the fire, so you can become rich; and white clothes to wear, so you can cover your shameful nakedness; and salve to put on your eyes, so you can see.

19 Those whom I love I rebuke and discipline. So be earnest and repent.

20 Here I am! I stand at the door and knock. If anyone hears my voice and opens the door, I will come in and eat with that person, and they with me.

21 To the one who is victorious, I will give the right to sit with me on my throne, just as I was victorious and sat down with my Father on his throne.

22 Whoever has ears, let them hear what the Spirit says to the churches."

VERSE 14

"To the angel of the church in Laodicea write: These are the words of the Amen, the faithful and true witness, the ruler of God's creation."

By reviewing the discussions on Revelation 1:20, 2:1, and 3:1, we are assured that the angel of the church in Laodicea is an angelic messenger or spirit who has been assigned to the church in Laodicea for the purpose of communicating revelation knowledge concerning Jesus.

Due to the Apostle Paul's extensive stay in Ephesus, during his 3rd missionary journey, Acts 19:10 states "that all the residents of Asia, both Jews and Greeks, heard the word of the Lord." Paul's ministry would have included Laodicea, since his letter to the Colossians (Col 4:13-16), which is also a city in Asia Minor, mentioned the church in Laodicea, as well as Epaphras (Col 4:12), a fellow minister of Paul's, as the possible founder and pastor of the Laodicean congregation. The city was formerly named Diosopolis and Rhoas, but was renamed Laodicea in honor of Laodice,[128] the wife of the Seleucid king, Antiochus II (261-246 B.C.), who founded it.[129] Since it was located on one of two imperial trade routes that connected it with Philadelphia, Sardis, Thyatira and Pergamum,[130] Laodicea was the richest of the seven cities and was considered the key center of banking and commerce within the Roman Empire. Though the city was the center of emperor worship,[131] the city's wealth was their real god. After suffering a devastating earthquake, the citizens refused financial aid from the Roman government and re-financed the rebuilding of their city at their own expense.[132] The city was also famous for its

---

128   The name of the city is also derived from two Greek words: λαός (lâ-ŏs′), meaning 'people,' and δίκη (dĭ′-kay), meaning 'justice.' Together, the city's name means 'justice of the people.'

129   Mounce, *THE BOOK OF THE REVELATION REVISED*, 106.

130   Ibid., 106.

131   Ibid., 108.

132   Ibid., 107.

production of "a soft, glossy black wool"[133] from which highly prized fabrics and garments were manufactured.[134] As the host of a renown medical school, Laodicea was also well known throughout the Empire for its production of 'Phrygian powder,' as the cure for weak eyes and various eye ailments.[135] The main disadvantage in Laodicea was its water supply. In needing to draw its water from distant hot water springs, some six miles away, the water arrived into the city lukewarm and nauseating to drink.[136]

Jesus first identifies Himself as the "Amen" — the Greek and English transliteration of a Hebrew word meaning "surely" or "so be it." The term appears in Chapter One in Jesus' salutation to the seven churches (Rev 1:6) and in the OT allusion, regarding His second coming (Rev 1:7). In its root version, the Hebrew and Greek words for Amen also share the following meanings:

- To build up or support; to be firm or faithful

- To trust or believe; to be trustworthy

- To turn to the right (position of power)

---

133   Ibid., 107.

134   Ibid., 107.

135   Ibid., 107.

136   Ibid., 107; see Hemer, *THE LETTERS TO THE SEVEN CHURCHES IN ASIA IN THEIR LOCAL SETTING*, 186-191, who after presenting several possible alternative ways to interpret Laodicea's lukewarm water, concludes with this same analysis.

Though "Amen" occurs 22 times in seven (7) books in the OT,[137] the most significant OT reference, with import for the church in Laodicea, occurs in Isaiah 65:16 where God is referred to in the Hebrew language as לֵהֵי אָמֵן (pronounced lō-**hay´** ah-**mayn´**) — "The God of Amen." The Hebrew "Amen" is rendered in most English translations as "truth" or "faithfulness,"[138] and appears as such in the Isaiah passage:

> *Then whoever invokes a blessing in the land shall bless by the God of faithfulness (truth, amen), and whoever takes an oath in the land shall swear by the God of faithfulness (truth, amen)... (NRSV)*

In the NT, each of the Gospels (as noted in the NRSV) and every Epistle concludes with the term "Amen" except the following:

- The Book of Acts – signifying that the work of the Holy Spirit will not be finished or concluded until Jesus (The Amen) comes;

- The Epistle of James – signifying that the work of faith will not be finished or concluded until Jesus (The Amen) comes;

- The Third Epistle of John – signifying that the individual believer's faithful accountability to the truth will not be finished or concluded until Jesus (The Amen) comes.

---

137 The 7 books in which the 22 instances of Amen occur in the OT are, as follows: Num 5:22 – Law of Jealousies; Deut 27:15-26 – Blessings and curses upon entry into the Promised Land; 1 Kings 1:32-36 – The anointing of King Solomon; 1 Chron 16:7-36 – David's first Psalm; Neh 5:1-13; 8:1-8 – The vow of the Israelites to free Israelite slaves; the opening of the Book of the Law to be read to the people by Ezra the scribe; Psalms 41:13, 72:19, 89:52, 106:48 – Ends of Book I, II, III and IV, respectively; Jer 28:6 – The false prophecy and death of Hananiah.

138 "The God of Faithfulness" occurs in the NRSV; "The God of Truth" occurs in the KJV, Holman CSB, NASB; and the Amplified cites both truth & faithfulness

Additionally, it is in 2 Corinthians 1:20 that Paul declares the following of Jesus:

> *For in Him every one of God's promises is "**Yes**" . . . it is through Him that we say the "**Amen**," to the Glory of God (cf. Deut 18:20-22; Rev 19:10, **author's emphases**).*

Given all the above references, we can safely conclude that Jesus is addressing Himself to the church in Laodicea as the truthfulness, the certainty and the conclusion of all divine proclamation. The word of any other god or human is a lie in comparison. However, the church's testimony, recorded in verse 17, does not express itself to the glory of the God of Amen, Truth or Faithfulness, but to the gods of their own wealth, health, and self-satisfaction.

In tandem to His attribute as "the Amen," as discussed above, Jesus further addresses the church by the very essence of His Character, which the church is indeed lacking: they are not faithful and true witnesses.[139] In other words, Jesus sees no reflection of Himself in the church, as a whole, as He did in the church in Philadelphia.[140] The church's testimony, as recorded in verse 17, is proof of this.

The Greek word ἀρχή (pronounced ar-**chay´** - ch=k sound) is translated "ruler" and can mean beginning, authority, or origin. As the Origin, the Beginning, the Authority, and the Ruler of God's creation, Jesus stands as the Source and the Sustainer of all life (John 1:1-4; Col 1:15-19). It is from God's "riches in glory by Christ Jesus" (Phil 4:19) that all His creation's needs are met and satisfied. In contrast to the city's much touted medical expertise, Jesus is also the Great Physician who can heal all wounds of the body, mind and soul of His creation (cf. Matt 9:12-13; Mark 2:17; Luke 31-32). As such, Jesus personifies the wisdom of God (1 Cor 1:24, 30), which

---

139   See discussion on Rev 1:5.

140   See discussion on Rev. 3:8.

was with Him in the beginning (John 1:1), by which the world was created, and from which all knowledge springs (Prov 8:22-36).

VERSE 15

"I know your deeds, that you are neither cold nor hot. I wish you were either one or the other."

What Jesus knows[141] about the works in the church in Laodicea is that the church is "neither cold nor hot." Except for its literal use in several NT passages, the Greek word ψυχρός (pronounced psū-**chrŏs´**), translated "cold," and its root word ψύχω (pronounced **psū´**-chō), which appears in Matthew 24:12, carry the figurative meaning of a gross loss of love for and faith in Jesus. For example, in the Matthew text, Jesus says, "Because of the increase of wickedness, the love of most will grow cold."

In contrast to both the literal and figurative meanings for cold, the Greek word ζεστός (pronounced zĕs-**tŏs´**), translated "hot," denotes the spiritual fervor that accompanies an active love for and an active faith in Jesus. Only here and in verse 16 is this Greek word employed, either literally or figuratively, within the entire NT. Jesus' indictment, however, is that the church in Laodicea is "neither cold nor hot."

Jesus' desire that the church be either cold or hot raises several questions. If cold is the loss of love for and faith in Jesus, and hot is the spiritual fervor of both love for and faith in Jesus, then why would Jesus wish that the church were one or the other, considering they are opposite responses to Him? Why would Jesus not stipulate that He wished the church were hot, which is the more favorable response to Him? Why one or the other?

To answer the above questions, let us re-visit Matthew's use of the word cold. In Jesus' end-time discourse (Matt 24:12), He states that it will

---

141   See previous discussions on Rev 2:2 and 3:1

be the increase of wickedness that will cause the love of most to grow cold. Since wickedness is paralleled with cold as its major characteristic, then we can safely assert that cold or wicked is what we all were before our conversion. In other words, we were all "dead (cold) in our trespasses and sins" (Eph 2:1-3).

However, herein lies the miracle of our conversion: for it was from this cold state of spiritual depravity and disregard for Jesus that the Holy Spirit quickened us to repentance and faith through the hearing of the Word. In other words, Jesus would prefer that the church be cold because she could at least be converted. On the other hand, if the church were hot, or on fire for the Lord, she could at least be used by the Lord as a faithful and true witness of the manifold Grace of God.

To be neither cold nor hot, therefore, was/is to both inconvertible (cf. Heb 6:4-6) and un-usable (Matt 5:13; Luke 14:34-35). It is this state that Jesus finds utterly nauseating.

VERSE 16

"So, because you are lukewarm—neither hot nor cold—I am about to spit you out of my mouth."

Given the above assessment of cold and hot, it should not surprise us that the Greek word χλιαρός (pronounced chlee-â-**rŏs´**), translated "lukewarm," is used only here in all of Scripture. From a Greek root meaning "tepid," the spiritual state of the Laodicean church is being compared with the insipid quality of the city's water supply. After its six-mile flow from the hot mineral springs, the water would arrive into the city lukewarm and nauseating to drink.

The critical nature of the church's spiritual condition was that in being neither cold nor hot, they were, in truth, standing at the door of complete apostasy. Though the previous six churches have manifested various stages of apostasy, i.e., abandoning first love, etc., luke-warmness stands on the very threshold of this irremediable state, as indicated by the most repulsive response from Jesus recorded in Scripture: "I am about to spit you out of My mouth." Lukewarm believers are not only identifiable by their worldly testimony, but also manifest the following lukewarm tendencies:

- Lukewarm believers are those who know the truth of Jesus, but hold this truth in unrighteousness (Rom 1:18, 21-25, 28, 32; Heb 10:26-27). In other words, they know better but choose not to do better; they know the Way but choose not to walk in the Way; they know their Master will return one day but conduct their lives as if He will not return today (Matt 24:45-51; Mark 13:35-37).

- Lukewarm believers subscribe to the notion that they have room for both Jesus and other entities of allegiance (Matt 6:24; Luke 16:13; cf. 2 Kings 17:32-33, 41; cf. Zeph 1:5).

- Lukewarm believers insert Scripture where there is no Scripture, e.g. "You take one step, God will take two;" and they truncate Scripture to suit their self-centered agendas, e.g. "All things work together for good . . . " (Rom 8:28 KJV truncated).

- Lukewarm believers are characterized by Paul as "having a form of godliness, but denying the power of it" and as "always learning but never able to acknowledge the truth" (2 Tim 3:5, 7).

- Lukewarm believers are those who become re-entangled in the defilements of the world and are

like a dog that returns to its vomit and like a sow
that, after washed, returns to wallowing in the mud
(2 Peter 2:20-22).

So characterized, it is little wonder that Jesus finds the lukewarm church nauseating. However, the grace in Jesus' indictment is that He does not say that He has already spit them out, but that He is "about to spit [them] out of [His] mouth," thus leaving room for His subsequent appeal for earnestness and repentance from the church (vs 19). Let there be no doubt that the Greek word μέλλω (pronounced **mĕl´-lō**), translated "about," connotes Jesus' definite intent to follow through on this judgment, if the church does not act on His counsel (vs 18).

VERSE 17

"You say, 'I am rich; I have acquired wealth and do not need a thing.'
But you do not realize that you are wretched, pitiful, poor, blind,
and naked."

This is the church's real testimony. It reveals that wealth, health, and prosperity are their gods and not Jesus. The church's testimony was a subscription to the motto of the city, which had distinguished itself on several occasions as being financially savvy and independently wealthy. The city also boasted of its medical expertise in providing a cure for eye ailments, as previously mentioned. As with the churches in Pergamum, Thyatira, and Sardis, the dominant culture of the city had made its way into the church in Laodicea, as well.

The testimony of the church is an allusion to Hosea 12:8 in which Ephraim's self-centered testimony before God was similar:

Ephraim boasts, 'I am very rich; I have become wealthy. With all my
wealth they will not find in me any iniquity or sin.

If we take into consideration that Hosea was married to a whore (Hos 1:2-3), and that God's prophetic ministry through Hosea and his marriage was to typify His undying love for the people of Israel (Ephraim is another name for Israel – Hos 2:14 – 3:5) who had played the whore in following other gods, then we can safely conclude that the above testimony is the testimony of spiritual whoredom or spiritual adultery — not the testimony of a faithful and true witness nor of the spotless and unblemished bride of Christ!

We should also note that the church's testimony is characterized by two "I" statements that resemble the pride and self-exaltation of Lucifer before he was cast out of heaven (Isa 14:12-15; cf. Ezek 28:11-19).

The following table allows us to compare the dynamics of the Laodicean testimony with that of the faithful and true witness, based on the Scriptures:

TABLE 2
LAODICEAN TESTIMONY VS. TESTIMONY OF THE FAITHFUL AND TRUE WITNESS

LAODICEAN TESTIMONY	FAITHFUL AND TRUE WITNESS
"I am rich"	**True Riches**
Psalm 49:6-9, 16-20; Proverbs 10:2; 11:4, 28; 13:7; 22:1; 23:4-5; 28:6, 11, 20, 22; Jeremiah 5:26-31; 9:23-24; Ezekiel 7:19; Zeph 1:18; Mark 4:18-19; Luke 6:24; 12:16-21; 1 Timothy 6:9-10; James 1:9-11, 17; 5:1-6	Proverbs 3:13-18; 4:5-9; 8:10-11, 18-21; Isaiah 33:6; 2 Corinthians 8:9; Colossians 2:2-3; 3:1-4, 16-17; 1 Timothy 4:8; 6:6-8, 17-19; Revelation 3:18
"I have prospered"	**True Prosperity**
Psalm 62:10; 73:3-12; Matthew 19:16-26; Mark 10:17-27; Luke 18:18-27	Matthew 6:25-34; 19:27-29; Mark 4:8-9, 20; 10:28-30; Luke 12:22-34; 18:28-30; John 15:1-8, 16; Colossians 1:9-10

LAODICEAN TESTIMONY	FAITHFUL AND TRUE WITNESS
"I need nothing"	**True Satisfaction**
Luke 12:16-21; James 5:1-3, 5	Psalm 22:26; 23:1; 34:9-10; 36:7-10; 63:1-6; 91:14-16; 107:9; Isaiah 58:11; 2 Corinthians 9:8; Ephesians 3:17-21; Philippians 4:11-13, 19; Colossians 2:9-10; 3:23-24; 2 Timothy 3:16-17

In summary, the Laodicean testimony betrays a corrupt heart condition: for "out the abundance of the heart the mouth speaks" (Matt 12:34; Luke 6:45 NRSV).

For all the church's material wealth, Jesus' five-point judgment finds them spiritually bankrupt. The gravest aspect of their spiritual bankruptcy is Jesus' assessment that they "do not know" that this is indeed their spiritual state. Such ignorance within the Body of Christ does not happen all at once but is the result of a time-worn habit of compromising the truth.

Though each of the judgments are indeed physical conditions, the following references will attest to their spiritual equivalency, as well:

- Wretched – Romans 7:24 (The only other time the Greek word occurs in the NT)

- Pitiable – 1 Corinthians 15:19 (The only other time the Greek word occurs in the NT)

- Poor – Colossians 2:1-3 (By inference, the church is poor because it is devoid of "all the riches of assured understanding and . . . knowledge of God's mystery, that is, Christ Himself, in whom are hidden all the treasures of wisdom and knowledge." The actual Greek word for poor occurs 32 times in the NT; it occurs for the last time in our current Revelation text)

- Blind – Matthew 15:14; 23:16-17, 19, 24, 26; Luke 6:39; 2 Peter 1:9 (Greek word occurs 52 times in the NT; it occurs for the last time in our current Revelation text)

- Naked – 2 Corinthians 5:2-4; Revelation 16:15; 17:16 (Greek word occurs 15 times in the NT; it occurs three times in the Revelation text, including its first occurrence in our current text)

The church's ignorance of their spiritual condition makes Jesus' judgment one of chastisement, not of destruction.[142] This will be borne out by His strong counsel in verse 18 as well as by His own words of exhortation in verse 19. However, the church will first need to accept the truth of their spiritual condition in order to conquer it.

VERSE 18

"I counsel you to buy from me gold refined in the fire, so you can become rich; and white clothes to wear, so you can cover your shameful nakedness; and salve to put on your eyes, so you can see."

Jesus' posture of "counseling" not only alludes to His prophetic name as "Wonderful, **Counselor** . . . " (Isa 9:6, **author's emphasis**) but also reflects His possession of the seven-fold attributes of the Holy Spirit (Isa 11:2), one of which is "the Spirit of counsel."[143]

As the Holy Spirit is the Spirit of Truth, who has been sent to guide believers into all truth (John 16:13), then all aspects of the Spirit's seven-fold fullness are conduits of truth. This is why Jesus could claim to be

---

142 Even under the Law, sins committed in ignorance or unintentionally required the stipulated sacrifices in order to be forgiven (Lev 4:1-35; 5:14-19) and Jesus' blood fulfilled this part of the Law when He prayed from Calvary, Father, forgive them for they do not know what they are doing" (Luke 23:34).

143 See previous discussion on Rev 3:1.

the Way, the Truth, and the Life: for He was given the Spirit of Truth without measure (John 3:34).

Speaking out of the Spirit of counsel, Jesus advises the church "to buy" from Him. Jesus is here contrasting the church's pre-occupation with worldly prosperity with the notion of spiritual commerce. Though, on the one hand, the church had become savvy in mastering the world's method for transacting business and acquiring material (temporal, corruptible, perishable) merchandise, she, on the other hand, had become bankrupt of the only currency that is needed to transact the Father's Business and to acquire the spiritual (eternal, incorruptible, imperishable) merchandise of the Kingdom.

Since Jesus' counsel to the church is "to buy from Me," then we can safely assert that some form of 'spiritual currency' is required to purchase the following spiritual merchandise:

1. "Gold refined by fire"

2. "White robes"

3. "Eyesalve"

The need for 'spiritual currency' is also implied in the passage to "Come, buy and eat; come buy wine and milk without money and without cost" (Isa 55:1d).

What is this 'spiritual currency'? The answer resides in the proverbial injunction to "Buy the truth and sell it not; also wisdom and instruction and understanding" (Prov 23:23 KJV). The injunction "to buy the truth" suggests that the truth is the currency of the kingdom, and is substantiated by the fact that:

• Jesus is the Truth – John 14:6

• The Holy Spirit is the Spirit of Truth – John 14:16-17; 15:26; 16:13

- Both Jesus and the Holy Spirit testify of the God of
  Amen (Truth) — Isaiah 65:16[144]

Since the wisdom of Proverbs instructs that the truth must be "purchased" (bought), then the truth must, in itself, have "purchasing" power. Just as it takes money to purchase the things that only money can buy (including the purchase of more money), so one must have (buy / acquire) the truth in order to purchase the things that only the truth can buy, including the purchase of more truth!

Because the truth is spiritual (John 6:63c; Rom 7:14a), then we can safely affirm that the Truth only purchases spiritual things. In other words, the truth is not only the "currency of the kingdom," but it has the "purchasing power" of securing more of itself as well as other spiritual treasures.

Since the church in Laodicea is spiritually bankrupt of the truth, i.e., "you do not realize . . . " then the critical question for her and us is "How does one buy the truth?"

Answer: In order to buy the essential currency of the kingdom, one must be employed in a spiritual process of surrender. Just as we are employed in the daily process of surrendering the temporal sacrifices of time, energy, and skills in order to obtain a pay-check, even more so are we to be employed in the daily (hourly, etc.) process of surrendering the necessary spiritual sacrifices in order "to buy the Truth." According to Scripture, the following four spiritual sacrifices (in their order) must be surrendered in order "to buy the truth:"

1. An Ear to Hear (see discussion on Rev 2:7 – church in Ephesus)

    - Inclined Ear – Psalm 78:1; 119:112; Proverbs 2:1-2;
      4:20; Isaiah 55:3

---

144   See discussion on verse 14.

- Open Ear – Job 33:14-17; 36:10-12, 15; Psalm 40:6;
  Isaiah 48:8; 50:4-5; Mark 7:34-35

- Attentive Ear – Luke 19:48

- Bowed down Ear – Proverbs 5:1-2

- Obedient Ear – 1 Samuel 15:22-23; Proverbs 25:12

2.   A Broken and Contrite Heart – Psalms 34:18; 51:17; Isaiah 61:1;
     2 Corinthians 7:9-12

3.   A Broken Will – Psalm 40:8; Matthew 26:39; John 1:12-13;
     Romans 12:2; Colossians 1:21

4.   A Broken Spirit – Psalm 51:17; Isaiah 57:15

Thus, it is only after we have inclined our ears to the truth of Jesus, and allowed it to break us in three places (heart, will, and spirit), that we, in truth, have bought the truth!

Since "buying the truth" is both a form of surrender and a form of acquisition, i.e., you surrender something in order to acquire something, then the aforementioned process of surrender is also the "purchasing" process for obtaining the truth, more truth, and all of the spiritual treasures one can buy with truth!

In God's economy, therefore, the concept of "buying" involves sacrificial surrender to the truth of Jesus. Another name for this process is repentance. In order "to buy the truth," therefore, once must repent or surrender to the truth. Only then does one possess the truth needed to purchase the other essential merchandise of the kingdom!

The first purchase of the truth of Jesus is "gold refined by fire." The phrase is symbolic of faith in Jesus that is tested and tried in the fire of trials and afflictions (James 1:2-4; 1 Peter 1:6-9; cf. 4:12ff).

The following two Scriptures (and there are many) validate that faith is the first purchase of the truth that Jesus is the Son of God:

For God so loved the world, that He gave His Only Begotten Son, that whosoever believes in Him should not perish, but have everlasting life (John 3:16 KJV).

But without faith it is impossible to please God; for he that comes to God must believe that He is and that He is a rewarder of them that diligently seek Him (Heb 11:6 KJV).

To believe in Jesus, therefore, is to obey, or engage, the purchasing power of the truth that Jesus is the Son of God.

As the gold of our salvation, faith must be tried in the fiery furnace of our trials and tribulations (cf. John 16:33; 1 John 5:4) in order to be purified and refined, much as fine metals are purified of their dross and refined to their highest gloss only by passing through varying levels of intense heat (cf. Isa 1:25; Zech 13:9; Mal 3:3).

The trouble with the Laodicean church is that they have deposited their faith in worldly wealth and have eclipsed Jesus as the God of all they are and of all they possess. What they do not know is that the faith that purchases the truth that Jesus is the Son of God is true faith: faith in anything or anybody other than Jesus is nothing more than wishful thinking premised upon a lie, i.e., sinking sand (cf. Matt 7:24-29; Luke 6:47-49; 1 John 4:1-6).

In tandem to the first purchase of faith is the second purchase of the truth of Jesus, i.e., "white robes," which is symbolic of the righteousness of Jesus. As was discussed in the letter to the church in Sardis, righteousness is often depicted in Scripture as a garment, and the "righteousness that is by faith [in Jesus]" (Rom 10:6) is characterized as "fine linen, bright and clean" (Rev 19:8). The garment of righteousness is imputed to believers by the seven-fold fullness of the Holy Spirit (Rom 4:13, 21-24; 10:4; 2 Cor 5:21; Phil 3:9; James 2:23). It is this garment that will adorn the bride of Christ, the church, at the Marriage Supper of the Lamb, and will characterize her as "without stain or wrinkle or any other blemish, but holy and blameless" (Eph 5:27).

"White robes" is in direct contrast to the silky and expensive fabrics produced from the black wool for which Laodicea was well known. Whereas the black wool garments were man-made and purchased in the world's marketplace, the "white robe" of Jesus' righteousness is the product of faith in the Truth of Jesus (Rom 3:21-22, 4:13-25), and is credited to the believer as a gift from God. The righteousness of Jesus was first anticipated in Abraham, about whom the Scriptures record, "And he (Abram) believed the LORD, and He credited it to him as righteousness (Gen 15:6; cf. Gal 3:6; James 2:23). However, Jesus is now "the end of the Law so that there may be righteousness for everyone who believes" (Rom 10:4 NRSV).

The church in Laodicea is guilty of the same indictment that the Apostle Paul levies against his Jewish brothers and sisters: "Since they did not know the righteousness of God and sought to establish their own, they did not submit to God's righteousness" (Rom 10:3). The difference between the two is that Paul's Jewish brothers and sisters had not yet come to faith in Jesus, meaning they were still cold and convertible, whereas the Laodicean church had come to faith in Jesus at some point but had habitually neglected, compromised and denied the truth of Jesus — the currency of the kingdom — in an effort to get along with or to impress the dominant culture. This progressive neglect of the truth of Jesus was what rendered the church neither cold nor hot, but lukewarm and naked.

Without the "white robe of Jesus' righteousness," the sinner is naked in sin before God. Just as Adam and Eve had to be re-clothed with coats of skin (Gen 3:7, 21), in order to cover the shame and nakedness of their disobedience, so we, their descendants, also require a garment that makes us acceptable in the sight of God. In both cases, the garment is provided by God and is not of our own making, which is the essence of self-righteousness.

When we consider, therefore, that the righteousness of Jesus was and is His sinless obedience and His perfect submission to the Will of His Father, then the church in Laodicea needs to "buy" the "white garment of Jesus' righteousness" as an act of obedience and submission to the Father's Will that "they believe in the One He [the Father] has sent" (John 6:29).

The final purchase of the truth of Jesus addresses both the church's spiritual blindness and her need for spiritual sight. Because the church has premised her testimony upon the pursuit and acquisition of materials things, she has, in truth, blinded herself to her spiritual need for the eternal things of God (cf. Col 3:1-2). She, in other words, has become absorbed, obsessed, and pre-occupied with the temporal. This pre-occupation with the temporal has been characterized by John as "the lust of the flesh, the lust of his eyes, and the pride of life" (1 John 2:16).

It is the "lust of the eyes" that ignites the other two lusts, as can be seen in the temptation in the Garden of Eden (Gen 3:6). To be pre-occupied with the temporal, therefore, is to be distracted by those things that can only be perceived through the natural eye. Since the natural eye is both finite and perishable, then all that it lusts after is also finite and perishable.

However, God's salvation is not premised upon finite and perishable things, but upon infinite and incorruptible treasures (1 Peter 1:3-5, 23). For example:

- Our faith is "the substance of things hoped for, the evidence of things not seen" (Heb 11:1 KJV)

- Our righteousness is patterned after Him "whom having not seen, you love. Though now you do not see Him, yet believing, you rejoice with joy inexpressible and full of glory" (1 Peter 1:8 NKJV)

- Our glory also resides in the truth that "it does not yet appear what we shall be: but we know that, when He shall appear, we shall be like Him, for we shall see Him as He is" (1 John 3:2 KJV)

Since our faith, our righteousness, and our glory are all premised upon eternal yet unseen realities, then we can safely assert that these spiritual treasures cannot be discerned nor perceived by the naked or natural eye. Another kind of sight is needed to see-the-unseen things of God! It is only as we believe in Jesus (faith) and obey His commands (righteousness) that the Holy Spirit will give us that new set of spiritual eyes that allows us to see more clearly the glorious revelation of God in Jesus Christ our Lord (cf. 1 Cor 2:9-10; 2 Cor 4:6).

In other words, when we are faithful and obedient to God's Word, God will reveal more of Himself to us as we show ourselves good stewards of what He has already revealed to us. These spiritual glimpses of the glory of God in Christ not only encourage our faithfulness and inspire our obedience, but they "purchase" for us the lively hope (1 Peter 1:3) that captures the vision of what shall be (1 John 3:3)!

In order to capture the vision of what shall be, the church in Laodicea is being counseled to buy the third spiritual treasure with the Truth that Jesus-is-the-Son-of-God, i.e., the eyesalve of hope for the unseen and eternal realities and riches of God's kingdom. Purposing to draw the church's attention away from the limited and futile eyesalve produced by the medical experts in the city, Jesus engages the term "eyesalve" as a symbolic reference to the Holy Spirit's anointing of hope, which alone cures the afflictions of both the spiritual eye (blindness) and the physical eye (lust).

When the natural eye, for example, is afflicted with lusts for the temporal things of life, the spiritual eye is blinded to eternal truths and realities (David and Bathsheba are a classic example). When, again, the natural eye becomes consumed with beholding the troubles of this world, the spiritual eye loses sight of the glory that lies beyond our present afflictions, oppressions, and persecutions (Rom 5:1-5; 1 Cor 4:17-18; Col 1:24-29).

However, when the spiritual eye is anointed with the eyesalve of hope, which, again, can only be purchased as we trust and obey the truth of Jesus, then the natural eye loses its addiction to the finite and perishable, and the spiritual eye becomes singularly focused on Jesus (Matt 6:22-24; Col 3:1-4)!

In summary, to buy the truth that Jesus is the Son of God is to purchase the power to believe this Truth (faith, or "gold refined by fire"), the power to obey this truth (righteousness or "white garments"), and the power to see the unseen and eternal realities of God (the Holy Spirit's anointed lens of hope or "eyesalve") that are guaranteed by the truth of God's Word.

VERSE 19

"Those whom I love I rebuke and discipline. So be earnest and repent."

The first sentence in this verse is an allusion to several OT passages: Deuteronomy 8:5; Job 5:17-18; Psalm 94:12; Proverbs 3:11-12. It is in Hebrews 12:5-15, however, that this phrase receives its fullest definition as the Lord's chastening process. His reproof and discipline are motivated by His love for us.

The first note of comparison between the text in Hebrews 12:5-15 and our current text is the Greek word translated "love." In Hebrews 12:6, the Greek word is ἀγαπάω (pronounced â-gâ-**pâ´**ō) from which we acquire the word "agape," meaning the unconditional love of God. However, in our current text, the Greek word for "love" is φιλέω (pronounced phĭ-lĕ´-ō), which carries the notion of brotherly love or friendship. It is the same word used by Jesus when He declared:

"You are My friends if you do what I command you" (John 15:14)

With this meaning, the first sentence in our current text could be rendered, as follows:

- "As many as I consider a dear friend . . . "
- As many as I have affection for . . .
- As many as I have kissed with grace . . .

The Greek word ἐλέγχω (pronounced ĕ-**leng**´-chō - ch=k sound), translated "rebuke" also means "to convince or convict someone of their error." The Greek word παιδεύω (pronounced pī-**dū**´-ō), translated "discipline" ('chasten' in the KJV), also means "to instruct" or "to lead in the right direction." Given Jesus' potentially nauseating response to the church's spiritual condition, it is nothing short of Grace that He still loves them enough to reprove and discipline them.

What should not be missed here is that just as Jesus has counseled the church to buy the truth of who He is, so Jesus premises His three-fold response to the church upon the truth of who He is, albeit to the unfaithful and to the lukewarm within His Body; and that three-fold response is His love, His reproof, and His discipline. All are manifestations of the undeniable truth that He is the Son of God: for "if we are faithless, He remains faithful – for He cannot disown Himself" (2 Tim 2:13)!

It is also important to note that discipline or chastisement becomes necessary when we fail to judge ourselves. According to 1 Corinthians 11:28, 31-32, self-judgment, or self-examination avoids the need for chastisement (cf. 1 John 1:9). Since discipline is Jesus' loving response to the believer's sinfulness, then we can safely conclude that discipline is accomplished by the persuasive application of both mercy and truth: "For by mercy and truth iniquity is purged" (Prov 16:6a; cf. Ps 85:10a KJV).

In order for the sweet communion of friendship to be restored, Jesus' loving initiatives of rebuke and discipline require a righteous response from those He loves. Jesus, therefore, commands the church to be "earnest and repent."

Earnest is translated from the Greek word ζηλεύω (pronounced zay-lū´-ō), which means "to have warmth of feeling for or against." In response to the church's lukewarm, fence-sitting posture, Jesus is commanding them to take a stand, to be either for Him or against Him, to be either hot or cold.

Repent is translated from the Greek word μετανοέω (pronounced mĕ-tâ-**nu**´-ō), which means to have a change of heart and mind from the error of one's ways and thoughts, and a turning to the ways and thoughts of God's truth concerning the matter.

Remember: repentance is another name for buying the truth!

VERSE 20

> *"Here I am! I stand at the door and knock. If anyone hears my voice and opens the door, I will come in and eat with that person, and they with me."*

Given the following invitations to hear and to open, we can safely assume that the imagery of "the door" is a reference to the ear. Some might consider "the door" to be a reference to the heart. However, before the heart can receive and believe the truth, the ear must first hear the truth:

> *So faith comes from what is heard, and what is heard comes through the Word of God (Rom 10:17 NRSV).*

Jesus, therefore, uses the truth "to knock" on the door of the church's lethargic ear to revive their love for and faith in Him. The truth that is received and believed will constitute the spiritual 'currency' that the church requires to purchase the spiritual merchandise of which they are in desperate need. His 'knocking,' in other words, is Jesus' gracious invitation to hear and 'buy' the truth presented in His counsel.

The above-cited imagery of the ear (the door) and the knock (the truth) are further endorsed by Jesus' injunction to "hear His voice (truth) and open the door (ear)."

The church's hearing must be done with the first of four spiritual sacrifices needed to purchase the truth of Jesus, i.e., an ear to hear (see discussion on verse 18 and in the Letter to the church in Ephesus), which is characterized by a five-point ear quality that is worthy to be repeated here:

- Inclined Ear – Psalm 78:1; 119:112; Proverbs 2:1-2, 4:20; Isaiah 55:3

- Open Ear – Job 33:14-17; 36:10-12, 15; Psalm 40:6; Isaiah 48:8, 50:4-5; Mark 7:34-35

- Attentive Ear – Luke 19:48

- Bowed down Ear – Proverbs 5:1-2

- Obedient Ear – 1 Samuel 15:22-23; Proverbs 25:12

We are further reminded that the church's response to "hear'" and "open" (which involves all five of the above-cited ear qualities) will serve as evidence that they are Jesus' sheep:

> My sheep hear My voice, and I know them, and they follow Me (John 10:27 KJV).

> Everyone who belongs to the Truth listens to My voice (John 18:37d NRSV).

If the church responds in hearing and heeding Jesus' counsel, a two-fold dynamic of fellowship is promised. The first phrase, "I will come in," is a direct reference to the indwelling presence and power of the Holy Spirit (John 14:15-17, 21, 23). The Holy Spirit is the Spirit of truth who has been sent to "guide us into all truth" (John 16:13); so the purchase of the truth of Jesus brings with it continuous fellowship with our Lord through the abiding and indwelling ministry of the Holy Spirit.

The second phrase, "and eat with that person," further endorses that the truth is the menu of our communion with the Lord. The word of God, or the truth, has been characterized in Scripture as a seven-course meal, and Jesus is the personification of each course:

1.   Living Water – John 4:10, 13; 1 Cor 10:1-4; cf. Isa 55:1

2.   Sincere Milk – 1 Pet 2:2; cf. Isa 55:1

3.   Bread of Life – John 6:48-59; 1 Cor 10:1-4; cf. Isaiah 55:2

4.   Fruit of the Spirit – Gal 5:22-23

5.   Strong Meat – John 4:32, 34; Heb 5:12-14

6.   Butter and Honey – Psalm 119:103; Isa 7:14-15; Ezek 3:3

7.   New Wine – Matt 9:17; Mark 2:22; Luke 5:37-39; John 2:3-10

The above references and symbols validate the use of the Greek word φιλέω (pronounced phĭ-lĕ´-ō) in verse 19, which carries the notion of brotherly love or friendship; for friendship includes sweet communion and the breaking of bread, i.e., the Communion Feast. The same Greek word φιλέω is used in the context of Jesus' restoration of Peter after providing him and the other disciples breakfast on the shore of the Sea of Tiberias or Galilee (John 21: 1, 12, 15-17).

VERSE 21

"To the one who is victorious, I will give the right to sit with me on my throne, just as I was victorious and sat down with my Father on his throne."

The identification of the one who is victorious or conquers[145] is the one who submits to and obeys Jesus counsel, as presented in verses 18-20.

Jesus' promise to those in the church in Laodicea who are victorious, i.e., "I will give the right to sit with me on my throne . . . ," poses the need to reconcile this current promise to two previous instances where references to Jesus' Throne are made.

The first instance is recorded in both Matthew 20:20-23 and Mark 10:35-40, in which the Mother of James and John in Matthew's text, and James and John themselves in the Mark text, request that they be allowed to sit at Jesus' right and left hands on His throne. Jesus, in both cases, responds "but to sit at my right or left is not for me to grant. These places belong to those for whom they have been prepared by my Father."[146] However, in the current promise to the overcomers in the church in Laodicea, Jesus is guaranteeing that He will give to those who are victorious the privilege to sit with Him on His throne, just as He conquered and sat down with His Father in His Father's throne.

The second instance is recorded in both Matthew 19:28 and Luke 22:28-30, in which Jesus articulates His promise to the apostles of their future reward in His kingdom: "Truly, I tell you, at the renewal of all things, when the Son of Man sits on His glorious throne, you who have followed Me will also sit on twelve thrones, judging the twelve tribes of Israel." However, in the current promise to the overcomers in the Laodicean church, Jesus does not restrict the number of thrones to twelve.

---

145 See discussion on Rev 2:7.

146 Mark's Gospel does not include "by My Father"

So, how are these two previous instances to be reconciled with Jesus' current promise? The answer resides in the fact that neither instance is the reference point for Jesus' current promise. Since Jesus is addressing His promise to an unspecified number of overcomers in the church in Laodicea, He is not referring to the seats at His right and left hands, because these are only two seats (Matt 20:20-23 & Mark 10:35-40). And by the same token, He is not referring to the twelve thrones promised to the apostles, as these are only twelve thrones (Matt 19:28; cf. Luke 18:28-30; 22:28-30).

Instead Jesus is referring to the reward of those who have been faithful stewards, as depicted in the Parable of the Talents in Matthew 25:14-23. In the case of the first two servants in this Parable, who received and doubled their five and two talents, respectively, Jesus not only commended them for having been faithful over a few things, but as their reward He promised to "appoint them" or "put them in charge" over many things. Since Jesus is Heir of all things (Heb 1:2), His reward to those who are victorious is to share the same inheritance He received from His Father for having conquered and overcome as a Faithful and True Witness, i.e., He now sits and rules from the throne His Father has given Him at His right hand (Ps 110:1; Matt 22:44; 26:64; Mark 12:36; 16:19; Luke 20:42; 22:69; Eph 1:20; Heb 1:13; 1 Peter 3:22; cf. Acts 7:55). Hence, Jesus refers to the place where those who are victorious will sit as "My Throne" in our current text, which fulfills His invitation in the Parable of the Talents to "enter thou into the joy of your Lord."

Another significant and strategic connection that Jesus' promise to the Laodicean overcomers has to the Parable of the Talents is that the Parable addresses and elevates the church's attention from material wealth to the spiritual riches that they have been exhorted to purchase. The "gold tried in the fire," "the white robes," and the "eyesalve" are their highest stewardship and are an allusion to the "few things" in the Parable over which they are commanded to be faithful. As a result, faithful and true stewards of these spiritual riches will inherit the reward of sitting on Jesus' throne and of entering into His joy as "heirs of God and co-heirs with Christ" (Rom 8:17) in His Father's kingdom!

Jesus' promise also confirms the millennial and eternal realities that "if we suffer, we will reign with Him" (2 Tim 2:12a) and "[we] will reign forever and ever" (Rev 22:5c). Furthermore, Jesus' promise beautifully alludes to His High Priestly prayer on the eve of His crucifixion:

> *Father, I want those You have given Me to be with Me where I am, and to see My Glory, the Glory You have given Me because You loved Me before the creation of the world (John 17:24).*

VERSE 22

"Whoever has ears, let them hear what the Spirit says to the churches."

This last installation of the invitation to have an ear to hear what the Spirit is saying to the churches carries with it all the import of the six preceding invitations, as the church in Laodicea in her lukewarm state is guilty of all the indictments against the preceding churches. It would also be worthy to review the ear quality needed to hear the Spirit, as presented in the discussion on Revelation 2:7 and in the discussion on verse 20.

As a final reminder, the word "churches," in the plural, affirms that the message to each church is the message to all churches, not only then but in every generation! The requirement is the same: to have an ear to hear what the Spirit is saying to the churches!

BIBLIOGRAPHY

Beale, Gregory K., *The Book of Revelation: A Commentary on the Greek Text* (The New International Greek Testament Commentary) Grand Rapids, MI: Eerdmans Publishing Co., 1999.

Brown, Francis (with the cooperation of S. R. Driver and Charles A. Briggs), *The New Brown-Driver-Briggs-Gesenius Hebrew and English Lexicon*, Peabody, MA: Henrickson Publishers, 1979.

Bullinger, E. W., *Number in Scripture: Its Supernatural Design and Spiritual Significance.* Grand Rapids, MI: Kregel Publications, 1967.

Carson, D. A. and Douglas J. Moo, *An Introduction to the New Testament.* Grand Rapids, MI: Zondervan, 1992, 2005.

Collins, John J., *DANIEL with an Introduction to Apocalyptic Literature.* Grand Rapids, MI: Eerdmans, 1984.

Douglas, J. D., ed., *The New Greek-English Interlinear New Testament.* Carol Stream, IL: Tyndale House Publishers, Inc., 1990.

Gardner, Joseph L., *Reader's Digest Atlas of the Bible.* Pleasantville, NY: The Reader's Digest Association, Inc., 1981.

Gregg, Steve, ed., *Revelation - Four Views: A Parallel Commentary.* Nashville, TN: Thomas Nelson Publishers, 1997.

Hemer, Colin J., *The Letters to the Seven Churches in Asia in Their Local Setting.* Grand Rapids, MI: Eerdmans Publishing Company, 2001.

Hodge, Charles, "The Protestant Rule of Faith," Pages 41-44 in *Readings in Christian Theology*. Edited by Peter C. Hodgson and Robert H. King. Philadelphia: Fortress Press, 1985.

Krause, Mark S. (2009) "The Seven Hymns of Revelation 4, 5 and 7," Leaven: Vol 17: Iss. 4, Art. 6. Available at: http://digitalcommons.pepperdine.edu/leaven/vol17/iss4/6

Michaels, J. Ramsey, *Interpreting the Book of Revelation*. Grand Rapids, MI: Baker Books, 1992.

Mounce, Robert H., *The Book of the Revelation Revised (The New International Commentary on the New Testament)*. Grand Rapids, MI: Eerdmans Publishing Company, 1997.

Mounce, William D., *Basics of Biblical Greek*. Grand Rapids, MI: Zondervan, 1993.

Scofield, Cyrus I., ed., *The King James Study Bible: Reference Edition* (Reproduction of the First Scofield Reference Bible). Grand Rapids, MI: World Publishing, no year date.

Unger, Merrill F. *The New Unger's Bible Dictionary*. Chicago, IL: Moody Press, 1988.

Witherington, III, Ben. *Revelation*. (Cambridge Bible Commentary). New York: Cambridge University Press, 2003.

INDEX

A

H

I

J

For more information about
Rev. Desiré P. Grogan
&
*Revelations from
The Revelation of Jesus Christ*
please visit:
www.empoweringthepew.org

or email:
dpgrogan@empoweringthepew.org

For more information about
AMBASSADOR INTERNATIONAL
please visit:

www.ambassador-international.com
@AmbassadorIntl
www.facebook.com/AmbassadorIntl